A DICTIONARY OF
ASIAN MYTHOLOGY

A DICTIONARY OF ASIAN MYTHOLOGY

DAVID LEEMING

OXFORD
UNIVERSITY PRESS
2001

OXFORD
UNIVERSITY PRESS

Oxford New York
Athens Auckland Bangkok Bogotá Buenos Aires
Calcutta Cape Town Chennai Dar es Salaam Delhi Florence Hong Kong
Istanbul Karachi Kuala Lumpur Madrid Melbourne Mexico City Mumbai
Nairobi Paris São Paulo Shanghai Singapore Taipei Tokyo Toronto Warsaw

and associated companies in
Berlin Ibadan

Published by Oxford University Press, Inc.
198 Madison Avenue, New York, New York 10016

Library of Congress-in-Publication Data

Leeming, David Adams, 1937–
A dictionary of Asian mythology / by David Leeming.
p. cm.
Includes index.
ISBN 0-19-512052-3—ISBN 0-19-512053-1 (pbk.)
1. Mythology, Asian—Dictionaries—Polyglot. 2.
Asia—Religion—Dictionaries—Polyglot. 3. Dictionaries, Polyglot. I. Title.

BL1005 .L46 2001
291.1'3'09503—dc21

00-062389

3 5 7 9 8 6 4 2
Printed in the United States of America
on acid-free paper

Contents

A DICTIONARY OF
ASIAN MYTHOLOGY

Introduction

The purpose of this dictionary is to provide a reference source for mythologies of the Asian continent. The major characters, places, and events of Asian mythology, as well as certain prevalent themes and cultural traditions, are listed alphabetically. There are, for example, entries for the god Śiva, Hinduism, Buddhism, Tibetan Buddhism, the theme of Sacrifice, the Hero Quest motif, and the story of the Chinese Cosmogony. The reader who chooses to read through the dictionary will follow a network of cross-referencing that will reveal a rich overall tapestry of mythology conveying the diversity, interrelatedness, and complex beauty that is Asia. The dominant mythologies here are clearly those of the national and/or geographic entities we now refer to as India, China, Tibet, Central Asia, Southeast Asia, and Japan. Iran stands as a continental divide of sorts between the traditions of the East and those of the West. The Aryans who invaded what is now Iran in the second millennium BCE brought with them a patriarchal "Indo-European" mythology similar to that of the Aryans who invaded India at about the same time, and in both cases, replaced or assimilated religious systems in which goddesses, for example, seem to have been important. But with the reforms of Zarathustra (Zoroaster) and the development of Zoroastrianism, the mythology of Iran came to have as much in common with the strongly dualistic Abrahamic religions of the Middle East as with those of Vedic and Hindu India. It is because of this divide that the Middle Eastern mythologies—those, for example, of the Sumerians, Babylonians, Canaanites, Assyrians, and those associated with Judaism, Christianity, and Islam—have not been included here, even though, technically, they are of the Asian continent. These mythologies might better be approached in a book on the mythology of the Middle East, which would also include Egypt, Asia Minor, and the Fertile Crescent.

Before pursuing the question of any mythology or mythological tradition, it is useful and even necessary to establish the definitions of terms being used in such a study. A *myth,* as used here, is a story—usually of unknown origins—by which a culture attempts to express its origins, its place in the universe, and/or its sense of identity and purpose. The term *mythology* refers specifically both to the study of myths and to the collected myths of a culture. Thus we speak of Greek mythology or Norse mythology, or, in the case of this book, of Asian mythology. Creation stories, stories of gods and goddesses, and stories of culture heroes are the most common forms of myth. To the extent that a *religion* is a system that lends authority to such stories, a religion is a mythological system. This is so whether we are speaking of so-called primitive animistic cults or the equally arbitrarily defined "great world religions."

The point is, a religious story is "holy scripture" to a believer and a *myth* to someone of another culture or belief system. Christians "believe"—often literally—in the virgin birth of Jesus and in his bodily resurrection. To a Hindu or a Buddhist, the stories of these events are clearly *myths,* because they describe phenomena that are too far outside of human experience to be believed. By the same token, the Christian sees the stories of the elephant-god Ganeśa or the resurrection of the ancient Egyptian god-man Osiris as perhaps "religious," perhaps even beautiful, but certainly bizarre and definitely *mythological* rather than literally true. In this book, then, there is little attempt to separate the terms *religion* and *mythology.* Religions, of course, are concerned with ritual, theology, ethics, and other elements as well as myth, but myths are the sacred stories of religion, the narratives that are used to support, explain, or justify rituals, theology, ethics, and so forth. When a myth or a mythological place or character is described in this book, then, there is no intention of implying falsehood or even illusion. In fact, to go one step further, as understood here, myths are stories that are literally or symbolically true to particular cultures and that contain elements in which outsiders with open minds can find archetypal or universal truth. In this latter sense, myths can be said to be the cultural vehicles for understandings that people in all corners of the world have shared. I may not believe that King Arthur pulled the sword from the rock, and a Zoroastrian might not believe that Jesus was born of a virgin, but we can both recognize the importance of crossing initiatory boundaries and of nurturing a higher state of being within ourselves.

There are those who would rightly question the appropriateness of defining a mythology by way of geographic boundaries. Asia is an immense region containing a great variety of cultures and a commensurate variety of religious systems and related mythologies. It is certainly possible, for example, to speak of the early indigenous mythologies of Japan or those of the Indus Valley in India, or of the emperor-god traditions of ancient China. And we can recognize valid categories, such as the peculiarly Japanese combination of the stories and characters of Shinto and Mahāyāna Buddhism. It is also reasonable to consider Vedic and Hindu mythology as a meaningful unit, and, as has been indicated, common Aryan roots can be established in the myths of ancient India and Iran out of which grew Vedism and Hinduism in India and Mazdaism and Zoroastrianism in Iran. Further, we can trace the movement of Buddhism from an Indian background, to Gautama Buddha, to Buddhist monks carrying their new message across Asia from India to Sri Lanka, Tibet, China, Southeast Asia, and Japan. During this long trek, Buddhist mythologies, affected by cultural differences, developed in many Asian forms over the centuries after the Buddha's death. But neither Vedic, Hindu, Zoroastrian, nor Buddhist myths are common to all of Asia, and again it must be pointed out that often they replaced, assimilated, or were partly assimilated by the many indigenous mythological traditions that were there before them. In short, to assume a common Asian mythology or mythological tradition would be as unrealistic, as to assume a common Middle Eastern or a common European mythology. Naturally, there are themes present in all Asian mythologies, but in most cases, these themes, or archetypal motifs, are common to mythologies all over the world. The Buddha and other Asian heroes are said to have been conceived miraculously; the same is said of Jesus, Theseus, and Quetzalcoatl. Many Asian mythological heroes go on quests; so do most heroes in other parts of the world. Thunderbolt-wielding judgmental patriarchal deities are important in many parts of Asia, but these deities have close relatives in other Indo-European cultures, such as those of the Semites in the Middle East and the people of Asia Minor, Greece, and Scandinavia. It is true that certain motifs, such as the earth-diver creation, seem to be peculiar to Asian societies and to their probable relatives in Native America, but earth-diver creation myths can be seen as cultural offshoots of a broader worldwide motif, one that suggests creation out of the void. In any case, earth-diver creations, while particularly prevalent in Central Asia, are by no means ubiquitous in the rest of Asia.

Having accepted the lack of any single Asian mythology, however, it is possible, even as we recognize the integrity of particular cultures and their mytho-religious systems, to take note of certain tendencies that seem to differentiate the mythologies of most of Asia (and perhaps Native America) from those of the rest of the world. First, it can safely be said that more than in the West, the mytho-religious systems of Asia stress the importance of moving beyond a personal individual life to a state of union with the Absolute source of being in the universe. Whether a practitioner of Daoism, Hinduism, Zen, or earlier forms of Buddhism, the Asian tends to see the world in both its evil and positive moments as a cosmic dance of which the individual is a part and in which one ideally "loses" oneself through meditation or some other discipline. To the extent that this is a unified view, it can be said that Asian mythologies suggest a universe in which everything is part of the Absolute, which itself is in every place but in no particular place. It may not be too extreme to suggest that all gods and goddesses in Asia are manifestations of the Absolute rather than personal or physical beings, so that, where people in the West tend to take their mythologies literally and to conceive of personal deities separate from themselves, Asians tend to see themselves as ideally liberated from ego and the delusion of the material world, free in the no-thing-ness of the Absolute. This may be one way of saying that the mystical mode is more widespread in Asia than it is in the western world.

A second related tendency is that underlying most Asian mythologies is an essential animism—a sense that as all gods, goddesses, and people are manifestations of the Absolute, so are all places and all objects. The world itself is sacred. All rivers and mountains and seas are holy. Whether the remnants of a sacrificed creator god or whether suffused with spirit beings, all elements of creation are seen as journeying companions through existence.

A third apparent tendency in Asian mythologies is the emphasis on a cyclical rather than a linear sense of time. Whereas people in the Abrahamic and ancient Norse and Greek religions, for instance, look ahead to the end of the world or the coming of a savior, or the discovery of "eternity," the Asian myths—aside from the special case of Zoroastrianism—remind us that we are already a part of eternity, which is a constant round of death and regeneration that can only be escaped by losing—rather than finding—the self.

It should be emphasized that these tendencies can very possibly be traced in part to the predominance in Asia of Buddhism, with its link to Vedism and Hinduism and its interrelationships with such indigenous religious traditions as Bön, Daoism, Confucianism, and Shinto. Once again, it must be said that Asian mythology as a single entity does not exist. Still, through immersion in the many mythologies of Asia, we may be able to achieve a sense of the separate but interrelated visions of reality characterizing that continent.

A

Aditi and the Ādityas—In Indian Vedic mythology (see Vedic Mythology), Aditi is "infinity," the source of all forms of consciousness including the divine characteristics of the gods themselves. Aditi is also "unity," whereas her sister Diti or Danu (see Diti) is that force which separates things. Aditi is the source of the divine within humanity. Diti reflects its flawed aspect. Vedic mythology celebrates Aditi as Earth, the goddess who is the source of all living things. She is the mother by the sage Kasyapa of the Ādityas, the "sons of Aditi," who are gods of the sun (one name for which is Āditya) and are the formative principles of the Universe. Among the personified Ādityas are Sūrya (see Sūrya), Mitra (see Mitra), Varuṇa (see Varuṇa), Aryaman (see Aryaman) and, perhaps most important, the great Vedic king of the gods, Indra (see Indra). In Buddhism (see Buddhism), Āditya is a name sometimes applied to the Buddha (see Gautama Buddha).

Advaita—Literally "nondual," *advaita* is the Hindu (see Hinduism entries) term for the state of nondifferentiation that is Brahman (see Brahman) or the absolute reality (see Advaita Vedānta).

Advaita Vedānta—One of several interpretations of Vedānta Hinduism (see Vedānta), Advaita Vedānta (see Advaita) was developed probably in the eighth and ninth centuries CE by the philosopher Śaṅkara. For followers of this branch of the religion, Brahman (see

Brahman) is the Absolute, the undifferentiated reality underlying all apparent reality. Even the differentiation between the individual (or self) and Brahman is ultimately illusory. The proper path for humans is to discover the oneness of the self (see Ātman) and Brahman. With this realization the individual achieves *mokṣa* (see *Mokṣa*) or release from the illusory state of worldly entanglements (see *Samsāra*).

Afterlife—Like most cultures around the world, Asian cultures have a sense of existence after death, but that existence is much less literal than the Elysian Fields and heavens and hells that mark Western mythology and religion. There is sometimes an underworld such as the one called Yomi (see Yomi) found in the Japanese story of Izanagi and Izanami, (see Izanagi and Izanami) or the Houses of Songs and Lies in Zoroastrianism (see Zoroastrian Afterlife). But often Asian afterlives are more philosophical states than literal places (see Fei-sheng, see Devayana). In most of the Indian cults, for example, afterlife is a state in which the individual develops into another being or is absorbed into the eternal flow or all encompassing void, the no-thing-ness that is, for example, the Buddhist nirvāna (see Nirvāna).

Agastya—Agastya (Agasti) was the great ascetic sage of Hindu mythology who defeated and controlled the monstrous Rāksaṣas of southern India.

Agni—A major Hindu god who appears originally in the *Ṛg Veda* (see *Ṛg Veda)* as one of the *asuras* (see *Asuras*) or Ādityas (see Aditi and the Ādityas)—Mitra, Varuṇa, Aryaman, Rudra, Uṣas, Indra—at the most obvious level, Agni is the god of fire. He is often opposed to Varuṇa (see Varuṇa), the god of waters, in philosophic dialogues. Sacrifice is associated with Agni; he carries sacrificial offerings to the gods. In a deeper sense he is the divine will without which nothing can happen in the universe. He is a hidden god—the divine fire in plants, in the earth, in animals, in the elements, in humans; he is the divine light by which we see, by which we are conscious. The sacrifice, of which Agni is at once the priest and the flame and the offering itself, is central to Hindu life. Thus, when he is depicted it is as a red man out of whose mouth shoot flames. He has three legs and seven arms and rides on a ram.

Many myths of Agni are related to his hidden aspect. In the *Mahābhārata* (see *Mahābhārata*), the gods roamed the world looking for Agni, who had hidden in the elemental waters. His hiding place was revealed by a frog, who had been burned by the god's heat. Agni was furious at the frog and decreed that he would no longer possess the sensation of taste. He then hid in a fig tree but was betrayed by the elephant, whose tongue he bent backward as punishment. After hiding in several other places and being betrayed by several other animals, whom he cursed, Agni was discovered in the *sami* tree, the wood of which is still used to create the fire of sacrifice. The gods asked Agni to father Skanda (sometimes said to have been fathered by Śiva), whose six heads represent what the Hindus see as the six seasons of the year (see Kārttikeya, see Śiva).

Ahiṁsā—Hindus (see Hinduism)—especially Brahmans (see Brahmans)—and Jains (see Jainism) practice essential nonviolence or *ahiṁsā* ("nonkilling") in relation to any living thing. In Jainism, where *ahiṁsā* is most strictly followed, the clear rule for monks is that all possible care must be taken not to harm living things while walking, acting, speaking, begging, or performing excretory acts.

Ahriman—see Angra Mainyu.

Ahura Mazda—The chief god of the ancient Iranians (see Mazdaism) and later the Zoroastrians (see Zoroastrianism), Ahura Mazda or Oromazdes or Ohrmazd first came to Iran during the Aryan (Indo-Iranian) invasions of the second millennium BCE as one of the *ahura* gods whose roots were in the ancient Indo-European past. His equivalent among the Aryans who invaded India at about the same time would have been Indra (see Indra) as revealed in the *Ṛg Veda* (see *Ṛg Veda*). It also seems likely that Ahura Mazda's nature is related to the Vedic Varuṇa (see Varuṇa). In both India and Iran the old gods seem to have been either *asuras* (*ahuras* in Iran) or *devas* (*daevas* in Iran). In the *Avesta* (see *Avesta*), the holy book of Zoroaster, or Zarathustra (see Zoroaster)—who lived perhaps as early as the middle of the second millennium BCE but probably not until the later part of that millennium—the daevas (see *daevas*) had become demons and a supreme god had emerged as Ahura Mazda (Ohrmazd). Ahura Mazda was the "Wise Lord," the sky-god organizer of the sun and the stars, the epitome of the true order of the universe. He is placed in opposition to an evil principle called Angra Mainyu, or Ahriman (see Angra Mainyu). According to one version of the myth—perhaps heretical for most Zoroastrians—Ahura Mazda and Angra Mainyu were both born of Zurvan, or Time (see Zurvan). When the evil principle escaped first from the primeval womb into the world, Zurvan was forced to divide Time in the world between good and evil until such time in the distant future when goodness would prevail. In fourth and fifth century *bas reliefs,* Ahura Mazda is depicted as a bearded male on a winged disk, a fact that seems to associate this supreme god with the sun, an appropriate association since light and fire are central factors in Zoroastrian ritual and dogma.

Ahuras—Ancient Iranian deities (see Ahura Mazda).

Ainu Mythology—Early non–Mongoloid inhabitants of the islands now called Japan, the non–Japanese-speaking Ainu were subjugated by the Japanese beginning in the early ninth century. The few Ainu who remain live in the northern islands. The essential dualism of Ainu mythology is expressed by a supreme deity in Heaven and evil deities who live in the world below. There is a fire goddess who presides over a kind of Last Judgment and there is a creation story that resembles the one in the Japanese *Nihongi* (see *Nihongi*). In this story a bird is sent down to earth to dry out some of the mud in the primordial slush so that islands can be formed for the Ainu (see Earth-Diver Creation). In one Ainu myth the creator is said to have sent a couple down to earth who gave birth to the first Ainu. The word *ainu* means human. Other myths say that the Ainu, who tend to have a great deal of body hair, are descended from the polar bear or a bear god. A bear sacrifice ritual is still practiced by the Ainu in which the sacrificed bear is sent "home" to the ancestors. The Ainu have a deluge myth in which a very few people escape to a mountain top. Many Ainu myths are contained in several heroic narratives, some as long as 15,000 lines, which were often sung by female shamans. (See *Kotan Utunnai,* and *The Woman of Poi-Soya.*)

Aizen-myō-ō—One of the *myō-ō* or *Vidyā-rāja* class of Japanese Buddhist deities, Aizen-myō-ō is the god of love. In fact, his name means "Love," and he represents the idea of love changed into the Buddhist desire for Enlightenment. Aizen is usually depicted with a red body possessing eight arms and three eyes on an angry face. A lion's head rests in his hair, symbolizing passion. He carries bows and arrows, which symbolize love as well as his role as a destroyer of evil.

Ālhā Epic—A popular epic cycle sung among the Hindi-speaking peoples of Northern India, the *Ālhā* epic tells of twelfth century wars in and around the city of Mahoba. Ālhā is the sole surviving warrior of Mahoba.

Alim Epic—Part of a larger epic cycle, the *Hudhud* (see *Hudhud*), this work is sung among the Ifugao people of the Philippines. Its primary subject is the Ifugao pantheon.

Altaic Mythology—The people living in the Altai Mountains of Mongolia possess a mythology that is influenced both by their own shamanistic (see Shamanism) past and their contact with Islam, Buddhism, Christianity, and even Zoroastrianism. Creation stories are especially important among the Altaic tribes. One story tells how the first man, Erlik, created by the god Ulgen from clay, was like the devil in the Hebrew creation, flung out of Heaven for attempting to usurp the creator's position. After Erlik's expulsion, Ulgen created the earth. As in the case of Satan in Genesis, the devil figure, Erlik, makes his way to earth and corrupts the first woman, bringing to humankind all the ills we now experience. In another Altaic creation myth, the first-man devil character tries unsuccessfully to fly higher than God and falls into the primeval waters and begs for God's help. God orders the devil to dive into the depths to find earth, and so the world is created. When the devil tries to hide some of the earth in his mouth so as to make his own world,

God discovers the trick and forces the devil to spit out the hidden material, which becomes the world's wetlands (see Earth-Diver Creation, Central Asian Mythology, Siberian entries, Turko-Mongolian Mythology).

Amaterasu—Considered to be the prime ancestor of the Japanese emperor, the Sun Goddess Amaterasu-ō-Mikami, queen of the *kami* (see *kami*) or the forces of Nature, is honored especially at her temple at Ise, Japan. As the Rising Sun, she gives spiritual power to her people. Amaterasu had a brother named Susanowo (see Susanowo). When Susanowo, the storm god, visited his sister in Heaven, he produced five gods by biting her necklaces and blowing a cloud over them. Amaterasu had created three goddesses by breaking her brother's sword, chewing on the pieces, and blowing a cloud over them. When later, in a drunken fury, Susanowo disrupted and destroyed much of Heaven and Earth and Amaterasu's home, the goddess hid in a cave, depriving the world of her light and warmth and causing the death of plants and animals. The gods and goddesses after several failed attempts to lure Amaterasu back into the world, asked the goddess Ama no Uzume to dance in front of the cave. She did so lasciviously, dropping her clothes in the process, that the gods were overcome with such loud laughter that Amaterasu became curious and opened the door to her cave. In so doing she noticed the reflection of herself in a mirror the gods had hung outside her door. Overcome by her own beauty, she left her cave to examine herself more closely, allowing the gods to rope off the door. Thus the world was bright and warm again, and life returned to it. It is said that in later years Amaterasu gave her jewels and mirror to her grandson Ninigi who went down to earth as the first ruler. Her brother Susanowo was banished from Heavens (see Izumo Cycle).

Ameretat—Representing immortality, Ameretat is one of the Persian Zoroastrian (see Zoroastrian entries) deities—the *Amesa Spentas* (see *Amesa Spentas*). She is particularly associated with Haurvatat or prosperity and with the Earth patroness Armaiti (see Haurvatat and Armaiti).

Amesa Spentas—The *Amesa Spentas* are the beneficent immortals or mortal saints (they also take human form by way of the qualities they represent) who, with Ahura Mazda, the Wise Lord (see Ahura Mazda), or within the prophet Zarathustra (Zoroaster) or other humans who adhere to divine truth *(asha),* form a spiritual pantheon of sorts in Zoroastrianism (see *Asha,* see Zoroastrian entries). These are the *Yazata* or "Venerables," gods created by God (Ahura Mazda). However analyzed, they are crucial to Zoroastrian thought. Specifically, they are Vohu Manah ("Good Thought"), Asha Vahishta ("Best Truth"), Khshathra ("Desirable Dominion"), Armaïti ("Beneficent Devotion"), Haurvatat ("Wholeness"), and Ameretat ("Immortality"). Sometimes Ahura Mazda himself is seen as the first of seven *Amesa Spentas.* Other Iranian deities, which have equivalents in India, are Hoama, Anahita, Mithra, Vāyu, and Verethraghna, all representing moral values or natural phenomena (see the individual deity entries).

Amida Buddha—Amida Nyorai (the Buddha Amitābha), the Buddha of Pure Light, is as close to the Western idea of God that we come in Japanese Buddhism (see Japanese Buddhism). Statues of Amida abound in Japan. Amida promises salvation to all who invoke his name. Pure Land originally developed in China and is based on the Indian (Sanskrit) Sukhāvatī. In the tenth century a monk named Genshin emphasized the idea of rebirth into Amida's paradise or "Pure Land." Thus the Japanese version of "Pure Land" Buddhism was born (see Pure Land Buddhism). It was developed further by the monks Honen and then Shinran in the twelfth and thirteenth centuries with emphasis on salvation through Amida's grace.

Anahita (Anahid)—The only important goddess of Zoroastrianism (see Zoroastrian entries), Ardva Sura Anahita ("The High, Powerful, and Immaculate One") is depicted as a beautiful young woman with full breasts. She is dressed in elaborate clothing, complete with jewels and a halo-crown of starry light. Anahita began as a goddess of the primal waters. As such she is associated with all bodily secretions as well as bodies of water. Later she teaches Zarathustra (see

Zoroaster) how to perform sacrifices and fight for justice among humans. Anahita aids Ahura Mazda in his work as Creator.

Ānanda—The cousin of Gautama Buddha, Ānanda became his primary disciple.

Ananta—The serpent Ananta, or Śeṣa, on whom the Hindu god Viṣṇu (see Viṣṇu, see Vedic cosmogony) sleeps, represents eternity or infinity. Sometimes Viṣṇu himself is called Ananta.

Ancestor Cults—In many cosmogonies of Asia, as in similar myths in other parts of the world, the creation of the world is followed by the creation of beings who become the ancestors of the human race. In Laos, for example, New Year celebrations feature the return of the first ancestors decked in elaborate masks. The worship of ancestors of particular clans or families is particularly important in Hinduism (see Hinduism) and Buddhism (see Buddhism) as well as in Shintoism (see Shinto) and Confucianism (see Confucianism).

Angkor—A collection of impressive ruins in Cambodia, Angkor was the center of Khmer civilization. There are several myths surrounding its origins. It is said that five goddesses *(devī)* came down to earth from the god Indra's (see Indra) Heaven. One remained behind for six years, on Indra's order, as the wife of a simple gardener. By weaving wonderful clothes to sell, the *devī* brought riches to her husband, and they had a son who became the great architect Viśvakarman (see Viśvakarman), as he is called in Sanskrit in India or, in Cambodia, an aspect of Viṣṇu (see Viṣṇu) called Braḥ Bisnukar (Viṣṇukarman). It seems that as a youth Braḥ Bisnukar set off to find his mother after she returned to Heaven. In Heaven he was introduced to Indra, who enrolled him in his heavenly workshops. There he learned to be the master of all human architects. When Indra named his own son, Braḥ Khet Mala, King of Cambodia, he sent Braḥ Biskunar to Earth to build Angkor so that the son could be reminded of the heavenly paradise of his father.

Angra Mainyu—Sometimes called Ahriman in Zoroastrian mythology (see Zoroastrian entries), Angra Mainyu is the twin brother of

Spenta Mainyu ("Holy Spirit") or Vohu Mainyu (the spirit of "Right Thought) or, according to some, of Ahura Mazda (the "Wise Lord") himself (see Ahura Mazda). As such, he is the source of the dualism peculiar to Zoroastrianism—the evil force that opposes the good, which is Ahura Mazda. Zarathustra (see Zoroaster) calls on his followers to concern themselves with this duality in the universe and to make the right choices accordingly.

Animism—Animism is the belief that all things are given life—that is, animated—by spirits. The word often refers specifically to the idea that aspects of nature—rivers, mountain, trees, and so forth—were originally parts of immortal beings. Animism plays an important role in many creation stories in Asia and elsewhere (see, for example, Chinese Cosmogony, Bön, Korean Mythology, Phi).

Aṇṇaṉmār—This folk epic of the Tamil Nadu region of India has been sung by professional storytellers at festivals since the fifteenth century. The narrative tells of a grandfather who leaves his famine-stricken home in search of work. When the man succeeds in gaining farm work for a Chola king, the king rewards him and his brothers with gifts of land. The brothers become jealous of their older brother and try to cheat him of his land—especially as his oldest son is childless and therefore weakened in the eyes of his peers. Although Śiva (see Śiva) and Viṣṇu (see Viṣṇu) provide a son for the childless man to adopt, the evil uncles eventually deprive the boy of his grandfather and father's land. The boy spends time in the wilderness protected by Viṣṇu until he marries a woman named Tāmarai and returns to reclaim his land in spite of the antagonism of his cousins. After twenty-one years, Tāmarai gives birth magically to twin boys, under Viṣṇu's protection against the evil cousins, who try to prevent the birth. The twins are hidden from the evil uncles and fed on tiger's milk by the goddess Cellāttā. As the twins are hidden, Tāmarai and her husband, who also have a daughter, appear to be sonless. Once more, the cousins take away their land and send the old couple into exile. Eventually the twins join their parents and lead them in an epic battle to regain their land. After the death of their parents and the defeat of their cousins, the twins rule all of the land in question. When the twins become involved in wars with certain hunters, many of their followers are killed, and in despair they kill themselves, only to be briefly revived by their sister. When all three finally die they are carried off to the home of the gods by Śiva's representative.

Antaragaṭṭamma—This epic of Dravidian (see Dravidians) India is of the type that is told in homes rather than at religious festivals. It concerns the whole question of caste. In the story a *brahman* (see *Brahmans*) girl is left in the wilderness by her parents because she menstruates before she has been promised in marriage. A man finds her and adopts her until a member of the "Untouchable" caste, who has seen her and fallen in love with her disguises himself as a *brahman* and succeeds in winning her hand. The couple has two children, who eventually discover their father doing the work of the Untouchables and tell their mother. Realizing that she has been deceived into marrying improperly and that she is, therefore, corrupted, the *brahman* wife becomes so enraged that she turns into a Māri—a Kālī-like goddess (see Kālī) called Antaragaṭṭama (she of the lolling tongue)—hungry for revenge. The many victims of her anger include her two sons and her husband, whose blood she drinks.

Āraṇyakas—*Āraṇyakas* are Vedic texts (see *Vedas*) in India meant to comment on the earlier *Brāhmanas* (see *Brāhmanas*).

Arhat—In Buddhism (see Buddhism), the *arhat* is literally the "worthy" one who is at the final stage before Enlightenment. He is, therefore, deserving of special respect. Usually the *arhat* is an ascetic. He is no longer attached to the world of form and the senses. For Hīnayāna and Theravāda Buddhists (see Hīnayāna Buddhism, Theravāda Buddhism) there can be only one Buddha in any era and in our era Gautama Buddha (see Gautama Buddha), "*the* Buddha" has already existed. Therefore, the state of the *arhat* is the highest achievable for others. The reformist Mahāyāna Buddhists (see Mahāyāna Buddhism) consider the *arhat* idea a self-centered concept and have generally substituted for it the ideal of the *bodhisattva* (see *Bodhisattva*), who *could* become a *buddha*, but who chooses rather to work with compassion in this world for the enlightenment of others.

Arjuna—The third of the five Pāṇḍava brothers (see Pāṇḍavas) who struggle against their Kaurava cousins in the great Hindu epic, the *Mahābhārata* (see *Mahābhārata*), it is Arjuna who is the recipient of Lord Kṛṣṇa's (see Kṛṣṇa) teachings in the part of the epic called the *Bhagavadgītā* (see *Bhagavadgītā*).

Armaïti—One of the *Amesa Spentas* (see *Amesa Spentas*) or major deities associated with the Zoroastrian (see Zoroastrianism) supreme god Ahura Mazda (see Ahura Mazda), Spenta Armaïti, or Spendarmat in Pahlavi, is the goddess of the Earth and is the essence of devotion and fidelity. Tradition says that she once appeared to Zoroaster (see Zoroaster).

Aryaman—Aryaman is one of the Vedic Indian Āditya*s* (see Aditi and the Ādityas). He is associated with rulership.

Aryans—The Aryans (Sanskrit: *ārya;* Old Iranian: *airya*) were Indo-European tribes who migrated from Eastern Europe to Central Asia in the third millennium BCE. They were patriarchal warriors who brought powerful male gods with them as they migrated eventually into Greece, Anatolia, the Fertile Crescent, Iran, and India. For some time (c. 2200–2000 BCE), the ancestors of the Vedic (after the *Vedas*—later Indian) and Iranian (Avestan—after the *Avesta*) Aryans lived together in the same region—probably around Balkh, and developed the religious positions that were the source for Zoroastrianism and Hinduism (see Zoroastrian entries, see Hindu entries). The Aryans who invaded India and Iran in the second millennium BCE were, therefore, closely related to each other. Thus we have the term Indo-Iranian, which is often used synonymously with Aryan. The Indo-Iranian gods were divided into *Asuras* (*Ahura* in Iran) and *Devas* (*daeva* in Iran). The protoreligion was based on a universal law that became the Vedicṛta (see *Vedas*) and the Avestan *asa* (see *Avesta*). The Vedic supervisor of the law was Varuṇa (see Varuṇa) and the Avestan head god was Ahura Mazda (see Ahura Mazda). During the migration to India and the wars involved with it, the cult of Indra (see Indra) as king of the gods developed. Fire worship was central to the Aryans and to their Vedic and Avestan expressions, as was the tradition of the holy drink—the Vedic *soma* (see *Soma*) and the Avestan *haoma*. Powerful sacred verses or *mantras* (see *Mantra*) and hymns were important to both groups. There was the hope of an afterlife (see Afterlife) and there were sacrificial rituals. Aryans generally looked down on the darker-skinned "barbarian" peoples they conquered—especially in India. The mytho-religious system of the Indo-Aryans is revealed by what we now call the Vedic texts, the best known of which is the *Ṛg Veda* (see *Ṛg Veda*). Hinduism developed from the Vedic tradition in India and Zoroastrianism out of the early Aryan religion and mythology expressed eventually in the *Avesta* in Iran.

Asha (Arta or Ashavahisht)—Asha is one of the *Amesa spentas* (see Amesa Spentas) in Iranian Zoroastrianism (see Zoroastrian entries). He is the guardian of fire and of moral and physical order.

Asuras—In a sense, *asuras* are demons in Hindu mythology. That is, they oppose the *devas*—the celestial gods. But when taken individually they are of equal status with the *devas,* and a great god such as Varuṇa (see Varuṇa) can be an *asuras*. In the Vedic tradition (see Vedism), *devas* and *asuras* are both offspring of the creator Prajāpati (see Prajāpati), or later of Brahmā (see Brahmā). But the constant struggle between these two forces is a theme of later Hindu mythology, in which the *devas* occupy Heaven, humans the earth, and *asuras* the dark depths.

Aśvins—The Aśvins are twin gods who engender the Pāṇḍava (see Pāṇḍavas) twins Nakula and Sahadeva in Pāṇḍu's wife, Madri, in the Hindu epic the *Mahābhārata* (see *Mahābhārata*).

Atharva Veda—The fourth *Veda* (see *Vedas*) of India, probably composed later than the *Ṛg Veda*, the *Sāma Veda*, and the *Yajur Veda*. The *Atharva Veda* consists of myths, magical formulae, spells, prayers, verses, and hymns and is named after Atharavan, a priest in charge of the worship of fire and *soma* (see *Soma*).

Ātman—In Advaita Vedānta (see Advaita Vedānta) and other branches of Hinduism (see Hinduism), Brahman (see Brahman) is the absolute that is transcendent—nowhere—but imminent—everywhere—as the Self or Ātman within all things. In the *Upaniṣads* (see *Upaniṣads*) Brahman is the ultimate whole, while Ātman is the individual soul that can merge with Brahman in mystical oneness, a state of ultimate consciousness or identity.

Aurobindo Ghose—The founder of Integral Yoga, a system combining older forms of *yoga* (see *yoga*), which works toward a consciousness change in the cosmos, Aurobindo (1872–1950) was also a nationalist, political thinker, and an expert on Indian mythology and religion.

Avalokiteśvara—The *bodhisattva* (see *Bodhisattva*) of compassion, Avalokiteśvara is associated with Tārā (see Tārā), the Tibetan Buddhist (see Tibetan Buddhism) goddess. It is sometimes suggested that Avalokiteśvara is a male form of the Chinese Buddhist goddess of mercy, Guanyin (See Guanyin, Kannon).

Avatar—The idea of the avatar or *avatāra* is central to Hindu mythology (see Hinduism entries), especially to the concept of the god Viṣṇu (see Viṣṇu). An *avatāra* is the earthly form assumed by a deity (see Avatars of Viṣṇu).

Avatars of Viṣṇu—The god Viṣṇu (see Viṣṇu) assumes various earthly forms in Hindu mythology (see Hinduism entries) in order to restore cosmic order. The first avatar was the great horned fish who saved Manu, the first human, from the deluge that occurred at the beginning of this world (see Manu). The second avatar was the great horned boar, who saved the goddess Pṛthivi ("Earth") from the demon Hiraṇyākṣa (see the Boar, see Pṛthivi). As the Tortoise, Viṣṇu is the cosmic foundation on which rests the churning stick used by the gods and demons in their act of creation in the ocean of milk (see Ananta). As the man-lion (see Narasiṃha), Viṣṇu was able to defeat the demon Hiraṇyakaśipu, brother of Hiraṇyākṣa, who was invulnerable to humans and animals but, apparently, not to a combination of the two. Hiraṇyakaśipu, also known as Hiraṇya, was no favorite of Viṣṇu since the demon persecuted his own son Prahlādā, a devotee of the god. When the *asura* (see *asuras*) Bali took over the world from the gods, he agreed that Viṣṇu, who had taken the form of a dwarf, could own whatever he could cover in three strides. The dwarf, Vāmana, immediately took on his real being as Viṣṇu and in three steps encompassed the whole world for the gods. When the *kṣatriya* (warrior) class persecuted the *brahman* (see *Brahmans*) class, Viṣṇu became axe-wielding Paraśurāma and defeated them, thus establishing the theological and social dominance of the *brahmans*. The two most famous avatars of Viṣṇu are Rāma (Rāmancandra), the hero of the Hindu epic the *Rāmāyaṇa* (see *Rāmāyaṇa* and Rāma) and Kṛṣṇa (See Kṛṣṇa), who appears in, among many other places, the epic *Mahābhārata* (see *Mahābhārata*) as a supporter of Arjuna (see Arjuna) and his Pāṇḍava (see Pāṇḍavas) brothers against their Kaurava cousins. Kṛṣṇa is particularly known for his preaching to Arjuna as his charioteer in the *Bhagavadgītā* (see *Bhagavadgītā*). Kṛṣṇa and Rāma have become, in effect, popular Hindu deities. It is said that the Buddha (see Gautama Buddha) is also an avatar of Viṣṇu, coming to preach gentleness. And finally, Viṣṇu will appear at the end of this age as a human, Kalki, riding on a white horse.

Avesta—The *Avesta* is the Bible of Zoroastrianism (see Zoroastrian entries). Most of the original *Avesta,* much of which predates the Zoroastrian reforms of the old Iranian religion (see Aryans) has been lost. The most important part of the *Avesta* is the *Yasna* ("Sacrifice," related to the Hindu *Yajna*), verses meant to be used by priests during sacrifice rituals. Contained in the *Yasna* are the *Gāthās*, "songs" said to have been written by Zarathustra (see Zoroaster), containing the essence of the prophet's philosophy. Also important in the *Avesta* are the *Yashts*, hymns that tell us much of what we know of Zoroastrian mythology.

B

Balarāma—The son of Vasudeva, the "lord of wealth" and Rohiṇī or "red cow," both of whom are associated with the moon, Balarāma ("lover of power") is Lord Kṛṣṇa's (see Kṛṣṇa) older brother and companion. Always a complement to his brother, Balarāma is white while Kṛṣṇa is black. As Kṛṣṇa is an avatar of Viṣṇu (see Avatars of Viṣṇu), Balarāma is an incarnation of the world serpent Śeṣa (see Ananta), on whom Viṣṇu (see Viṣṇu) sleeps. Like Kṛṣṇa, he is placed in the care of Nanda ("Joy"), the cowherd. Balarāma's birth was extraordinary. He was conceived in Devakī (see Devakī), whose children her brother, the demon Kaṃsa, threatened to kill. But by the power of Viṣṇu, Balarāma was moved to Rohinī's womb for birth.

Balinese Mythology—A visitor to Bali will be struck by the importance of the stories from the Hindu epic the *Rāmāyaṇa* (see *Rāmāyaṇa*) in various rituals. In fact, Bali is the only Hindu-Buddhist civilization in Indonesia. The official religion is Bali Hinduism (see Hinduism). Old Balinese and Sanskrit texts on the island indicate Indian influence from perhaps as early as the first millennium BCE. These texts reveal the presence in Old Balinese mythology and religion of such familiar Hindu figures as Gaṇeśa (see Gaṇeśa), Durgā (see Durgā), various Buddhas, Viṣṇu (see Viṣṇu), and Śiva (see Śiva). All the sacred texts of Bali are dedicated to the goddess of speech and wisdom, Sarasvatī (see Sarasvatī), who is the wife of Brahmā (see Brahmā). The Balinese say that the Hindu world center, Mount Meru (see Meru), is in fact their own sacred mountain, Gunung Agung (see Mountain Mythology). The Balinese also have Anantaboga, their own version of the primeval Indian serpent Ananta (see Ananta). There are also remnants in Balinese mythology of pre-Hindu gods such as the popular trickster-like Twalen, who is assimilated into Hinduism as a brother of the great god Siwa (see Śiva).

Ballad of the Hidden Dragon—This Chinese ballad—probably sung first in the eleventh century and written down in the twelfth—was of the *zhukongdiao* type. That is, it was composed of alternate sections of poetry and prose. The subject of the hero of *The Hidden Dragon* is Liu Zhiyuan during the years before he became Emperor in 947 CE. In the ballad, the trials of the hidden dragon (that is, the future emperor) are narrated. After many years of exile and separation from his betrothed, Liu Zhiyuan is reconciled with all those who have harmed him.

Banāras—Banāras (Benares, also Kāśi or Vārānasī) is a *tīrtha,* a spiritual pilgrimage city on the sacred Ganges (see Ganges) River in Northern India. Pilgrims come from all over India to bathe in the river at Banāras. The Buddha (see Gautama Buddha) preached near Banāras in the Anandavana (the "forest of Bliss"), and deities have always been worshipped there. The god Śiva, as Viśvanātha, "Universal Lord" (see Śiva), is the dominant god at Banāras. The *Skanda Purāṇa* (see *Purāṇas*) tells how Śiva's *liṅga*, or sacred phallus (see *Liṅga*) of light arose from the earth itself to pierce the skies above at Banāras. It is also said that Śiva sent all the gods to his sacred city, which he entered in glory after Viṣṇu (see Viṣṇu) had helped him rid it of its king.

Bantugan—An epic-like narrative poem or *darangan* of Philippine Moro culture.

Bardo Todrol (Bar-do'i-thos-grol)—The *Bardo Todrol* or *Tibetan Book of the Dead,* refers to the brief period between death and rebirth, during which the consciousness remains near the body seeking release into a form of Enlightenment. If the consciousness fails to achieve enlightenment it remains in the physical world as an unhappy ghost of sorts until the Lord of the Otherworld reviews the demons and desires of the individual's former life (see Tibetan Buddhism).

Bear Sacrifice—See Ainu Mythology.

Benzaiten—A transplant to Japan of the Hindu Sarasvatī—the sacred river personified as the goddess of Speech and Wisdom and wife of Brahmā (see Sarasvatī)—Benten, as she is most often known, is the Japanese Buddhist and Shinto goddess of Good Speech and Music. Sometimes she is depicted with two arms, sometimes with eight. She always carries objects symbolic of her meaning—for example, the lute for music, the sword and jewel for wisdom and sacred vows. She is one of the Seven Gods of Good Fortune (see Seven Gods of Good Fortune).

Bhaga—One of the Vedic Ādityas (see Aditi and the Ādityas), Bhaga is the dispenser of wealth and the brother of the Dawn (see Uṣas).

Bhagavadgītā—"The Blessed Lord's Song," the *Bhagavadgītā,* was composed about two thousand years ago and is generally considered to be the most beautiful religious writing in India. Since it is part of the epic the *Mahābhārata* (see *Mahābhārata*), the *Gītā* is technically *smṛti* (see *smṛti*) or traditional literature rather than *śruti* (see *śruti*), or revealed sacramental text. In effect, however, the *Bhagavadgītā* has attained the level of *śruti.* More than any other Hindu text, it is consulted as a source of truth and wisdom. The poem itself, which is placed in Book VI of the *Mahābhārata*, is made up of seven hundred Sanskrit verses divided into eighteen sections. The source of the wisdom contained in these verses is the Lord Kṛṣṇa (see Kṛṣṇa), who, as an avatar of the god Viṣṇu (see Viṣṇu, Avatars of Viṣṇu), teaches the Pāṇḍava (see Pāṇḍavas) hero Arjuna (See Arjuna). The sermon takes place in the middle of the battlefield. Kṛṣṇa is at first in his form as mortal ally and charioteer of Arjuna. The Pāṇḍava hero has suddenly been overcome by questions about the mass killing that the battle will entail. Kṛṣṇa answers that Arjuna must follow his proper social role or *dharma* (see *Dharma*) as a member of the warrior caste, without considering the outcome. Sometimes becoming Viṣṇu himself, Kṛṣṇa tells Arjuna that, in any case, the individual is immortal, only appearing to control his destiny. The essence of Kṛṣṇa's teaching is that the individual is ultimately linked to an ultimate divine reality. In terms of the mythology contained in the *Gītā,* Kṛṣṇa-Viṣṇu reveals himself as the personal embodiment of supreme primal power—of the impersonal Brahmān (see Brahmān). He appears to Arjuna as the container of every kind of place and being, of the gods themselves, even as Time and the Universe itself. In the epic poem, therefore, the relationship of Arjuna to Kṛṣṇa stands as a metaphor for the real relationship between humanity and divinity in the world.

Bhakti—The Sanskrit word for something approximating "devotion" or "reverence," *bhakti* is expressed traditionally through Hindu ritual sacrifices, ascetic practices, and hymns and prayers. Different kinds of *bhakti* apply to the worship of particular deities. Thus followers of Śiva (see Śaivas) have one kind of *bhakti* and devotees of Devī as Śakti (see Śakti, Śāktas), or creative goddess power, have another. Worshippers following a *bhaktimarga*, a *bhakti* path, generally believe in only one personal god, the *Īśvara* or Iṣṭadevatā. The goal of the *bhakta* is union of some sort with the deity in question.

Bhīma—See Pāṇḍavas.

Bhīṣma—An incantation of Dyaus (see Dyaus) in the Indian epic, the *Mahābhārata* (see *Mahābhārata*), Bhīṣma is a son of the sacred Ganges (see Ganges) and a moral leader of great stature.

Birhor Mythology—The Birhors are a Central Indian tribe who do not subscribe to the classical Hindu caste and religious system but who, like most of the nonclassical tribes of the region, sometimes make use of Hindu deities and heroes in their myths. The Birhors tell their own version of the *Rāmāyaṇa* epic (see *Rāmāyaṇa*), for example, in which the monkey hero Hanumān (see Hanumān) has a Birhor uncle. The Birhor creation myth is of particular interest because it is an earth-diver story such as those found in Central

Asia and native North America (see Earth-Diver Creation). In the Birhor version, the creator, Singbonga, arises from the depths of the primal waters through the stem of a lone lotus. Sitting on the lotus, he decides to create the world and sends a series of animals into the depths to find mud with which to work. It is the leech who succeeds in this task after other creatures fail. The leech swallows some mud and spits it into the creator's hand. Out of this mud Singbonga makes various animals and, after several false tries, the human being.

Bishamon—Sometimes known as Tamon-tenno, Bishamon is the Japanese Buddhist-Shinto (see Shinto entries) equivalent of the Indian god-king Vaiśravana (See Vaiśravana), one of the four guardians of the world's directions. The four god-kings were adopted by Japanese Buddhism (see Japanese Buddhism) as protectors of the law. By the ninth century, Bishamon was being worshipped in certain Buddhist monasteries as a curer of sickness, and by the fifteenth century he was known as a dispenser of wealth. Bishamon wears armor and holds a spear. Often he is depicted standing on a monster he has slain. He is one of the Seven Gods of Fortune (see Seven Gods of Fortune).

Boar—The ancient *Taittirīya Saṃhītā* and *Śatapatha Brāhmaṇa* of India tell how the creator Prajāpati (see Prajāpati) became a boar and spread out the earth, who thus became Pṛthivi (see Pṛthivi)—the "extended one"—and gave birth to many gods. In the *Viṣṇu Purāṇa* and *Kālikā Purāṇa* (see *Purāṇas*), Viṣṇu (see Viṣṇu), as Nārāyana (see Nārāyana), in association with Brahmā (see Brahmā), is the earth-diver (see Earth-Diver Creation) who in the form of the Great Horned Boar saves Pṛthivi, the earth, by raising her from the primeval waters on what is, in effect, his phallic tusk (see Avatars of Viṣṇu).

Bodhi Tree—The Bodhi or Bo Tree is the sacred tree, the tree of Wisdom or Enlightenment *(bodhi)* under which the Buddha sat to gain Enlightenment (see Gautama Buddha) in Bodhgaya, Bihar.

Bodhidharma—Zen Buddhism (see Zen Buddhism), a Japanese version of the meditative and ecstatic form of Mahāyāna (see Mahāyāna)

Buddhism, is said to have been brought to China from India by the fifth century CE Bodhidharma, the twenty-eighth successor to Gautama Buddha (see Gautama Buddha), the Buddha Sākyamuni. There are many legends or myths associated with Bodhidharma. One story says that when he came to China, the sage crossed the Yang-tse on a reed and that he spent nine years without moving in the absorbing meditation now called *zazen* (see *zazen*). Bodhidharma became the founder of Chan, the Chinese version of Zen, a version that also owes much to the philosophy of Daoism (see Daoism). Another story tells how Bodhidharma was poisoned before he could return to his native India. Although he had been buried in China, he was seen walking along the road to India wearing only one sandal. When his grave was opened, there was nothing there but one sandal. In Japan, Bodhidharma is called Daruma and doll replicas of him are given out as rewards for concentration.

Bodhisattva—Depending on the sect of Buddhism (see Buddhism), the word *bodhisattva* has essentially two meanings. Literally, a *bodhisattva* is a person who is seeking Enlightenment *(bodhi).* In early Pāli (see Pāli) Buddhism—Buddhism contained in the Pāli as opposed to Sanskrit texts; for example, Theravāda (see Theravāda Buddhism) and other forms of Hīnayāna Buddhism (see Hīnayāna Buddhism), the so-called "small vehicle" of India, Burma, Sri Lanka, Cambodia, and Laos—the word refers to particular beings, saints (see *arhat*) in past eons who were on the path to full Enlightenment or Nirvāna. It refers especially to the pre-enlightenment stages of Gautama Buddha (see Gautama Buddha), the Buddha Sākyamuni, who is commonly called simply "the Buddha." In later or Mahāyāna Buddhism (see Mahāyāna Buddhism)—the "great vehicle" of Nepal, Sikkhim, Tibet, China, Mongolia, Vietnam, Korea, and Japan—the *bodhisattva* is the compassionate person whose life is dedicated to the salvation of others and to becoming a Buddha only in some far distant eon. The Mahāyāna Buddhists thus stress the possibility for many people of the "bodhisattva path" (in Sanskrit the *Bodhisattvayāna* or *bod-*

hisattvacarya) leading to enlightenment, and there are many celebrated *bodhisattvas* (See Buddhism, Avalokiteśvara).

Bön—Bön is the ancient indigenous pre-Buddhist religion of Tibet. It was shamanistic (see Shamanism) and animistic (see Animism) in nature. After the rise of Buddhism it was assimilated to some extent into the practices of the new religion (see Tibetan entries).

Book of Changes—See *Yijing (I Ching).*

Brahmā—Brahmā is the primary creator god in Hindu mythology. With Viṣṇu (see Viṣṇu) the "preserver" and Śiva (see Śiva) the "destroyer" he forms a *trimūrti*—a trinity of sorts. In terms of worship, however, he does not have the importance of the other two gods. If there is a worshipped trinity in India, Devī, the "Goddess" (see Devī) in her many forms would make up the third part with Viṣṇu and Śiva. Still, Brahmā is of great mythological importance. As the creator in the *Purāṇas* (see *Purāṇas*), he is derived from the creator god Prajāpati (see Prajāpati) of the ancient *Brāhmaṇas* (see *Brāhmaṇas*, Vedic Cosmogony), and sometimes he is considered the same being as Prajāpati. The name Brahmā is the masculine Sanskrit form corresponding to the neuter Brahman or Brahma—the Absolute on which the whole universe is based (see Brahman). But Brahmā, although a creative aspect of Brahman, is not Brahman. In fact, Viṣṇu is more likely to be seen as a physical expression of the Absolute, as in the myth of his sleeping on the primal serpent (see Ananta, Vasuki, Śeṣa) in the primal ocean of milk—out of time and out of space. It is in this myth that Brahmā appears seated, as the first conscious deity, on a lotus that emerges from Viṣṇu's navel. This Brahmā has four faces and four arms that hold the sacred books—the *Vedas* (see *Vedas*)—that exist before creation and give him the authority to create. In the post-Vedic *Laws of Manu* (see *Laws of Manu*), however, Brahmā creates a cosmic golden egg-womb *(hiraṇyagarbha)* from his seed. After a time in the primordial waters, Brahmā takes form from the egg as the cosmic man Puruṣa (see Puruṣa). Brahmā's other methods of creation are many. He copulates, masturbates, and thinks things into being. Sometimes the elements of creation develop animistically (see Animism) from dismembered or sacrificed parts of his body Brahmā's wife is Sarasvatī (see Sarasvatī) who, in the *Ṛg Veda* (see *Ṛg Veda*) is the primal Word or Vāc—that is, the articulation of the Creator, or his *śakti* (see *Śakti*). She is the "mother" of the *Vedas*.

Brahman—Brahman is the Hindu Absolute of the Vedānta tradition (see Vedānta). In the Vedic (see *Vedas*) hymns the neuter noun *brahman* (or brahma) refers to the power of the word and a *brahman* (see *Brahmans*) or *brāhmaṇa* is a member of the priestly caste who understands the word. In the *Upaniṣads* (see *Upaniṣads*) Brahman becomes the eternal first cause, present everywhere and nowhere, always and never—the ultimate unknowable mystery or riddle of the universe. The closest one can come to revealing what Brahman is is to say or write the sacred syllable "Oṃ" (see *Oṃ*). Brahman can be incarnated in Brahmā (see Brahmā), and Viṣṇu (see Viṣṇu), and Śiva (see Śiva), or Devī (see Devī), but when the Absolute takes no form there is no existence. To put it another way, everything that is owes its existence to Brahman.

Brāhmaṇas—These ancient texts are part of Hindu writing designated as *śruti* (see *Śruti*) or sacred knowledge. Each of the four *Vedas* (see *Vedas*) is made up of poetic hymns and prayers (*Saṃithās*) to which are attached one or more *brāhmaṇas,* theological revelations in prose. They describe certain rituals and myths and then provide explications or *arthavādas*. The religion of the *Brāhmaṇas* is one centered in rites of sacrifice rather than in the gods themselves. *Āraṇyakas* (see *Āraṇyakas*) and *Upaniṣads* (see *Upaniṣads*) can be thought of as extensions of the *Brāhmaṇas*. The word *brāmaṇa* also refers to the *brāmaṇa* caste (see Brahmans).

Brahmanism—Brahmanism refers to the whole way of life associated with the Brahman caste in Hindu India (see Brahmans). Specifically, Brahmanism is a development of earlier Vedism (see Vedism), which was the religion of the Indo-European Aryans who entered India in the second millennium BCE. Brahmanism, like Vedism, reveres the ancient rituals and sacred texts or *śruti* (see *śruti*)—the *Vedas* (see *Vedas*) and the *Brāhmaṇas*, *Upaniṣads*, and

Āraṇyakas (see *Brāhmaṇas*, *Upaniṣads*, and *Āraṇyakas*) that grew out of them—but it also places a great deal of trust in the myths contained in less sacred texts or *smṛti* (see *smṛti*) such as the epics, the *Mahābhārata* (see *Mahābhārata*) and the *Rāmāyaṇa* (see *Rāmāyaṇa*), the *Purāṇas* (see *Purāṇas*), and various books of Hindu law.

Brahmans—The highest caste in Hindu India, *brahmans* or *brāhmaṇas* (sometimes *brahmins*) are de facto priests whose primary duty is to see that proper rituals and rules—especially those spelled out in the *Brāhmaṇas* (see *Brāhmaṇas*)—are followed and properly executed. The *brahman* is the earthly counterpart of Bṛhaspati (see Bṛhaspati), the priest among the gods.

Bṛhaspati—Bṛhaspati might be called the chaplain of the Hindu Gods. His role is that of the *brahman* (see Brahmans) priest in Heaven, the one who, as the "lord of sacred speech" or *mantras* (see *Mantra*) is "master of the ritual sacrifice."

Buddha—"The Buddha" is a term usually applied to the Buddha Sākyamuni (see Buddha Sākyamuni) otherwise known as Gautama Buddha (see Gautama Buddha, Buddhism).

Buddhas—A *buddha* is literally a person who has been enlightened or awakened to ultimate reality (see *Arhat*). The Sanskrit/Pāli (see Sanskrit, Pāli) term *buddhi,* which is related to the term *buddha,* conveys the sense of special intelligence or knowledge (see Buddhism). The term "the Buddha" usually refers to Gautama Buddha (see Gautama Buddha, *Bodhisattva*). But there are other Buddhas. The Jains (see Jainism) would consider their founder Mahāvīra (see Mahāvīra) a *buddha* and the Pure Land Buddhists (see Pure Land Buddhism) in Japan have their Amida Buddha (see Amida Buddha).

Buddha Sākyamuni—Sākyamuni (Śākyamuni in sanskrit) "the Buddha," is, in effect, the family name of Gautama Buddha (see Gautama Buddha), whose father was a king of the Śākyas. The Buddha is sometimes referred to simply as "Sākyamuni" (see Buddhism).

Buddhacarita—The *Buddhacarita,* or "Deeds of the Buddha," in Sanskrit (and in Tibetan and Chinese translations), is a second-century CE epic-like biography of Gautama Buddha (see Gautama Buddha) compiled by the sage Aśvaghoṣa.

Buddhism—For some, Buddhism is a religion. For others it is a philosophy or a culture. There are so many kinds of Buddhism and so many contradictions within the overall tradition that it is almost impossible to define, but there are important common threads. The so-called "Three Jewels" (*Triratna*)—Buddha (see Buddha, Gautama Buddha), *dharma* (see *Dharma*), and *saṅgha*—are essential elements for Buddhists. In most sects there is the presence of certain of the teachings or concepts of Gautama Buddha, the Buddha Sākyamuni, who lived in Nepal and India some 2,500 years ago. Of primary importance to these teachings are *śūnyatā,* the sense of selflessness achieved by way of inner searching—often in a monastic setting—and a goal of *nirvāna* (see *Nirvāna*), or Enlightenment. *Dharma,* or proper behavior and truth, in the Buddhist world is manifested in the life and teachings of the Buddha. *Saṅgha*, or "community," is the holy community of Buddhists, a place of spiritual refuge. *Saṅgha* can refer to a community of nuns or monks or to any group of devoted and spiritually committed Buddhists. At the basis of *saṅgha* are the "Four Noble Truths" of the Buddha's teaching. These are (1) the acceptance of *dukkha,* or transience and the suffering which comes with it; (2) the realization that it is *tanhā*, or the "thirst" for permanence that leads to suffering; (3) the understanding that by eliminating *taṅha, dukkha* can be overcome and *nirvāna* achieved; and (4) the *Aṣṭangika-mārga,* or "Eightfold Path" to the elimination of *taṅha* taught by the Buddha in the first sermon after his Enlightenment.

The Eightfold Path contains the elements necessary to Enlightenment. These are (1) perfected understanding of the Four Noble Truths; (2) non-attachment; (3) perfected speech; (4) perfected conduct; (5) the pursuit of livelihood in such a way as to do no harm to others; (6) the production of good *karma* (see *Karman*); (7) the development of meditative mindfulness; and (8) perfected concentration.

A major division between Buddhists centers around the question of *boddhisatvas* (see *Boddhisattva*) and whether emphasis should fall on the individual salvation or that of the larger society.

There are two major paths or "vehicles" *(yāna)* in Buddhism. The older Hīnayāna (see Hīnayāna Buddhism) or "Lesser Vehicle," so termed by the reformist Mahāyāna (see Mahāyāna Buddhism) or "Larger Vehicle" group, is represented, for instance, by the Theravāda (see Theravāda Buddhism) and Sarvāstivāda sects which developed in India before the Common Era and have spread to various parts of the Asian continent. The Hīnayāna approach stresses the ideal of the *arhat* (see *Arhat*), the enlightened one who has attained *nirvāna*. The Mahāyāna groups stress the ideal of the *bodhisattva,* not as the earlier stages of Gautama Buddha's movement toward Enlightenment, but as the person concerned with achieving Buddhahood only in some distant eon as he works compassionately in this world for the salvation of others. It should be noted that within the larger divisions of Hīnayāna and Mahāyāna exist many diverse understandings and doctrinal divisions.

The original literature of Hīnayāna Buddhism is written primarily in the Middle India dialect of Sanskrit called Pāli (see Pāli). The *Pāli Abhidhamma Piṭaka,* for instance contains sermons *(suttas)* and Theravādan doctrine. The primary Mahāyāna scriptural form is the *sūtra* (sermon of the Buddha), which is traditionally recited or chanted as a form of worship. The best known of the *sūtras* is probably The Lotus Sūtra (the *Saddharmapuṇḍarīka Sūtra*), which has a strong narrative aspect and stresses the relationship of all people to the deeds of the Buddha himself.

More esoteric forms of Buddhism include the Tantric tradition (see Tantric entries) and Zen Buddhism (see Zen Buddhism). Tantric Buddhism is influenced by Brahamanism (see Brahmanism) and is concerned with yogic (see *Yoga*) paths to salvation stressed in rituals and in texts called *tantras.* Zen, primarily practiced in Japan, developed from Chinese Ch'an Buddhism and emphasizes meditation rather than the worship of idols.

The myths of Buddhism are associated with the life of Gautama Buddha and are found primarily in the Pāli-language canon of the Theravāda tradition in first century BCE Sri Lanka, although stories have emerged from other traditions as well.

Buddhist Cosmology—The so-called three-world system is a prominent one in Buddhist thought. The ancient Theravāda Buddhist (see Theravāda Buddhism) tradition saw a flat world with Heaven above and Hell below. Later, a ten-thousand world vision emerged, and still later Buddha fields, where true wisdom is taught. Such a field is the "Pure Land" of Pure Land Buddhism (see Pure Land Buddhism). The Buddhist cosmology also contains the ideal of *nirvāna* (see *Nirvāna*), which, like the Pure Land, is a state of being rather than a particular place.

Bundahisn—Literally, "The Book of Primordial Creation," the ninth and tenth century *Bundahisn* is the primary sourcebook for Zoroastrian (see Zoroastrionism) theology and mythology in the Middle Persian or Pahlavi period.

Buryat Mythology—See Central Asian Mythology.

C

Candainī Epic—Performed in central India (Chhattisgarh) by men of the Raut (cowherd) caste in a combination of dance and song, this epic is the story of Candainī, a raja's daughter who leaves her husband because the goddess Pārvatī (see Pārvatī) has made him impotent. Candainī falls in love with Lorik, a local man, who fights and defeats an Untouchable who has been making unwelcome advances. Candainī and Lorik have an affair and leave home for Hardi Gahr. On the way they have many adventures. Candainī almost loses her lover in an all-female country. She does, in fact, lose him to his wife when they return to their original country.

Catakaṇtarāvaṇaṉ—A Tamil epic that owes much to the great epic the *Rāmāyaṇa* (see *Rāmāyaṇa*) but that features a woman, Rāma's (see Rāma) wife Sītā (see Sītā), as the main character. In this epic, Sītā leads the battle against the demon called Catakaṇtarāvaṇa (Satakaṇtharāvana, or 100-headed Rāvaṇa) (see Rāvaṇa). The epic begins with Catakaṇtarāvaṇa announcing that he will take revenge against Rāma and his people for their recent defeat of his relatives in Lanka. Sītā begs Rāma's permission—and receives it—to lead the battle against the demon. After many days of difficult battle, with Rāma as her charioteer and the monkey king Hanumān (see Hanumān) as her general, Sītā—driven by her immortal connections—defeats the demon king and his allies.

Central Asian Mythology—Little is known of pre-Buddhist, pre-Muslim Central Asian mythology. But from shamanistic practices remaining among several groups—for example, the Samoyed and Buryat peoples—it seems clear that there were stories of spirits in both Heaven and Hell with whom shamans (see Shamanism) could communicate in order to practice certain cures. One myth—again judging from such peoples as the Samoyeds and Buryats—would seem to have been an earth-diver creation (see Earth-Diver Creation) in which an animal is sent by the creator to find an earthly substance in the depths of the primal waters. Often a devil figure assists the creator in this venture and sometimes tries to usurp his position in the universe. There also seem to have been myths of the separation of sky and earth and the resulting loss of direct communication between humans and gods. The Samoyeds and others still have a sun god, a moon cult, and many spirits. For many Central Asians, the world was held up by a giant whose feet were in Hell. Hell was a place populated by spirits who sent evil to the world. The indigenous peoples of Siberia possess complex pantheons and creation stories and, like most Central Asians, are shamanistic (see Siberian entries).

Chan—See Zen Buddhism, see Bodhidharma.

Changxi—The Chinese goddess of the Moon, Changxi (Hengnge or Henge)—the Lunar Toad—is protected by the moon after she steals and swallows an immortality herb from her husband Yi (see Yi), the Excellent Archer, who is known for shooting down nine of the ten suns that used to pass the sky one after the other each day (see Chinese entries).

Charioteers—Charioteers often have symbolic importance in Hindu mythology. As the driver of the hero's vehicle of war, the charioteer is more a guide than a servant. In fact, he sometimes represents the hero's particular source of divine guidance, his or her divine alter ego, as it were. Thus Kṛṣṇa (see Kṛṣṇa) is the logical charioteer for the Pāṇḍava (see Pāṇḍavas) hero Arjuna (see Arjuna) in the *Mahābhārata* (see *Mahābhārata*). As an incarnation of the god Viṣṇu (see Viṣṇu, *Avatars* of Viṣṇu), he not only drives the hero's chariot but also, as the teacher in the *Bhagavadgītā* (see *Bhagavadgītā*), guides him along the proper divine path. In the Tamil folk epic, *Catakaṇṭarāvaṇaṉ* (see *Catakaṇṭarāvaṇaṉ*), it is in his incarnation as Rāma (see Rāma) that Viṣṇu, in effect, guides the heroine, Rāma's wife, Sītā (see Sītā) as her charioteer in her war against the demons.

Chinese Buddhism—When Buddhism (see Buddhism) first came to China in the first century BCE it came in the many forms that had emerged in India and was brought by people who knew little Chinese and absorbed by people who knew little Sanskrit (see Sanskrit). In addition to this problem there was opposition from both the Confucian (see Confucianism) and Daoist (see Daoism) schools of religious and philosophical thought. It was not until the late fifth and early sixth centuries CE that Buddhism of a Mahāyāna (see Mahāyāna Buddhism) sort was able to weave itself fully into the fabric of Chinese life. By then it had become a spiritual complement to secular Confucianism and had provided the idea of Enlightenment to Daoism. In time, the three schools of thought would be seen as a complementary unity.

Chinese Cosmogony—Although there are several versions of early Chinese creation myths, which in all likelihood developed in the pre-Buddhist period, the best known is one text that was written down in the third century CE, the *Sanwu Liji*. According to this myth, there was once only a kind of chaos, which resembled an egg. In this egg was born Pangu (P'an-Ku) (see Pangu), who remained in it for eighteen thousand years. When the egg finally broke, the heavy elements, called *yin*, became earth and the lighter ones, *yang*, became the sky (see *Yinyang*). As the earth sank and the sky rose, Pangu grew and was as tall as the distance between *yin* and *yang*. It is written in the sixth century CE *Shuyi Ji* that when Pangu died various parts of his body became aspects of the world (see Animism). His eyes became the sun and moon, his body hair became trees and plants, and his head became a sacred mountain (see Chinese Deities).

Chinese Deities—In Chinese mythology it is sometimes difficult to separate history and myth, mortals and immortals (see Chinese Mythology). The most important gods who survive in today's popular culture are considered to be the first Chinese emperors: the Three August Ones (see Chinese Emperors) and later emperors such as the Han dynasty warrior Huangdi (see Huangdi), who was also God of War. Even historical figures are well insulated by legends. Furthermore, characters who possess the supernatural qualities of deities are considered to be human. Thus Pangu, born in the cosmic egg of creation and himself the animistic source of this world, is known as the First Man (see Chinese Cosmogony). Perhaps the nearest expression of the kind of absolute godhead we find in Hinduism, for example, might be the figure of Earth-Sky or Tiandi (see Taiyi Tiandi, Di, Tian) known in the Daoist tradition as the Jade Emperor (see Chinese Flood). In the Daoist (Taoist) tradition an individual, through certain spiritual and physical disciplines, could achieve the state of the "immortals" (Xianren) (see Daoism). Some Daoists consider their founder, Laozi (Lao tse) (see Laozi), a god. In his form as the Laojun (Lord Lao) he is part of a divine triad presided over by the Yuanshi Tianshun and the Yuanshi's follower, the Daojun (Lord of the Dao). These divinities embody Daoist principles. The role of the Yuanshi is that of father and revealer of truth to the Daojun, who passes the truth on to the Laojun, who as Laozi teaches the proper "way", the Dao, to human beings.

Goddesses occupy an important place in pre-Buddhist Chinese mythology. Fubao was the mother of Huangdi by way of a miraculous conception (see Chinese Emperors). She was the goddess of spirits and divine possession. The mother of the Emperor Yu also conceived miraculously when she swallowed the *yiyi* seed. Yu was born when Fubao's side split open to release him. Jiandi, the mother of the Yin dynasty, conceived miraculously by swallowing a blackbird's egg. Perhaps the most important of the ancient goddesses is Nügua, the serpent sister-wife of the August One, the Emperor Fuxi. She was the divine matchmaker and the creator of the first humans. It was she who repaired the sky after the monster demon Gonggong smashed one of its supporting pillars (see Chinese Emperors, Nügua, Virgin Birth).

Easily the most popular Chinese goddess, who is derived from the male Buddhist Boddhisattva Avalokiteśvara (see Avalokiteśvara), is Guanyin, the goddess of Mercy. Guanyin is also the patron saint of Tibetan Buddhism. In ancient times of suffering and poverty, Guanyin used her breast milk to feed the rice plants and, therefore, the people (see Guanyin, Kannon).

Chinese Demons—Demons or *gui*, are prevalent in the Chinese mythological world. *Gui* also refers to the secondary soul that is separated from the higher soul *(hun)* at death. The superior soul becomes spirit *(shen),* and if not treated properly in a ritualistic sense, *gui* can become a ghost or bad demon. Important demons are Chiyou, who fought against the Yellow Emperor, Huangdi (see Chiyou, Huangdi); Gonggong (see Gonggong), who destroyed one of the pillars of the world with his enormous horn, causing turmoil on earth; and the Four Evils, which any new sovereign had to overcome upon assuming rule. Chiyou had gigantic teeth, was part animal and part man, and had extra eyes and arms. Gonggong was a serpent-human combination, whose follower, the monstrous Xiangliu, ate nine mountains with his nine heads and then vomited up the swamps of the world.

Chinese Emperors—The stories of the ancient rulers of China are part of a mythology created by scholars at the end of the last millennium BCE. The myth of the three *Huang,* or the August Ones, and the *Di* (see *Di*), the five emperors *(Sanhuang Wudi),* was the story of a golden age in which there was harmony between gods and rulers. These first eight monarchs were followed by the mythical Xia and the partly historical Yin and Zhou dynasties. From the time of Qinshi Huangdi in the third century CE, Chinese emperors took the title *Huangdi,* combining, they hoped, the power of the three August Ones and the ancient five emperors, who were thought by some to have been deities on earth. Chinese emperors, therefore, like the Japanese emperors, were, in a sense descended from the gods (see Huangdi). The August Ones were Fuxi, Shennong, and sometimes the wife of Fuxi, Nügua (see Nügua), and sometimes a fire-god named Zhurong or Suiren. Fuxi was the inventor of the trigrams that became the hexograms of the Yijing (see Yi Jing or *I Ching*). It is said that Fuxi took the form of a snake. He often is depicted holding a square. His wife Nügua, whose tail is that of a snake, holds a compass. These are symbols of creativity and social order and the fact that the tails of the two figures are usually entwined is indicative of the necessary union of *yin* and *yang* (see Yinyang). Shennong is depicted as a plowman, which indicates his association with agriculture. He is also associated with healing.

Of the Five Emperors, the best known is the Yellow Emperor (Huangdi), whose real name was Xianyuan. Like many heroes, the Yellow Emperor was conceived miraculously. His mother, Fubao, received the energy of lightning as she walked in the countryside. The color yellow perhaps signifies a connection with the sun. It was Huangdi who defeated the monster rebel Chiyou (see Chiyou). At the end of his life Huangdi and his entourage were carried up to the gods on a dragon. The Emperor Zhuanxu, or Gaoyang (the Great yang), also defeated a monster rebel, Gonggong (see Gonggong). It was Gaoyang who separated heaven and earth. The Emperor Gu, or Gaoxin, had several wives who are the sources for several royal lines. The Emperor Yao is considered by some Confucians to be the model ruler and the ancestor of the Han dynasty. The Emperor Shun, a pious commoner, underwent several tests of wisdom and morality before succeeding to Yao's kingdom. When he became emperor he defeated the forces representing certain vices that threatened his own royal virtues. The Emperor Yu (see Yu) succeeded Shun and with his father, the demiurge Gun, attempted to stop the great flood (see Chinese Flood). Yu succeeded in ending the flood by digging channels, this signifying the civilizing techniques much admired by the Confucians who contributed to his myth. Yu was the father of the first of the Xia emperors and stands, therefore, at the edge of Chinese history. It was at the end of the Xia dynasty and also at the end of the Yin dynasty that evil emperors effectively ended the golden age.

Chinese Flood—Like most cultures the Chinese have their flood myth. The great flood was sent by the high god Tiandi (Sky-Earth) during the reign of Yao (See Chinese Emperors). As is usually the case with such floods, the cause was the general wickedness of the human race. The single advocate for the human race, which was now stranded on mountain tops plagued by wild beasts, was the demiurge Gun. Gun unsuccessfully pleaded the human case with Tiandi and finally decided, Prometheus-like, to do something on his own. Gun's *de facto* second creation contains aspects of the earth-diver motif (see Earth-Diver Creation) that is common in Central Asia and North America. He tells an owl and a tortoise that Tiandi has magical earth substance that could be used to stem the flood. After managing to steal some of the material, Gun dropped it into the waters, where it became land. Although the people were happy, Tiandi was not, and he sent the fire god Zhurong to kill Gun and to retrieve the magic soil. The flood returned, but Gun's body, guarded by his followers, regained life. Tiandi had Gun's body cut by a sword. But out of the incision came Gun's son, the great dragon Yu, who stemmed the flood (see Yu). Gun himself became a yellow dragon and lived at the bottom of the waters.

Chinese Mythology—Chinese mythology, as it has developed over the ages, is a mixture of history, legend, and myth. This is most clearly seen in the mythology of the early emperors (see Chinese Emperors and Chinese Deities). The actual myths of ancient pre-Buddhist China are, for the most part, only known to us in later Confucian works, in which scholars have attempted to place the old stories in a historical context and to use them to illustrate moral and other social principles. In the first millennium BCE collection entitled *Shanhai Jing,* for example, demons and gods were listed for the benefit of travelers. Other sources for ancient myths are the late fourth century BCE poems of Qui Yuan. Daoists and later Buddhists contributed their own perspective to Chinese mythology as well (see for example, Guanyin, Daoism, and Chinese Buddhism). Daoism contributed the philosophy of a natural order, reflected in the art of *fengshui,* for instance, a system of aesthetic arrangement of space so as to not offend the spirit of that space. Buddhism, among many other things, contributed the idea of the cyclical life of souls (see Chinese Cosmogony, Yi).

Chiyou—A monster with horns and a heavily armored head, sometimes a human body and sometimes an animal one, Chiyou ate sand and, as a blacksmith, was the inventor of war and armaments. He was a direct descendant of Shennong, the second of the so-called Three Augusts or legendary emperors of Chinese mythology (see Chinese entries). Chiyou was also a dancer and a jouster. The best-known story about him involves his fight with Huangdi (see Huangdi), also known as the Yellow Emperor. Huangdi's army was made up of various wild animals, Chiyou's of demons. In the battle the two principals used supernatural powers and the natural elements against each other and finally Chiyou was defeated and decapitated by the Winged Dragon. The struggle between Huangdi and Chiyou reflects the cyclical aspect of Chinese mythology. One virtue is overtaken by another until another emerges to take over the previous one. This process is an aspect of the *yinyang* of Chinese myth and philosophy (see *Yinyang*).

Chuang-tzu—See Zhuangzi.

Churning of the Ocean of Milk—The Indian epic the *Mahābhārata* (see *Mahābhārata*) contains a story in which, at the suggestion of Viṣṇu (see Viṣṇu) as Nārāyana, the gods and demons churn the primeval ocean in order to obtain the ambrosia (*soma*—see *Soma*) that guarantees their immortality. To churn the salt ocean the immortals placed Mount Mandara, uprooted by the serpent-demon Ananta or Vasuki (see Ananata) on the back of the great tortoise and used it as the churning stick. Ananta became the churning cord. As the gods and demons churned the sea clouds, lightning came out of Ananta's mouth and flowers came down from the spinning mountain top and formed garlands on the gods. The motion of the whole process caused a crushing of animals and great trees and a fire resulted, which was put out by the great god Indra (see *Indra*). From the smashing of the trees and plants and the juices exuding from the process, the source of ambrosia flowed into the sea. The sea became milk and eventually the milk became butter that would be used for ritual purposes. Urged on by Viṣṇu, the gods and demons continued churning until *soma* arose from the sea and provided immortality for the gods.

Confucius—Master Kong, or Kongzi, lived in the Lu state of China in the sixth century BCE. Legends about the great sage are contained in the conversations between Confucius and his followers in the *Analects.* Confucius was a government worker, a traveler, and a lover of the arts. Gradually gaining a reputation as a wise man, he attracted many disciples as he searched for balance and a better society based on an essential humanism. Although not particularly interested in religion as such or with myth, he accepted the idea of a supreme divinity that is Heaven. Although undermined by the communist revolution, Confucianism—the teaching of Confucius—has dominated Chinese philosophy for some two thousand years, sometimes confronting but usually interacting well enough with Buddhism (see Buddhism) and Daoism (see Daoism).

Cosmic Egg—In many creation myths—including some in China, Japan, and especially India (see Brahmā)—the great precreation void takes the form of an egg, often a golden one. The analogy between cosmic birth and earthly birth is obvious here. The cosmic egg story seems to answer the perennial chicken versus egg argument.

Cosmic Tree—The tradition of the cosmic world tree is found in many parts of Asia. In insular Southeast Asia the cosmic tree unites the sky with the earth and symbolizes wholeness. In the Korean myth of Čumong (see Čumong, Korean Mythology), the hero's legitimate son is recognized when he is able to find half of his father's sword at the base of a pine tree growing out of a heptagonal stone. Also in Korea, it was believed that a sacred tree connected the three worlds of existence. Among the Turko-Mongol peoples of central Asia, cosmic trees are of great importance. For the Tartars, a giant pine tree grows out of the navel of the earth and reaches to the home of the supreme ruler in heaven. Without the cosmic tree the world above would not be able to communicate with the world below and without it the shaman would be unable to make his journeys to the spirit world (see Shamanism).

Cosmogonic Myths—A cosmogonic myth or *cosmogony* is a particular culture's story of the creation (see, for example, Chinese Cosmogony, Indian Cosmogony, and Creation).

Cow—See Kāmadhenu.

Creation—A creation myth is a cosmogony, a story that describes the origins of the universe. Creation myths concern themselves with the creation of the world and of human beings. All cultures have creation myths. A creation myth is a good reflection of a given culture's sense of itself—not only its origins but also its priorities and its meaning. Creation myths are etiological in that they "explain" things during the prescientific age—how the world was formed and where the people came from. Although each creation myth reflects an individual culture, there are basic patterns that emerge when we compare creation myths from around the world, and Asian creation myths are no exception to this rule. Creation myths, for example, often have flood myths attached to them. There is nearly always a creator or creatrix and a first man and woman. Creation stories describe in various ways the essential struggle between chaos and form. In creation myths no-thing becomes some-thing; chaos becomes cosmos ordered by Logos—the ordering force of the universe. Often creation emerges from a cosmic egg, sometimes from primal maternal waters in which an earth-diver finds the building material for the world creation. All of these themes and others are found in Asian creation myths (see Earth Diver Creation, Chinese Cosmogony, Indian Cosmogony, Japanese Cosmogony).

Čumong—A primary hero-god of ancient Korean mythology (see Korean Mythology).

D

Daevas—In the reformed Iranian religion as proclaimed by Zarathustra (see Zoroaster, Zoroastrian entries), the world is presided over by the supreme god Ahura Mazda (see Ahura Mazda), the Wise Lord, and the *daevas (daivas),* whose name ties them to the Hindu *devas* or gods, have been relegated to an inferior level of being associated with unreality and even falseness. They have become, in fact, devil-demons of sorts, who attempt to steer humans away from the supreme wisdom that is Ahura Mazda (see Asuras).

Daikoku—Mahākāla in Sanskrit, Daikoku-ten is the Japanese Buddhist (see Japanese Buddhism) god known as "The Great Black One." He had once been the protector of wealth and happiness, but by the ninth century the Tendai (see Tendai Sect) and Shingon (see Shingon Sect) sects of Buddhism saw him as the protector and provider of their monasteries. Daikoku was also taken up by non-Buddhists and identified with the ancient Japanese god Okuninushi no kami (see Okuninushi), the Great Spirit Master. Later still he was seen as part of a group called the "Seven Gods of Happiness" or "Fortune" (see *Seven Gods of Fortune*). Daikoku is often depicted as a hunter who carries a sack and a rice mallet. He stands on a large bag of rice, perhaps signifying agricultural wealth.

Dainichi—The Buddha Dainichi Nyorai or the Buddha Mahāvairocana is known as the "Illuminator." In the tradition of esoteric Buddhism *(mikkyō)* as developed in Japan (see Japanese Buddhism) in the early ninth century, especially by the Shingon sect (see Shingon Sect), Dainichi is the embodiment of the Absolute—the supreme Buddha with whom humans may unite through proper discipline and meditation. For the Shingon Buddhist and for many Shinto (see Shinto entries) followers, the universe is the Dainichi Nyorai in much the same way that Brahman (see Brahman) is the universe for some Hindus (see Hinduism).

Dakṣa—Although sometimes identified with the Indian Vedic creator (see Vedism) Prajāpati (see Prajāpati), Dakṣa later came to be thought of as the son of that later version of Prajāpati, the creator god Brahmā (Brahmā). He also serves as the father of Pārvatī (see Pārvatī), the wife of Śiva (see Śiva). In the *Mahābhārata* (see *Mahābhārata*), the story is told of Dakṣa's presiding over a sacrifice that is destroyed by Śiva. Dakṣa represents that aspect of the "good Hindu" who follows the proper rites and performs the sacrifice with perfection, but who is lacking in devotion (see *bhakti*). In the epic version of the myth, Dakṣa and the gods perform the sacrifice and dole out the offerings but fail to invite the god Rudra-Śiva (see Rudra) or to assign him any offerings. Enraged, Śiva proves his power and comes into his own in relation to Viṣṇu (see Viṣṇu) and the other gods by destroying the sacrifice and maiming several of the gods. The gods beg him to throw the fire of his anger into the waters and finally he does so. He then heals the maimed gods and brings back the sacrifice and, thus, order, under his aegis. In some versions of the story, Dakṣa is decapitated during the destruction and his head thrown into the fire. In the restoration of the sacrifice, Dakṣa is given a ram's head to replace his original. Many have seen in the destruction of Dakṣa's sacrifice a symbol of the destruction that will come at the end of the world under the direction of the Destroyer, Śiva. The myth also suggests that no sacrifice can be valid without the devotional aspect of Śiva the meditative yogi.

Dance of Śiva—The great Hindu god Śiva (see Śiva)—at once the Destroyer and the perfect yogi—is often depicted as a dancer. Traditionally the dance is magical and trance-inducing. It is a high form of cosmic yoga (see *yoga*). Śiva is Nāṭarāja, the Lord of the Dance, and the dance is, in a sense, the breathing of creation. As he whirls in the meditative and gentle movement called *lāsya*, with his consort Pārvatī (see Pārvatī), the elements of the living world are the flashes of light made by his movements. These elements are destroyed in turn by the violent turnings of the *tāṇḍava.* In his dance Śiva-Nāṭarāja holds various symbolic objects. In his top right hand is the hourglass drum connoting the rhythm of the dance of life, which is sound, the means by which understanding is transmitted. Sound is connected in India to the essential element ether, out of which comes air, fire, water, and earth, the necessary elements for creation. In the upper left hand the dancer holds the fire, the agent of the destruction of creation in the sacrifice and in the cosmic cycle. The lower right hand gives the sign of peace and the lower left hand points to the left foot raised in a sign of devotion and release. Sometimes Śiva dances on the body of a demon symbolizing human forgetfulness or ignorance.

Dānu—See Diti.

Daodejing—See Daoism.

Daoism—Daoism (Taoism) is in some ways a religion and in others a philosophical system. The founder of Daoism, Laozi (Lao tse) was to some a god and to others the greatest of philosophers (see Laozi). He is said to have contributed the popular work called the *Daodejing (Tao Te Ching),* probably in the later years of the first millennium BCE. Another source for Daoist thought is the *Zuangzi* (Chuang-tzu) attributed to the second of the great Daoist thinkers, Zuangzi (see Zuangzi). At the center of Daoist thought is the Dao (Tao) or "Way," the totality of existence conceived of as a whole. The way to mystical freedom is by way of letting go of conventional concerns and achieving union with the Dao. Once union has been achieved, such conditions as poverty and wealth will become meaningless, and ordinary societal values will no longer apply.

Dayak Myths—The Dayak people of Borneo, like many people in the world, see their territory as sacred space surrounded by chaotic foreignness. They are the people of the Supreme Being, who has a male aspect, Mahatala, associated with the Sun, and an Underworld female aspect, Jata. Jata is represented by the coiled watersnake biting its own tail, forming a sacred *maṇḍala* (see *Maṇḍala*) of sorts that supports the Dayak world. The snake rests on the primeval chaotic waters between the upper and lower worlds. The people communicate with Mahatala by way of ascetic disciplines on certain sacred mountains (see Mountain Mythology). The Supreme Being created the world out of the sun and the moon. According to several so-called *bakowo* ("hiding away") myths, the universe will come to an end as a result of human failings. Following the destruction of the universe, only a maiden will remain—hidden in a rock or a tree, symbolizing the Underworld. A ritual reflection of this myth is the hiding away *(bakowo)* of girls for a set time at the beginning of puberty. The annual ritual cycle of the Dayak reflects the mythological sense of the progress of the universe from beginning to end.

Descent of the Ganges—In both the great Hindu epics the *Mahābhārata* (see Mahābhārata) and the *Rāmāyaṇa* (see Rāmāyaṇa), there are versions of the story of the descent of the sacred river Ganges or Gaṅgā (see Ganges) from Heaven to Earth. The *Purāṇas* (see *Purāṇas*) tell us the source of the river is Viṣṇu's (see Viṣṇu) big toe. But it is Śiva (see Śiva) who controls the flow of the river. In the myth the King Sagara wishes to have Gaṅgā come to earth to purify the ashes of his sixty thousand dead warrior sons. It is not until many generations later that the sage Bhagīratha, a descendant of Sagara, goes to the Himālayas and succeeds in doing sufficient austerities to Gaṅgā to convince the river to come down to earth. But in order to prevent the force of the flow from destroying the world, the sage must perform austerities to Śiva. Finally the great god agrees to allow the river to fall on his head. When it falls Gaṅgā forms the three Himālayan rivers that in turn make up the river Ganges. The significance of this myth lies in the relationship between the Ganges as the "blood" of the earth and Śiva as its heart.

Descent to the Underworld—In mythologies from all parts of the world, the motif of the descent to the Underworld (see Underworld) is common. Sometimes the hero—for example, the Greeks Herakles, Orpheus, and Theseus—makes the descent in search of destiny or of a lost lover or relative. In some cases a god or goddess—for example, the Summerian-Babylonian Inanna—descends. As part of the traditional hero journey, the myth of the descent seems to signify several things: for instance, a return to Mother Earth in preparation for rebirth into a higher divine hero state or the facing of death before full selfhood can be achieved. Psychologically, the descent is the "night journey" or "dark night of the soul," which points to the fact that to be whole the self must rule his or her inner world. The motif of the descent to the Underworld may not be as prevalent in the Eastern traditions as in the Western. It is nevertheless clearly present. In India there is the popular story of the beautiful Sāvitrī (see Sāvitrī), who follows Yāma (see Yāma), the Vedic (see Vedism) god of death, to the gates of the Underworld and convinces him to release her husband Satyavān from death. In the *Upaniṣads* (see *Upaniṣads*), the story is told of the young Brahmān Naciketas, who in the Underworld manages to obtain from Yāma the knowledge that beyond death itself is the Absolute, the Brahman (see Brahman). In China, the goddess Guanyin (see Guanyin) is also a heroine who dies and returns from the Underworld where she demonstrates her powers. Having been killed by her wrathful father's servant, Guanyin rides on the back of a tiger to the Land of the Dead (see Underworld). There she relieves the shades of their eternal sorrow with her beautiful singing. Enraged, the king of the Land of the Dead sends her back to earth, where she lives on an island from which she sends mercy and solace to those who pray to her (see Chinese Deities). In Japan it is the creator god Izanagi who makes a disastrous descent to the Underworld in search of his wife Izanami (see Izanagi and Izanami).

Devakī—The mother of the Hindu Lord Kṛṣṇa (see Kṛṣṇa), Devakī was the sister or cousin of King Kaṃsa (see Kaṃsa) who, like the

Greek Kronos, killed his children as they were born because of a prophecy that one of them would kill him. Kṛṣṇa was saved when he was exchanged with the daughter of the herdsman Nanda (see Nanda), who served as his surrogate father.

Devas—Celestial Hindu gods (see Asuras).

Devayāna—The Hindu *Upaniṣads* (see *Upaniṣads*) tell of the narrow bridge (see also Zoroastrian Afterlife), the way of the gods or the wise, by which the good Hindu after death discovers *Brahman* (see Brahman). In terms of philosophy, Devayāna is the path to truth.

Devī—Devī is the Hindu Goddess. Although we speak of the *trimūrti* of Brahmā (see Brahmā), Viṣṇu (see Viṣṇu), and Śiva (see Śiva), in fact it is Devī who in practice joins Viṣṇu and Śiva as one of the three most important *bhakti* (see *bhakti*) or devotional deities in India. Some would say that she is the most important divinity, the fullest embodiment of the Absolute Brahman. In the *Mārkaṇḍeya Purāṇa*, in which many of Devī's myths appear, we find the *Devīmāhātmya,* in which the origin of the goddess is described. It seems that the world was being threatened by a gigantic water buffalo bull monster named Mahiṣa. He was king of the *asuras* (see *Asuras*), who had conquered Heaven. Following Brahmā, the gods take refuge with Viṣṇu and Śiva, and together project their angry energy in the form of sheets of light, which form one light and become the eighteen-armed Goddess, the perfect amalgamated personification, therefore, of the power and energy of godhead. Devī emerges as the ultimate feminine principle, the Life Energy itself, the original *Śakti* (see *Śakti*), the psychic and spiritual energy without which even Śiva is nothing material. Devī can, in fact, be worshipped as *Śakti* (see Śāktism).

In her form as the violent avenging warrior goddess, Śiva's consort Durgā (see Durgā), Devī kills the monster and saves the world. It is the world that concerns Devī; she is the key to a successful existence in this reality. Although as the blood-thirsty Kālī (see Kālī) she brings disease, war, and destruction, it is because death and destruction are necessary to the cycle of life. For those who worship her, Devī is for the most part benevolent. Sometimes she is the wife of Śiva as Pārvatī (see Pārvatī), Daughter of the Mountain. As Satī (see Satī), the daughter of Dakṣa (see Dakṣa) and the wife of Śiva-Rudra (see Rudra), she throws herself into her husband's funeral pyre, setting the example of self-immolation or *satī* for Hindu widows. But Devī can also take form as Śrī (see Śrī) or Lakṣmi (see Lakṣmi), the wife of Viṣṇu. The name Śrī refers to prosperity and Viṣṇu to the sacrifice, indicating that prosperity cannot be separated from the necessary rituals of sacrifice. In the *Mahābhārata* (see *Mahābhārata*), Lakṣmi is incarnated as Draupadī (see Draupadī), the wife of the Pāṇḍava (see Pāṇḍavas) brothers. In the *Rāmāyaṇa* (see *Rāmāyaṇa*), she is Sītā (see Sītā), the loyal wife of the Viṣṇu avatar (see Avatars of Viṣṇu) Rāma (see Rāma). Philosophically, Devī is also the yogic sleep within Viṣṇu—that which keeps the world within the god. When she is outside of Viṣṇu she becomes not only Devī herself but Līlā (see Līlā) or "Divine Creativity", and Māyā (see Māyā) or "Divine Illusion."

Devnārāyaṇ—Devnārāyaṇ is the hero of the epic named for him in Rajasthan in the northwest of India. Performed by and for agricultural castes, the epic concerns twenty-four brothers who are killed by the Goddess (see Devī), who becomes incarnated in the household of the brothers. Viṣṇu (see Viṣṇu) is incarnated there, too, as Devnārāyaṇ, and he defeats the enemies of the descendants of the twenty-four brothers. Before returning to Heaven, he establishes his own cult among the cowherds, a fact that associates him with his great avatar (see Avatars of Viṣṇu), Kṛṣṇa (see Kṛṣṇa).

Dharma—The Hindu concept derived from the *Vedas* (see *Vedas*) of social obligation or duty that is at the basis of all Hindu social laws and ethics (see *Laws of Manu*). Dharma is sometimes personified as a god and is the father of one of the Pāṇḍava (see Pāṇḍavas) brothers in the *Mahābhārata* (see *Mahābhārata*).

Ḍholā Epic—This popular epic of Northwestern India is sung in nightly episodes at village festivals. There are fifty episodes in all, which tell the story of the Navargarh kingdom. The king, Raja

Pratham, has a wife, Manjhā, who becomes pregnant miraculously by way of a grain of rice provided by a guru. The king's other wives convince him that Manjhā's son will kill him, and so begins a string of events known in fairy tales and myths in many parts of the world. The king orders a servant to kill the queen in the forest but the servant cannot bring himself to do so and kills a deer instead, presenting the deer's eyes to the king as proof of the slaying of Manjhā. Manjhā, of course, has a son, Nal, who, with his mother, is taken in by a merchant. The merchant and his sons are arrested by the king when Nal cannot present him with more than one cowrie shell used in gambling games. Nal arrives at court and promises to deliver more shells if the king will release the merchant and his sons. The king agrees. Nal then goes in search of the shells and is told by an old woman that they are in the possession of Motinī, the daughter of a demon king called Ghūmāsur. After Nal meets Motinī and successfully gambles with her she agrees to marry him and turns him into a fly in order to hide him from her wicked father. Nal finally overcomes the demon by destroying the magic duck that is the source of his strength.

When Nal returns with Motinī to the merchant and his sons, the sons fall in love with Motinī and throw Nal into the sea. Eventually, however, the king is offered Motinī as a substitute for the promised shells, and he falls in love with her. Motinī refuses to marry him until the story of Nal—the *Nal Purāṇa*—is told. At this point, Nal himself, alive and disguised as an old man, arrives and tells his own story. The king realizes who he is, brings back Manjhā, and the union of Motinī and Nal is celebrated. Soon Motinī produces a son of her own, and he is named Ḍholā. What follows is the story of Nal's conflict with the god Indra (see Indra) over a raja's daughter, Damyantī. After many trials, Nal is able to win another raja's daughter, Mārū, for his son. After more difficulties and separations, Ḍholā and Mārū are happily united.

Dhyāni Buddhas and Bodhisattvas—In the Mahāyāna Buddhist (see Mahāyāna Buddhism) tradition, Gautama Buddha (see Gautama Buddha) was preceded by other Buddhas in other ages (see

Buddhism). Among these are the five Dhyāni (meditation) Buddhas: the white colored Vairocana (see Dainichi) who rides on a dragon and is particularly popular among the Shingon sect in Japan; the yellow Ratnasaṃbhava, who rides on a horse; the red Amitābha, particularly revered in Japan (see Amida Buddha, Japanese Buddhism), whose place is the Pure Land or Sukhāvatī (see Pure Land); the green Amoghasiddhi, who rides with his thunderbolt on an eagle; and the blue Akṣobhya, who also carries a thunderbolt and rides on an elephant. There is, however, little in the way of further characterization of these Buddhas. We know much more about the Dhyāni Bodhisattvas (see *Bodhisattva*) who result from the meditation of the Buddhas. The green Bodhisattva Samantabhadra is popular in Nepal. A companion of Gautama Buddha, he rides on an elephant, and stands for happiness. Vajrapāṇi was also a companion of the Buddha. His sign is a thunderbolt, and he gives kindness to true followers and pain to those who deny the Buddha. Avalokiteśvara (see Avalokiteśvara) achieved enlightenment, but in the best Mahāyānist tradition, decided to remain on Earth to bring mercy and enlightenment to other human beings. Avalokiteśvara emanates from the Amida Buddha, carries a pink lotus, and works constantly to help those in need. He carries refreshment to those in Hell and converts the evil. In China he became the goddess Guanyin (see Guanyin).

Di—Di or Shang-ti was the supreme creator god of the Shang dynasty of China during the second millennium BCE (see Tian, Taiyi, Tiandi).

Diffusion and Parallelism—Mythologists have long been aware of the fact that certain motifs or archetypes and even whole plots are found in cultures that are not geographically connected. Some thinkers—the psychiatrist Carl Jung, for example—have postulated what might be called the "parallel development" of myths because of a common "collective unconscious"—the idea being that humans inherit certain mythic tendencies just as they inherit certain physical characteristics. So it is that we find the motif of the hero's quest in all parts of the world because the hero is a reflection, in his various cultural clothes, of a larger psychic human need.

Others have attributed the transmission of common motifs and themes to a process of diffusion, whereby ideas are carried from culture to culture by humans involved in such activities as war and trade.

Diti and the Daityas—In Hindu mythology the sister and opposite of Aditi (see Aditi and the Ādityas), Diti (Dānu) is the mother of the demonic Daityas such as Vṛtra (see Vṛtra) and other enemies of the gods. She represents dualism and division. Aditi is universality and godliness in humans, Diti is that which is individual and mortality-based.

Dragon King—In Vietnam, the Dragon King is Long-vuong or Thuy-tê. He is the lord of the seas and lives in a magnificent aquatic palace surrounded by beings of the sea. Traditionally, the Dragon King is important for giving gifts to those who release his children after unwittingly catching them in their nets or on their hooks. In one story, a student, Giap-Hai, saves a turtle from some fishermen and discovers that the shell contains a beautiful woman who turns out to be the Dragon King's daughter. The pair are married and with the help of the Dragon King, Giap-Hai passes his scholarly exams with great distinction.

Dragons—The most important of Chinese mythological beasts (see Chinese entries), dragons are positive expressions of *yang,* the male principle balanced by the female *yin,* represented by the phoenix (see Yinyang). The dragon and the phoenix were symbols of Chinese emperors and empresses from the Han Dynasty on. The dragon was especially associated with the sea and other forms of water. Dragon dances mark the beginning of the Chinese lunar year (see Dragon King).

Draupadī—The wife of all five Pāṇḍava (see Pāṇḍavas) brothers in the Indian epic the *Mahābhārata* (see *Mahābhārata*), "fire-born" Draupadī is an incarnation of Śrī (see Śrī, Lakṣmi) or "Prosperity," the wife of the god Viṣṇu (see Viṣṇu), which is appropriate to a kingdom such as that of the Pāṇḍavas, which follows the principles of *dharma* (see *Dharma*), or proper social law. Draupadī's situation as the wife of five men is not common and occurs only because of a promise made by Kuntī (see Kuntī) or Pṛthā, the mother of the brothers. In any case, although she favors the hero Arjuna (see Arjuna), Draupadī is a faithful wife to all five brothers and provides each with a son. When Yudhiṣṭhira, the oldest brother and the king, gambles away his kingdom and his brothers and even their wife, it is Draupadī who convinces the Pāṇḍava enemies to grant the brothers their freedom. The event that leads to their release is a high point in the Draupadī myth and clearly establishes her as Śrī and as the source, with Kṛṣṇa (see Kṛṣṇa), of Pāṇḍava power. When the gambling victors, the Kauravas (see Kauravas), attempt to strip Draupadī in order to humiliate her and her husbands, Kṛṣṇa intervenes and miraculously prevents the stripping. As always in the events of Hindu mythology, there is a symbolic meaning to this incident. It suggests that the dissolution of the universe, represented by Śrī-Draupadī, will not yet take place. A cult based on Draupadī as an incarnation of the Goddess (see Devī) exists to this day in parts of India.

Dravidians—Dravidians are people who speak non-Indo-European languages, primarily in Southern India and Northern Sri Lanka. These languages include Tamil and Malayalam. When we speak of Dravidian culture, we generally refer to an indigenous pre-Hindu culture such as the one described in the Tamil *Tolkāppiyām*, written in the first and second centuries CE, Dravidian culture in all likelihood developed from the Indus Valley culture in south India in the Neolithic period and, in terms of religion, was probably earth-centered and possibly dominated by a goddess cult (see Tamil Mythology and Indus Valley Mythology).

Durgā—Durgā, "the inaccessible," is the beautiful multiarmed warrior form of Devī (see Devī), the Goddess, the wife of the Hindu God Śiva (see Śiva). It is Durgā who saves the gods and the universe by defeating and killing the buffalo demon Mahiṣa as described in the *Devīmāhātmya* in the *Mārkaṇḍeya Purāṇa*. Until very recently, annual sacrifices of water buffalo were made to honor Durgā, and Durgā is the center of an annual festival celebrating victory over evil in many parts of the Hindu world.

Durvāsas—Durvāsas means "Naked" and suggests the image of the Hindu Brahman (see *Brahmans*) sage as ascetic. An incarnation of the god Śiva (see Śiva), the perfect yogi and the destroyer, he is capable of great destructive power and of an inner power to overcome evil. He was once given a magic garland by the Goddess (see Devī), whom he particularly revered.

Dwarf—See Avatars of Viṣṇu, Vāmana.

Dyaus—The Sanskrit (see Sanskrit) word for the Vedic (see Vedism, Vedic Mythology) Indian personification of the sky, Dyaus is at the root of the common term for God—for example, *Deus, Dios, Zeus*.

E

Earth-Diver Creation—In earth-diver creation (see Creation) myths an animal or god is sent by the creator to retrieve substance from the depths of the primal waters. This substance, in any number of possible ways, becomes the earth. Earth-diver creations are particularly prevalent among Native American peoples, who very likely originally migrated to North America across the Bering Strait from Asia. Not surprisingly, then, earth-diver creations are found in the mythology of the Ainu people of Japan (see Ainu Creation), the Birhor people of India (see Birhor Mythology), and in the mythology of Hinduism (see Purāṇic Cosmogony, Boar). In addition, it is found in the Chinese flood myth (see Chinese Flood), and especially in the creation stories of many Central Asian (see Central Asian Mythology) groups—particularly the Buriat, the Samoyed, and Altaic peoples (see Altaic Mythology).

Emma—Emma-O', derived from the Sanskrit Yama (see Yama), is the Japanese Buddhist Lord of Jigoku, or Hell (see Jigoku). Emma judges souls and places them in hells appropriate to their crimes. In this context there are a total of eight hells. These have been described by people who were for one reason or another released from punishment. The hells are a popular subject for Japanese scrolls. Emma's primary enemy is Jizō (see Jizō), always a supporter of the dead souls against Emma and usually the victor over his dark adversary. As Jizō's popularity has grown and Emma's diminished, Emma has become a demon.

Emperor Yu the Great—See Yu.

Erintsen Mergen—An oral epic of the Mongols, the *Erinchin,* as it is often called, is the story of a seventeenth-century Ordo chieftain, Erintsen, who successfully wars against Mongol rivals. Eventually, however, his people came under the control of the more powerful Manchus.

Eschatology—Eschatology is the branch of mythology or religion that is concerned with questions such as death, judgment, and heaven and hell. Resurrection and underworld (see Underworld) myths, for instance, are, therefore eschatological myths.

Excellent Archer—see Yi.

F

Feisheng—*Feisheng* in Daoism (see Daoism) is the act of ascending to Heaven and achieving immortality.

Fish and the Flood—The story of Viṣṇu's (see Viṣṇu) avatar (see Avatars of Viṣṇu), the Fish Matsya, is related to the story of the Viṣṇu Boar (see Boar) avatar in two ways: both animals are horned and both stories concern Viṣṇu's rescue of the world from the waters, in this case a flood. The *Śatapatha Brāhmana* tells a story from Vedic (see Vedic entries) times of how Manu (see Manu), the human progenitor, found a small fish in the water he was using for his morning ablutions. The fish asks Manu to protect him from larger fish and promises to save his protector from a predicted flood. Manu places the fish in a jar and when it is large enough to protect itself, he releases it into the ocean. The fish has warned Manu—now a Noah-like figure—to build a boat and when he has done so, the fish allows Manu to tie his boat to its horn for protection against the rising waters. Some say that the serpent Vasuki (see Vasuki) served Manu as the connecting rope. A version of the Matsya story is also told in the *Mahābhārata* (see *Mahābhārata*).

Flood—In all parts of the world, including Asia, flood myths are found, usually as aspects of the larger creation story. Generally the flood marks a new beginning, a second chance for a sinful humankind or for creation itself. The flood waters become a second version, as it were, of the primeval maternal waters—a vehicle for rebirth as well as a cleansing element. (See the Fish and the Flood, Chinese Flood Myth, Zoroastrian Flood, Indonesian Flood, Nithan Khun Borom.)

Four Ages—According to the Hindu (see Hinduism) *Purāṇas* (see *Purāṇas*), each eon or *kalpa* is made up of four ages or *yugas*. These cosmic ages take their names from the four essential dice throws: the *Kṛta* or *Satya,* the *Tretā,* the *Dvāpara,* and the *Kali.* The first age is the golden age of truth. Each succeeding age of the dice game of life marks a deterioration of values. Thus the *Kali* age—the present time—finds humanity at a low ebb that precedes the ritual sacrificial dissolution of the world by fire and resubmersion in the primal waters, in preparation for the birth of a new *kalpa.*

Fudō—The "Immovable One" at the center of the "Kings of Knowledge"—the *myo'o*—Fudō was brought to Japan by the esoteric Shingon sect (see Shingon Sect) of Buddhism (see Buddhism, Japanese Buddhism) in the ninth century. Fudō is the concrete form of the Supreme Buddha, the Buddha Dainichi Nyorai (see Dainichi). In the current age Fudō is worshipped independently and is usually depicted as a blue-black or sometimes yellow or red figure. Holding a rope and a sword as weapons against evil, Fudō stands for purity and resolution.

Fuxi—One of the *Sanhuang* or "Three August Ones" in Chinese legend and myth (see Chinese Deities, Chinese Emperors), the Emperor Fuxi (Fu-Hsi) was the brother-husband of Nügua (see Nügua). He is usually depicted in the form of a snake.

G

Gaṇeśa—One of the most popular of Hindu gods (see Hindu Mythology), Gaṇeśa, or Gaṇapati, the elephant-headed son of Pārvatī (see Pārvatī) and Śiva (see Śiva) is the subject of many myths. He is worshipped by Hindus called Gāṇapatyas, who even produced their own version of the *Bhagavadgītā* (see *Bhagavadgītā*) called the *Gaṇeśagītā,* in which Gaṇeśa replaces Kṛṣṇa (see Kṛṣṇa) as the source of wisdom. The *Bṛhaddharma Purāṇa* (see *Purāṇas*) tells how Pārvatī, the "Daughter of the Mountain," wished for a child. Her husband Śiva, both as a yogi ascetic and as an immortal who, therefore, had no need of descendants, heaped scorn on her desire. But when Śiva saw how unhappy he had made the goddess, he agreed to her wish. He did so, however, while preserving his own distance from the conception of the child. Tearing off a piece of Pārvatī's dress, he told her to make her own baby from it. This Pārvatī did, and soon the child was nursing at her breasts. But in this version of the story, as in many others, Śiva takes a dislike to the child. Some would even say he was jealous of it. Either as a result of a curse by Śanaiścara (Saturn) or the evil gaze of Śiva, the child's head falls off. Failing in his attempt to calm his now very unhappy wife by replacing the detached head on the body, Śiva sends Nandin, his faithful bull attendant, to take the head of Indra's (see Indra) elephant Airāvata so that it might be attached to the body of Pārvatī's child. After a terrible struggle with Indra and other gods, Nandin succeeds in his mission and Śiva places the elephant's head on Pārvatī's son. He was now short and fat with a red face, but in some deeper sense he was very beautiful. He was named Gaṇeśa or Lord of his father's *gaṇas* ("hosts") by Brahmā (see Brahmā) and was given a rat as his mount. It is said that, directed by the poet-sage Vyāsa (see Vyāsa), he wrote the *Mahābhārata* (see *Mahābhārata*). It is Gaṇeśa who brings wealth and success in life. In one of the many versions of his birth story, Gaṇeśa appears in the hand of Pārvatī during her bath. Gaṇeśa was, among many other things, the guardian at Pārvatī's door.

Ganges—The Ganges, or Gaṅgā, is the sacred "white river" of purification and salvation among Hindus (see Hindu entries, Descent of the Ganges). In the *Mahābhārata* (see *Mahābhārata*) the personified Gaṅgā is the mother of the hero Bhīṣma (see Bhīṣma).

Garuḍa—Garuḍa is the god-bird mount of the Hindu (see Hindu entries) god Viṣṇu (see Viṣṇu). He represents both the sun and fire and is known as the enemy of the snakes (see *Nagas*). The *Bhāgavata Purāṇa* (see *Purāṇas*) tells how the *Nagas* present Garuda with an offering each fortnight in order to protect themselves from his tendency to otherwise devour them.

Gāthās—The sacred songs attributed to Zarathustra (see Zoroaster), the poet-priest and founder of Zoroastrianism (see Zoroastrianism), the *Gāthās* stress the dualism that is at the basis of the religion—the struggle between the good Ohrmazd (see Ahura Mazda) and the evil Ahriman (see Angra Mainyu).

Gautama Buddha—Gautama Buddha or the Buddha Sākyamuni, or simply "the Buddha," whose personal name was Siddhārtha ("the one whose goals are achieved") lived in present-day Nepal during the late sixth and early fifth centuries BCE. He was born into the royal family of the Sākyas (thus, Sākyamuni: "wise one of the Sākyas"). Eventually he became the *de facto* founder of an outgrowth of Brahmanism (see Brahmanism) called Buddhism (see Buddhism). Little is known about Gautama's life, but a rich mythology has developed around it. The first "biography" was not set down until about 80 CE in the so-called Pāli (see Pāli) Canon in Sri Lanka. Mythic narratives of the Buddha's life had developed over the centuries, however, both orally and in writing—in various *jātaka* or previous life tales contained in Buddhist Sūtras (scriptures), for instance, and in traditional tales told at various Buddhist pilgrimage sites. As is the case with other great religious leaders—Jesus, Zarathustra (see Zoroaster), Muhammad, for example—the Buddha's life was raised by myth to the level of the sacred and the superhuman.

The mythic Buddha's story begins in the heavens, where the future Buddha—the Bodhisattva (see Bodhisattva)—who had already lived thousands of lives, preached to the gods. When he realized that it was time for him to enter the world as the Buddha, he allowed himself to be miraculously conceived in Queen Māyā (see Māyā) of the Sākyas. He entered her womb in a dream as a beautiful white elephant, causing all of nature to rejoice. The child was born without pain or blood from the side of the queen as she stood in a Lumbinī grove. Upon birth, the child possessed adult qualities. He surveyed each of the four directions and then announced his possession of the world. Soon after he received the name of Siddhārtha, the Buddha's mother died of joy, her role as birthgiver duly accomplished. When Prince Siddhārtha was twelve, *brahman* (see *Brahmans*) sages revealed to his worldly father, King Suddhodana, that the boy would one day be a great ascetic. As if playing out the archetypal refusal of the call for his son, the king decided he would rather that Siddhārtha be a world monarch, and he provided him with sumptuous palaces, beautiful women, and riches. Siddhārtha was married to Yasodharā, who produced a son, Rahula. But Siddhārtha's vocation was strong, and he sensed the imperfections of the world. When he asked his charioteer to take him into the city, the King first had everything ugly or unclean removed. But, miraculously, there appeared before the young prince an old man on the verge of death. On other trips he met other people marked with signs of pain and mortality and imperfection. Finally he met an ascetic beggar who had left worldly pleasures in search of a deeper peace. In spite of the efforts of his father and the love he felt for his wife and son, Siddhārtha left his palace and city and became the ascetic monk Gautama. After a long period of wandering and fasting, he accepted milk-cooked rice from the maiden Sujātā and bathed in the river before moving to the central act of his life, the ordeal under the world tree (see Bodhi Tree) or tree of Enlightenment. There he sat down to die or to achieve total Enlightenment. At first the demon Mārā tried to tempt the Buddha away from his intention. He tempted him with lust, with power, and some say with the supposed enslavement of the wife and child he had left behind. Then Enlightenment *(bodhi)* came to Gautama and he became a Buddha. He understood death and rebirth and existence itself. After seven days of further meditation and four more weeks near the tree, the Buddha decided to put off his entering Nirvāna (see Nirvāna) in favor of preaching his wisdom to the world. He went first to Banāras (see Banāras) and there preached his brand of mercy and universal love. Many miracles followed. The Buddha tamed a wild elephant sent by his cousin Devadatta to undermine his work. He converted his family, including his cousin Ānanda (see Ānanda), who became his chief disciple. As he was dying, the Buddha reminded his followers that they must work for liberation from the impermanence of life. His funeral pyre caught fire of its own accord, and Gautama Buddha entered Nirvāna. In one popular depiction, he sits on a lotus flower between the Hindu gods Brahmā (see Brahmā) and Indra (Indra) and creates a vast number of lotuses all with himself seated in their centers.

Gayomart—In an ancient myth, Gayomart is the primal human aspect of the Zoroastrian (see Zoroastrianism) founder Zarathustra (see Zoroaster). Zarathustra is also revealed in Saoshyant the savior (see Saoshyant). Gayomart is the sacrificial victim of Zoroastrianism. He and the great Bull were created by Ohrmazd and both killed by the evil Ahriman. At his death, Gayomart announced that humanity would find life in him. And, in fact, as the blood of the Bull gave rise from the earth to plant and animal life, the seed that was Gayomart was the source of the plant that divided into the first male and female humans, Mashye and Mashyane.

Gesar Saga—An eleventh-century Tibetan (see Tibetan entries) epic of the King of Ling, the story became the national epic of Ladakh as the *Kesar Saga*. At his birth Gesar announces his identity as the Lion King. He will inevitably confront the evil Trotun who has long ravished the kingdom. To avoid a prophecy of his defeat at the hand of a magical king, Trotun convinces the nobles of the land to exile Gesar, and the hero spends time wandering with his mother in the mountain wilderness. During this period, the beautiful Brougmo (Cho-cho-dogur-ma in Ladakh) is growing up in Ling. Eventually she finds the exiled hero, and together, on magical horses, they overcome evil and bring unity and prosperity to the kingdom of Ling.

Gītāgovinda—See Govinda.

Gokuraku—A name for paradise or Sukhavātī as opposed to *jigoku* (see Jigoku), or Hell, in the Pure Land Buddhism of Japan (see Pure Land).

Gond Mythology—The Gonds are one of many groups in Central India who are outside of the traditional caste system of Hinduism (see Hinduism) and whose mythologies differ in various ways from the classical Hindu tradition (see, for example, *Birhor Mythology*). The creation story of the Gonds contains a theme common also to other Central Indian tribes, namely that of the brother and sister saved from the Great Flood (see Flood), who then became the progenitors of humankind. The heroes of Gond mythology are the Pāṇḍava (see Pāṇḍavas) brothers of the *Mahābhārata* (see *Mahābhārata*) and Lingal (see Lingal).

Gonggong—A demon deity in Chinese mythology (see Chinese Mythology, Chinese Deities, Chinese Emperors), Gonggong lost an epic battle to Zhurong (see Zhurong) and in his despair tried to kill himself by running into Mount Buzhou, one of the supports of the sky. This caused a tear in the sky and a subsequent flood (see Chinese Flood) and storm of flames. By upsetting the balance of the sky, Gonggong caused the rivers of China to run toward the east (see Nügua).

Gopīs—In the Hindu (see Hinduism) *Bhāgavata Purāṇa* (see *Purāṇas*), Kṛṣṇa (see Kṛṣṇa) is a cowherd *(gopā)* and the cows are symbolic of love and devotion to Kṛṣṇa. The female cowherds or milkmaids are *gopīs*. Their erotic love for Kṛṣṇa is symbolic of devotion to the great avatar of Viṣṇu (see Viṣṇu, Avatars of Viṣṇu, Govinda).

Govinda—Literally, the "cow herder" *(gopā),* Govinda is another name for the Hindu (see Hinduism) Lord Kṛṣṇa (see Kṛṣṇa). The *Bhāgavata Purāṇa* (see *Purāṇas*) tells how Govinda, merely by favoring them with his ambrosia-filled glance, revived the cows and cowherds who had been killed by drinking from a pool infected by the poison of the evil snake Kāliya (see Kāliya). Composed in about 1100 CE by the Bengali poet Jayadeva, the Sanskrit *Gītāgovinda,* which has been called the *Song of Songs* of Hinduism, is both mystical and erotic. It celebrates the power of Kṛṣṇa-Govinda as a lover. Through the *Gītā,* the devoted worshipper can learn of the ecstatic love of Viṣṇu (see Viṣṇu), whose avatar (see Avatars of Viṣṇu) Govinda is (see *Gopīs*).

Guandi—See Huangdi.

Guanyin—A form of the bodhisattva (see Bodhisattva) Avalokiteśvara (see Avalokiteśvara), Guanyin in China becomes female and one of the most popular of Chinese deities (see Chinese Deities). In Japan she is the sometimes masculine, sometimes feminine Kannon (see Kannon). Guanyin is the provider of children (see Descent to the Underworld).

Gun—Gun was a descendant of the Chinese Yellow Emperor (see Chinese Emperors, Chinese Deities), Huangdi (see Huangdi), and the father of Yu (see Yu), one of the greatest of ancient Chinese heroes. Both Gun and Yu play significant roles in the ending of the Chinese Flood (see Chinese Flood).

H

Hachiman—The Japanese chronicles entitled *Kojiki* (see *Kojiki*) tell us that Hachiman, the Shinto (see Shinto entries) god of war, was in real life Ojin Tenno, a fourth-century emperor of Japan. From the late eighth century on, Hachiman was sometimes identified with Kannon (see Kannon) or even with Amida Buddha (see Amida Buddha). This last fact is in keeping with a tendency in Japan to see Shinto deities as local embodiments of Buddhist (see Japanese Buddhism) ones.

Hainuwele—The Wemale people of Ceram in Indonesia tell an origin myth in which the first animals and plants are the result of the sacrifice of the maiden Hainuwele. A man called Ameta cuts his finger while collecting sap from the newly discovered coconut tree and a baby girl, Hainuwele ("coconut branch"), emerges from the mixture of blood and sap. Hainuwele grows into mature girlhood in a few days and joins the ritual *Maro* dance that is being performed by the nine first human clans. Traditionally the men dance in circles around the women, who give the men betel to chew as they dance, but Hainuwele gives the people valuable gifts—coral, jewels, gongs, porcelain, and other things, all made from her excrement. On the ninth night of the dance the people, now jealous of Hainuwele's wealth, cause her to fall into a hole at the center of the dance circle, and they cover her over with earth. This is the first instance of human death. When Ameta later searches for Hainuwele, he discovers her body and dismembers it, planting various pieces in the earth. From these plantings come the staple tuberous vegetables of the Wemale people. And when the goddess Mulua Satene, angry at the murder of Hainuwele, an aspect of herself, strikes several of the people with the arm of the dead maiden, these people become the first animals.

Hanumān—The greatest of the Hindu (see Hinduism) monkey gods, Hanumān takes his immense strength from his father, the Vedic (see Vedic entries) wind-god Vāyu (see Vāyu), who is also the father of Bhīma, one of the Pāṇḍava (see Pāṇḍavas) brothers in the *Mahābhārata* (see *Mahābhārata*). Hanumān is worshipped as a protector to this day in shrines in many parts of India. In Hindu mythology (see Hindu Mythology), his primary deeds are recorded in the *Rāmāyaṇa* (see *Rāmāyaṇa*). In that epic, Hanumān leads the war to free Sītā (see Sītā), the wife of Rāma (see Rāma), an avatar of the god Viṣṇu (see Viṣṇu, Avatars of Viṣṇu), from the demon Rāvaṇa in Lanka. As the son of the Wind, he is able to make the passage from India to Lanka (Sri Lanka/Ceylon) in one leap. He demonstrates his powers of self-denial and his loyalty to Rāma by not rescuing Sītā himself so that Rāma can have the honor of doing so.

Haoma—Haoma is the ancient Iranian version of the Vedic (see Vedic entries) Soma (see Soma). It was the "drink of immortality" stolen in ancient times from the gods and used in ecstatic rituals by the early Indo-Europeans, including the people of the pre-Zoroastrian (see Zoroastrianism) reforms in Iran. Zarathustra (see Zoroaster) rejected the use of *haoma,* and it has found its way back into his religion only as a nontoxic substitute drink used in certain rituals by priests.

Hara—Hara (the "destroyer") is one of the many names of the Hindu god Śiva (see Śiva).

Hare Krishna—The International Society for Krishna Consciousness, or ISKCON, or Hare Krishna in the United States, is the result of the philosophy of Swami Prabhupada, the twentieth-century worshipper of the Hindu Viṣṇu avatar (see Viṣṇu, Avatars of Viṣṇu) Kṛṣṇa (see Kṛṣṇa). The practitioners of the movement work toward "Krishna Consciousness" as a means of salvation from the horrors and entanglements of the current age. Methods employed in this process include self-discipline, especially in connection with sexuality; specific rituals; and the singing recitation of the Kṛṣṇa mantra (see Mantra)—"Hare Krishna, Hare Krishna; Krishna, Hare, Hare; Hare Rama, Hare Rama, Rama, Rama; Rama, Rama, Hare, Hare" (see Rāma), accompanied by dancing.

Hari—Hari is a name of the Hindu (see Hindu entries) god Viṣṇu (see Viṣṇu). It is associated with the divinity of Viṣṇu and his avatar (see Avatars of Viṣṇu) Kṛṣṇa (see Kṛṣṇa). But the *Viṣṇu Purāṇa* (see *Purāṇas*) tells us that Hari is any divine presence—the vehicle by which Brahman (see Brahman) is made known.

Hari-hara—Especially in the Advaita Vedantism (see Advaita Vedānta) branch of Hinduism (see Hinduism), Viṣṇu (see Viṣṇu), who is also Hari (see Hari), is combined with Śiva (see Śiva), who is also known as Hara (see Hara), to form *Hari-hara,* a representation of the oneness of all things—Time being Hara and Space being Hari—united as a kind of manifestation of the Absolute, Brahman (see Brahman).

Harivamśa—This is a supplement to the Hindu epic the *Mahābhārata* (see *Mahābhārata*). It is a genealogy of the god Viṣṇu (see Viṣṇu), who is sometimes called Hari (see Hari, Hari-hara).

Haurvatat—One of the *Amesa Spentas* (see *Amesa Spentas*), of the Mazdian (see Mazdaizm) pantheon of Zoroastrianism (see Zoroastrianism), Haurvatat represents prosperity and is associated with Ameretat (see Ameretat) or immortality. Both are grouped with the earth goddess Spenta Armaiti or Spendarmat (see Armaiti).

Heavenly Weaver Girl—In a Chinese stellar myth (see Chinese Mythology, Chinese Deities), the Weaver Maiden was the daughter of the August Sun. She was obsessed by her weaving, which helped to maintain the order of the universe. When her father married her to the Heavenly Cowherd, she became so obsessed with her husband rather than with her weaving that the Sun had to separate the couple. So it is that they live as stars at opposite ends of the heavenly river that is called the Milky Way. On the seventh day of the seventh moon of each year, the Weaver Maiden crosses the Milky Way on a bridge of magpies and visits with her husband. This myth may reflect an aspect of Chinese peasant life, in which the husband often spent weeks away from home working in far-away fields while the wife attended to domestic chores at home.

Heike Monogatari—The *Heike Monogatari* is one of the greatest Japanese war epics *(gunki monogatari).* It was written from oral sources early in the thirteenth century. The epic concerns the rise and fall of the Heike or Taira clan of *samurai* and the eventual ascendancy of the rival Genji or Minamoto clan.

Hero quests—A common motif in world mythology, including Asian mythology, is that of the hero quest, in which a hero—the representative of a culture—seeks some significant goal or boon for his people. Often the voyage involves archetypal stages such as the miraculous conception or birth, the search for truth or riches or a lost loved one, a struggle with monsters, and the descent to the underworld (see Virgin Birth, Saoshyant, Karna, Gautama Buddha, *Rāmāyana,* Kṛṣṇa, Guanyin, Descent to the Underworld). The hero quest can be said to reflect our own search for identity in the face of internal and external denials of the call.

Hikajat Pòtjoet Moehamat—Pòtjoet Moehamat is one of the heroes of an epic poem of Aceh in northern Sumatra in Indonesia. The poem was transcribed from the oral form in the eighteenth century and is the legendary record of a civil war between Pòtjoet and his ally Béntara Keumangan and Djeumalōj Alam, a king who claims descent from the prophet Muhammad. In fact, the dominant hero of the epic is not Pòtjoet but Bentara, whose death at the hands of the king stirs up the people to support the war and Pòtjoet Moehamat's cause.

Hikayat Bayan Budiman—Also called *Hikayat Khoja Maimun,* this is one of several Malay epics containing the story of Sultan Ibrahim Ibn Adhem (see *Hikayat Sultan Ibrahim Ibn Adhem*).

Hikayat Sultan Ibrahim Ibn Adhem—The Malay epic about the famous Sultan of Iraq was written down in the seventeenth century. Ibrahim was a wise and just king much given to spiritual ways and asceticism. Having built a great wall around his city, Ibrahim invites the people to inspect it for flaws. When an old man tells him that there is a flaw in the wall as in all material things, the Sultan leaves his throne and becomes a traveling mendicant. Led by the vizier, the people beg their sultan to return, and he agrees to do so but as an Islamic (see Islam) mystic, or *sufi,* rather than as king. Various signs, however, lead him back to the road and eventually to marriage with a young maiden named Siti. After forty days, Ibrahim again takes to the spiritual and literal road and makes his way to Mecca to devote his life to Allah in worship. Eventually, his son Muhammad Tahir, born to Siti after his departure, goes to Mecca in search of his father. Ibrahim sends his son away saying he will join his family in the hereafter. Tahir travels to Iraq, where he advises his father's ministers and then returns to his mother. Both mother and son are much honored for the rest of their lives.

Hīnayāna Buddhism—Literally "Smaller vehicle," Hīnayāna is the name Mahāyāna (see Mahāyāna Buddhism), or "Large vehicle," Buddhists use for early forms of Buddhism (see Buddhism, Theravāda Buddhism), characterized by strict adherence to the teachings of Sākyamuni Buddha (see Gautama Buddha).

Hindu Mythology—Hindu (see Hinduism) mythology is a network of intermingling connecting threads, which, if it could be perfectly understood, would provide a clear narrative map to the rich tapestry that is Hindu thought. As in the case of the medieval cathedral, the decorations of the given Hindu temple confront the viewer as a mysterious mythic story in which everything has philosophical or religious significance. The postures of the figures depicted, the objects held by them, the way they relate to each other all have specific meanings. So it is with Hindu mythology as passed down orally and as written in the great epics and religious texts. No story is told for its own sake; every myth has meaning in relation to other myths and to the Vedic (see Vedic entries) tradition that is its ultimate source. This overall source is dominated by the idea of cosmic sacrifice and related human rituals, by a universe and individuals that are repeatedly sacrificed so that they might be reborn.

As Hinduism developed over the centuries from the period of the Aryan (see Aryans) invasions (c. 1500 BCE), so did its mythology—the narrative expression of its religious and philosophical understandings of the universe. The complex dance of the cosmos, reflected in human life, is acted out by a variety of deities, demons, and humans who, like the universe itself, possess qualities that are at once "good" and "evil," nurturing and destructive. The myths are found in many Sanskrit sources—especially the ancient *Ṛg Veda* (see *Ṛg Veda*), the other *Vedas* (see *Vedas*), the *Brāhmaṇas* (see *Brāhmaṇas*), the *Upaniṣads* (see *Upaniṣads*), the epic poems the *Mahābhārata* (see *Mahābhārata*) and the *Rāmāyaṇa* (see *Rāmāyaṇa*), and in the *Purāṇas* (see *Purāṇas*) of the Common Era.

In the *Ṛg Veda* there is a pantheon made up of the sovereigns Varuṇa (see Varuṇa) and Mitra (see Mitra) and the warrior Indra (see Indra) as well as the two ritual deities Agni (see Agni) and Soma (see Soma), or "the plant of immortality." Indra takes on a position of particular importance as the upholder of cosmic order by defeating the demonic *asura* (see *Asuras*) Vṛtra (see Vṛtra, Indra, and Vṛtra). Two sun gods are Sūrya (see Sūrya) and Savitṛ. Uṣas (see Uṣas) is goddess of the dawn. Yama (see Yama) is god of the dead and Vāyu (see Vāyu) is god of the wind. Rudra (see Rudra) is an outsider of sorts but will develop later into the powerful god Śiva (see Śiva). Viṣṇu (see Viṣṇu) and Devī (see Devī) are present in Vedic scripture but have not yet achieved their greatest power.

A dominant creation myth of the *Ṛg Veda* (see Vedic Cosmogony) is the animistic (see Animism) one of the sacrificial dismemberment of the primal man or Puruṣa (see Puruṣa), a myth that conveys the centrality of the ritual sacrifice in Hinduism. Puruṣa the first man is the sacrifice out of which all things originate, including the caste system. His mouth became the *brahmans* (see *Brahmans)*, those who teach with words; his arms became the *kṣatriyas,* the warrior caste; his thighs, the ordinary populace; and his feet, the servant classes. Indra and Agni were born of his mouth, Vāyu of his breath.

In the *Brāhmaṇas,* it is Prajāpati (see Prajāpati) who is the creator, sometimes by way of cosmic incest with his daughter, sometimes by way of masturbation. By the time we get to the *Mahābharata,* it is Brahmā (see Brahmā) who takes the place of Prajāpati as creator. The presence of Agni (fire) is important in these early creation stories. Agni "eats" even as the creator creates and his is the appropriate element to consume the dead human, who can then be reborn, as fire eats only the body and not the soul (see Ātman). In the *Purāṇas*, Brahmā creates good and evil. Eventually Brahmā will lose stature in favor of the great yogi Śiva; and Viṣṇu and his avatars (see Avatars of Viṣṇu), particularly Rāma (see Rāma) and the Lord Kṛṣṇa (see Kṛṣṇa); and the Goddess, or Devī, who is at once Pārvatī (see Pārvatī) the wife of Śiva, Kālī (see Kālī) the devourer, the violent Durgā (see Durgā), and various other forms (see *Śakti*).

Hinduism—Hinduism is the dominant philosophical system of India and of the Indonesian island of Bali. *Hindu* is a word derived etymologically from the Persian pronunciation of the Sanskrit *sindhu,* meaning "river" and referring to the Indus River Valley or India itself. Hinduism is more a flow of traditions, practices, and customs than it is a religion in the usual sense of the word. Unlike Buddhism (see Buddhism), Jainism (see Jainism), and Sikhism (see Sikhism), all of which are tributaries of Hinduism, Hinduism can point to no particular founder. If there is a dominant characteristic of Hinduism it is its ability and willingness to absorb all physical and philosophical experience and all gods and goddesses in a happy polytheism (see Hindu Mythology). It is true, however, that in practice, many Hindus tend to concentrate their worship on one of three particular deities—Śiva (see Śiva), Viṣṇu (see Viṣṇu), or the Goddess (see Devī). And in a mysterious way, with its all-encompassing absolute Brahman (see Brahman), Hinduism might be said to be *ultimately monist,* at least to some schools of thought (see Advaita Vedānta).

The beginning of an understanding of the complexities of Hinduism requires a historical context. Perhaps the earliest source of Hinduism was the religion of the Indus Valley (see Indus Valley Mythology) people of the Neolithic, before the invasion of Aryan (see Aryans) peoples from the north. The Indus Valley culture is sometimes referred to as Dravidian (see Dravidians), after the language probably spoken by the people there, or Harappan after one of the two major cities in the area. Indus Valley archeological evidence suggests a goddess-dominated religion with composite human-animal male figures, a tradition of ritual purification in pools, and a system of ritual sacrifice. Ancient seals depict an ithyphallic yogi-like figure with buffalo horns, a figure mirrored in later Hindu representations of the great god Śiva. The dominance of the Goddess is reflected in later Hinduism's emphasis on the various forms of Devī.

The Aryans, who arrived perhaps as early as about 1500 BCE, brought with them an Indo-European religious system and pantheon that bears much resemblance to the patriarchal systems of other Indo-Europeans such as the Greeks and the Iranians. They also brought the beginnings of what would become the characteristic Hindu caste system, a system that would be dominated by the two upper classes—the priestly *brahmans* (see *Brahmans*) and the warrior *kṣatriyas*. Preclassical Hinduism or Vedism is expressed most fully in the sacred knowledge called *Vedas* (see *Vedas,* Vedic entries), characterized as *śruti* or "that which is heard" (see *Śruti*). First transmitted orally, the *Vedas* were eventually transcribed—traditionally by the sage Vyāsa (see Vyāsa), who was also said to have written down the great Hindu epic the *Mahābhārata* (see *Mahābhārata*). The *Vedas* developed over many centuries and are made up of several kinds of texts. First are the four *Saṃhitās* (collections): the ancient *Ṛg Veda* or "chant *Veda*" (see *Ṛg Veda*), the *Sāma Veda* and the *Yajur Veda* (liturgical Vedas), and the *Athara Veda* ("Atharavan's *Veda*"). Offshoots of the Vedic texts were developed by schools of Vedic priests. These texts are called *Brāhmaṇas* (see *Brāhmaṇas*), *Āraṇyakas* (see *Āraṇyakas*), and *Upa-*

niṣads (see *Upaniṣads*). The *Brāhmaṇas,* the most important of which is the *Śatapatha Brāhmaṇa,* are expositions of the absolute Brahman by priests or *brahmans* (see Brahmans), and are concerned with the proper practice of rituals. In the *Brāhmaṇas* the *Ṛg Veda* one-time only world-forming sacrifice of the transcendent primal male Puruṣa (see *Puruṣa*) is essentially replaced by the cyclical death and resurrection sacrifice of Prajāpati (see Prajāpati), himself the source of the creator god Brahmā (see Brahmā), in a sense, a personification of the absolute Brahman. The original Puruṣa would evolve into the person of the god Viṣṇu. The theology that emerges from the *Brāhmaṇas* is called Brahmanism (see Brahmanism).

The *Āraṇyakas* ("books of the forest") are more mystical texts, centering on the inner life and the universal Brahman. They precede the *Upaniṣads* ("mystical understandings"), which move away from Brahmanic teachings about proper ritual to a belief that the individual must seek *mokṣa* (see M*okṣa*), or "release" from the life death continuum or *saṃsāra* (see *Saṃsāra*). To achieve *mokṣa* the disciple must learn—perhaps from a *guru*—the connection between the transcendent absolute or *Brahman* and the inner absolute *Ātman* (see *Ātman*). It is important to understand that the concept of life and the universe as developed in Vedic philosophy is the essence of Hinduism.

During the eight or nine hundred years after the late Vedic *Upaniṣads*—that is, from about 500 BCE—the great epics the *Mahābhārata* (see *Mahābhārata*), including and especially its *Bhagavadgītā* (see *Bhagavadgītā*) section of about 200 BCE, and the *Rāmāyaṇa* (see *Rāmāyaṇa*) play important roles in the development of a Hinduism dominated by the concepts of *bhakti* (see *bhakti*), or "devotion," and *dharma* (see *Dharma*), or "duty." Much mythical material of this classical Hinduism is also contained in works called *Purāṇas* (see *Purāṇas*), or "ancient stories," written between 400 and 1200 CE (see Hindu Mythology, Tantrism). The epics and the *Purāṇas* come under the category of *smṛti* (see *Smṛti*), "that which is remembered," rather than the more sacred *sṛuti*. If the epics and *Purāṇas* take what might be called mythological liberties, they are, nevertheless, firmly based in Vedic tradition and philosophy. The epics and the *Purāṇas* are, like the *Upaniṣads,* concerned with paths to salvation or *mokṣa*. They are also primary sources for Hindu mythology, which is important for everyday "popular" Hinduism.

Several schools of Hinduism have emerged during the many centuries in which attempts have been made to consolidate the many streams of the overall tradition into one "flow." Of these schools, two have achieved a certain dominance or orthodoxy. Both base their teachings on the Vedic philosophy, but the Mīmāṁsā school stresses the ritual tradition of the *Vedas,* while the Vedānta (see Vedānta, Advaita Vedānta) school emphasizes the more mystical understandings of the *Upaniṣads*. It must be emphasized, too, that many Hindus are particularly devoted to one of three deities, Śiva, Viṣṇu, and Devī, in their several forms or, in the case of Viṣṇu, avatars (see Avatars of Viṣṇu) or even to lesser deities such as Gaṇeśa (see Gaṇeśa).

It is tempting for adherents of monotheistic traditions to see all of the Hindu gods as incarnations of the one Absolute or Brahman, and in a sense they are. But Brahman is not "God" in any personal sense. Still, at the level of creation there is a *trimūrti* of gods working as one being and as aspects of that one Absolute. Brahmā (see Brahmā) is the creator, Śiva the destroyer, and Viṣṇu the preserver. These three roles are important at several levels, the most important of which is the Hindu understanding of the cosmic sacrificial cycles or *yugas* (see *yugas*), the throws of the cosmic dice of existence, whereby the universe is destroyed and re-created over and over again. It should be noted, too, that even by the last books of the *Ṛg Veda* the gods seem to take on the characteristics of each other, depending on the context of the hymn in question. One has the distinct sense in Hinduism that a single supreme Absolute expresses itself in many forms or gods.

Hoke-kyo—See *Lotus of the Good Law.*

Hou Ji—The Chinese divinity of the harvest.

Hsuan-tsang—see *Xuanzang*.

Huangdi—Huangdi (Guandi) is usually the famous Yellow Emperor of ancient China. But Huangdi is also the title for emperors in general (see Chiyou, Chinese Emperors). Huangdi was also a popular Chinese god who historically was a late Han dynasty warrior depicted in the Ming dynasty *Romance of the Three Kingdoms*. As a deity, Huangdi is associated with War and with Justice.

Hudhud—This is an oral epic recited over a period of many days by the Ifugao people of the Philippines.

I

I Ching—See *Yijing*.

Idaten—The Japanese god who protects monastic sects (see Japanese Buddhism). Particularly important to followers of the Zen (see Zen Buddhism) tradition, Idaten is known for his great speed. He wears a Chinese helmet and carries a sword.

Impetuous Male—See Susanowo.

Inari—Inari is a Japanese god associated with fertility and agriculture and especially rice. The fox is his particular animal symbol.

Indian Cosmogony—See *Vedic Cosmogony,* Laws of Manu, Prajāpati, Puruṣa, Brahmā, *Viṣṇu Purāṇa* Creation, Hinduism, Hindu Mythology, *Upaniṣad* Cosmogony.

Indian Mythology—See Hindu Mythology, Hinduism, Vedic entries, Indus Valley Mythology, Buddhist Mythology, and individual myths—especially those of Śiva, Viṣṇu, and Devī.

Indo-Chinese Mythology—The Austroasiatic and Austronesian peoples—the indigenous people of southern Indo-China—believe that everything was created by Ndu or Adei, the most important of the *yang* (spirits, sacred beings), who, although he provided milk and rice and otherwise provides for the people through particular expressions of *yang,* is, like the Hindu Brahman (see Brahman), a nonpersonal absolute that is everywhere and nowhere. Ndu/Adei can take form, however. There are many stories of Ndu's entering the world to assist humans. A story is told, for instance, of the culture hero, the orphan (Ddoi/Drit), who was refused rice by his uncle. As he wanders hungry along the road the young man meets Ndu in the form of an old man. Ndu gives the boy magic seeds for an abundant harvest of rice and brings about the death of the uncle, and he even provides a bride. Also important among tribes such as the Sre and the Jörai are female figures. There is a female sun and an old woman called Mother Bush or Dung-Dai, who is sometimes the wife of Adei.

The Sre people envision a world of many levels with the earth in the middle. Ndu was helped in the creation by the spirit Bung, who brought up plants from the lower worlds through a hole. For the Jorai, the earth is like a basket within another upside down basket that is the sky. Adei is king of the sky. The people emerged into the earth from a lower world, also by way of a small hole. Students of Native mythology of the American Southwest will note the likeness of this myth to the emergence creation myths typical of this area.

In the Jörai mythology, humans and animals conversed in ancient times and humans could fly. There was no death, and humans were like *yang*. It was only when men abused their paradise that Adei left them and they had to work to live. The Sre say that Ndu offered humans the water of immortality but that they found the water too cold and therefore only dipped their hands and feet and hair in it. So it is that people die but their hair and nails keep growing.

The Austrasians have a flood (see Flood) myth in which we are told that the only survivors of the deluge were a brother and sister who protected themselves in a drum. These two became the first human ancestors. Among the Austronesian tribes, it is a mother and son who survive. In both cases it is incest that becomes the basis for new life. As incest is taboo, sacrifices are necessary to purify what is essentially a flawed existence from which Ndu/Adei remains aloof and in which animals and humans are no longer in direct communication. All of the indigenous people of the Indo-Chinese region await an apocalypse or "cold darkness" at some future time.

There are many Austrasian and Austronesian myths in which the connection between the world of the *yang* and that of humans is reestablished by beings who take animal form or by spirits sent down to earth in human form. In one story the sun attracts a young man to the upper world by sending a spirit in the form of a beautiful woman to seduce him. In other stories a particular species of monkey is thought to be a remaining link between heavenly beings and earthly ones.

Shamanism (see Shamanism) is important in indigenous Indo-China. Shamans, like mythic heroes such as Drit, have the ability to take flight, to voyage in dreams between the worlds and to the ends of the earth. The shaman can use his dream voyage to confront tormentors of the sick in the other world and thus to achieve cures.

Indian Flood—See Fish and the Flood.

Indo-Iranian Mythology—See Aryans.

Indonesian and Malaysian Divinities—Among the many indigenous peoples in Indonesia and Malaysia there are several examples of dual gods and sometimes of trinities. In Sumatra, the Toba Batak see the Absolute Mula Jadi na Bolon as three persons representing the upper, middle, and lower worlds. In Nias there is a two-person divinity representing the dual nature of the universe—good and evil, light and dark. For the Ngaju people of Borneo, Jata is the feminine side of a dual godhead. She represents the lower world and the moon. Mahatala, the male aspect, is the upper world and the sun. Together Jata and Mahatala form the Absolute Tambon Haruei Bungai (see Southeast Asian entries; Indonesian, Malaysian, Philippine Origin Myths, and Dayak Myths.)

Indonesian, Malaysian, and Philippine Origin Myths—In the origin myths of insular southeast Asia, animals, humans, and plants are interrelated players. In Kalimatan, the Indonesian section of Borneo, the first woman springs from a tree destroyed in a struggle between the male and the female hornbill. In Ceram the heroine-goddess Hainuwele (see Hainuwele) is born of a mixture of blood and coconut sap. More generally, the first people descend from the heavenly region. Often, as in the case of Hainuwele, edible plants come from the body of a sacrificed hero or heroine (see Animism). Origin myths of the overall area usually include an explanation of the prevailing social order. Clan systems, for instance, are explained by myths of the descent of the first people at particular geographical locations. Nobility as opposed to commonness is explained by connections with particular deities. The origin myths often include stories of the adventures of culture heroes. In the Celebes, for example, the High God Patoto'e, sent his son La Toge 'langi to Earth, where he took the title Batara Guru. On his way to Earth, the hero traveled in a bamboo stalk, where he formed the world and its species. After a period of fasting, Batara Guru sent for his wives and servants, and thus the first human beings were categorized according to class. As his principal wife, Batara Guru took the daughter of the king of the Underworld (see Underworld). When his first earthly daughter died, rice was formed from her body. Descendants of Batara Guru became the culture heroes of various groups (see Stone and the Banana).

Indra—The Indra of the *Ṛg Veda* (see *Ṛg Veda*) is the king of the gods, the Vedic (see Vedic entries) version of the old Indo-European warrior god Zeus-Jupiter-Odin, the god of the warrior class *(kṣatriyas)*. He is, in effect, the Dyaus (see Dyaus), the heavenly representative of the Aryan (see Aryans) invaders of the Indian subcontinent during the second millennium BCE. He is the destroyer of cities—the conqueror. Like Zeus he wields the thunderbolt and sleeps with mortal women. Like Zeus he kills his father and is challenged by his son. One creation story tells us that Indra created the universe by separating Heaven and Earth. Later both Varuṇa and Viṣṇu will be credited with this deed. Indra is also the provider of *soma* (see Soma), the ambrosial drug mixed with milk in the ritual sacrifice. Indra is the sun and fertility, represented as Śiva (see Śiva) would later be represented, by the erect phallus. Perhaps most important, Indra represents the new order of Vedic India in the myth of the slaying of the great demon Vṛtra (see Vṛtra, Indra and Vṛtra).

In time Indra would be a figurehead only and sometimes the object of lessons and jokes (see Parade of Ants). By the time of the *Brāhmaṇas* (see *Brāhmaṇas*) in about 900 BCE, his power has waned. He is now besotted with *soma* and Prajāpati (see Prajāpati) is the supreme creator. Once the god of fertility, he is now a womanizer who is even at one point punished by castration. His place on the throne is dependent on the help of the now much more powerful Śiva and Viṣṇu (see Viṣṇu). Joseph Campbell and others have seen the process of Indra's decline as a process by which the Aryan invaders were somewhat assimilated by the older Dravidian (see Dravidians) religion already in place in India (see Indus Valley Mythology, Hinduism, Hindu mythology).

Indra and Vṛtra—As the king of the gods in the *Ṛg Veda* (see *Ṛg Veda*), Indra's (see Indra) primary task is to establish order. This he does in various ways. He frees the cows from the *Paṇis* (see *Paṇis*)—the pre-Aryan (see Aryans) demons of India, and he does so by killing the dragon demon Vṛtra (see Vṛtra) and Vṛtra's mother (see Diti). The Paṇis and the dragons both symbolize the "restraining" cultures that attempted to prevent the Aryan conquest of India. Energized by soma (see Soma) and using his thunderbolt to kill the *asura* (see *Asuras*) Vṛtra, who had enclosed the waters, Indra freed the waters and brought forth the sun and light and the new order.

In the *Mahābhārata* (see *Mahābhārata*) we find a quite different Indra. The king of the gods is now king in name only and has limited powers. Anxious that his enemy Tvaṣṭṛ (see Tvaṣṭṛ), the architect of the gods, has created the three-headed son Triśiras (see Triśiras) to overpower him, Indra slays the demon with his thunderbolt. In revenge, Tvaṣṭṛ creates the dragon Vṛtra, who defeats Indra—swallowing him and his whole world. It is only with the help of Viṣṇu (see Viṣṇu) and Śiva (see Śiva) that he and the world are freed.

Indus Valley Mythology—In the middle of the third millennium BCE an urban culture developed in the Indus Valley of western India. This culture was related in terms of myth and religion to the

Elamite culture of southwestern Iran and to village cultures of Afghanistan, Turkmenistan, and Baluchistan. The center of the Indus Valley culture were the cities of Harappa and Mohenjo-Daro, until a gradual decline beginning early in the second millennium BCE led to a movement of the culture to the Ganges–Yamuna Valley in the north and Gujarat and the Deccan plateau in the south. After the Aryan (see Aryans) invasions in the middle of the second millennium, there was an amalgamation of Indus Valley and Aryan traditions leading to the complexities of Vedic (see Vedic entries) religion and myth and to the Dravidian (see Dravidians) village culture of south India.

Archeological evidence from related cultures suggests that Indus Valley mythology was centered in the idea of female power and Goddess (see Devī) cults. There is direct evidence of Goddess dominance on Indus seals, which, like the seals of ancient Sumer, bring together goddesses, sacred snakes, and such symbols of male power and virility as horned bulls and rams and mythical animals such as unicorns. There is also ample indication on the seals of rituals involving sacrifice to what appears to be a horned goddess. At the ruins at the ancient settlement of Mehrgarh, dating back to as early as 6000 BCE, goddess figurines have been discovered that would seem to confirm the importance of the female power during the 600–2500 BCE period (see Hinduism, Hindu Mythology).

Iranian Afterlife—See Zoroastrian Afterlife.

Iranian Pantheon—See Amesa Spentas.

Islam—The word *Islam* comes from the Arabic root *slm* meaning a *Muslim* is a person who submits to the order and peace that is the law of Allah as described in the holy book, the *Qur'an*. Islam was founded in Arabia by the Prophet Muhammad, the "messenger" of Allah, in the seventh century CE. In 630 CE (AH 8), Muhammad and his followers took control of Mecca, the holy city of the Ka'bah ("cube") or "House of Allah," in the eastern corner of which is located the Black Stone. According to one myth this "cornerstone of the House" fell from Heaven or was brought by angels. In theory, the Muslim does not pray to the stone as an idol but to

God at the stone. The Ka'bah, however, was considered a sacred place by Arabs even before the rise of Islam and probably was worshipped.

In the Holy Book we are told of five aspects of the faith: belief in Allah (God), angels, the *Qur'an*, the messengers of God (prophets), and the Day of Judgment. Based on these five beliefs are the "Five Pillars of Islam": the public expression that "There is no god but Allah and Muhammad is his prophet"; the obligation of prayer five times a day while facing Mecca; almsgiving; fasting during Ramadan (the ninth month of the Islamic lunar calendar); and the *hajj,* or once in a lifetime pilgrimage to the Ka'bah at Mecca. Islam is a religion that is as much or more concerned with social order as with religious ritual or myths. There are, of course, myths of creation (Allah created the world in two days), the afterlife (see Afterlife) and the end of the world, as in the other Abrahamic religions, Christianity and Judaism. And there are myths surrounding the Prophet's life. But the primary concern has always been practical and rational Islamic law in this world. Its very simplicity and directness has always made Islam a religion with great appeal. The religion has traveled easily from continent to continent, including, with special success, to Asia.

By the middle of the eighth century CE, Islam dominated Turkistan, and under the Samanids in the ninth and tenth centuries, Islam made inroads into the domains of the shamanistic (see Shamanism) and Christian peoples of the steppes of Central Asia. Meanwhile, the religion had also made many converts in China. With the invasions of the Mongols and their tolerant attitude toward Muslims in the thirteenth and fourteenth centuries, Muslims became part of the ruling class in China. After the fall of the Mongols, however, Chinese Muslims were tolerated but not particularly welcomed into the mainstream of society.

Muslim traders and settlers came to the Indian subcontinent within a generation of the Prophet's death. By the end of the seventh century CE, Muslims had conquered parts of Afghanistan, and from the tenth century, Muslims began to conquer parts of the

North Indian plain. Parts of Bengal, Assam, and Orissa were taken early in the thirteenth century, and parts of Kashmir in the fourteenth. In the early sixteenth century, the Muslim Mughal dynasty was established on the ruins of the Muslim sultanate of Delhi by Babur, a descendant of Tamerlane and Gengis Khan. The dynasty would rule Northern India and eventually control most of the south as well until the last Mughal emperor was expelled by the British in 1858. Perhaps the greatest of the Mughals was Akbar, who reigned from 1556 to 1605 and was able, through tolerance and generosity, to win over his Hindu (see Hinduism) subjects. It was Akbar's grandson, Shah Jahnan, who built the Taj Mahal.

Islam remains the dominant religion of Central Asia, Pakistan, and Afghanistan, and Muslims are a significant minority in India. Muslims are a majority in Indonesia and Malaysia.

Izanagi and Izanami—The *Kojiki* (see *Kojiki*) and the *Nihongi* (see *Nihongi*), the primary sources for Japanese (see Japanese entries) pre-Buddhist or Shinto (see Shinto entries) mythology, tell of the mythological age that began with events surrounding the first couple, Izanagi and Izanami. When at the beginning of time chaos was overcome by the separation of Heaven and Earth, the first parents were created. Izanami was the passive principle—the "female who invites." Izanagi was the active principle—the "male who invites" (see *Yinyang*). When the first couple thrust a jeweled spear into the maternal waters below, the central island of Japan was formed. The couple decided to marry and did so after developing a courtship ritual in which the male was dominant and in which the details of the procreative act were discussed. From their union came the islands of Japan and eventually the sun goddess, the source of all Japanese emperors, Amaterasu (see Amaterasu).

The Izanami-Izanagi cycle contains a particularly dark myth in which Izanagi goes to the Land of the Dead (see Underworld) in search of his wife, who had been killed, in effect, by giving birth to fire. When he arrives, he finds that Izanami, like Persephone in the Greek underworld, had already eaten of the fruit of the Dead and therefore could not return with her husband to life. Izanami orders Izanagi not to look at her body, now deformed by death, but he disobeys, and Izanami, insulted, chases him to the very gates of Yomi (see Yomi), the Underworld. Having wrongly visited the Underworld, Izanagi is plagued by bad luck until he is able to wash in sacred waters, after which he isolates himself on a distant island. His wife becomes queen of the Underworld.

Izumo Cycle—The Impetuous Male, Susanowo (see Susanowo), brother to the Japanese sun goddess Amaterasu (see Amaterasu), after his banishment from the heavens, goes to Izumo across the water from Korea. He builds a palace there at Suga and marries the daughter of an earth spirit for whom he has killed a notorious eight-headed monster. Susanowo and his wife then become parents to many important gods—especially Okuninushi (see Okuninushi) and the "Spirit Master" of Izumo.

J

Jahangir—The oldest son of Tamerlane (Timur), Jahangir is the fourteenth-century villain/hero of the Mongolian verse epic named for him.

Jain cosmology—Jains (see Jainism) believe in a three-part cosmos comprised of upper, middle, and lower worlds. At the bottom are seven hells for people whose lives were marked by bad *karman* (see *Karman*). Divinites live in the upper world. The middle world is a place where the individual can learn to be awakened and liberated. At the center of the Middle World is Mount Mandara or Meru (see Meru). Like the Brahmanic (see *Brāhmaṇas*) cosmology, which it generally resembles, the Jain system recognizes a cosmic cyclical time made up of *kalpas* or recurring ages.

Jainism—Founded in part by Vardhamāna Jnātṛputra, or Mahāvīra (see Mahāvīra) in the sixth century BCE, Jainism remains an important religious philosophy and tradition in India. It seems likely that Jainism first came fully into being with the joining of the followers of Mahāvīra and those of an earlier prophet, Pārśva. Over the centuries the Jains have evolved into two primary communities, the Digambara (the sky-clad or naked) and the Śvetāmbara (the white-clad). There are four orders of Jains—monks, nuns, laymen, and laywomen. In general, Jains practice an extreme form of the disciplines practiced by Brahmanic (see Brahmanism) and

Buddhist (see Buddhism) monks. Jain monks and nuns must, above all, practice *ahiṁsā* (see *Ahiṁsā*) or nonviolence to any living creature, be it man or insect. The monastic vows or *mahāvratas* are all directed toward a goal of liberation from internal and external bonds. Strict and complex rules of fasting, eating, begging, wandering, confession, and study apply. It is by means of the strictest asceticism that the Jain monk may achieve the remains of *karman* (see *Karman*) so that his soul, or *jīva* (see *Jīva*), might achieve its true nature and ascend to the Upper World beyond the bondage of death and rebirth (see Jain Cosmology).

Jalandhara—According to a Hindu myth (see Hinduism entries), Jalandhara was a Herakles-like *asura* (see *Asuras*) born of the union of Gaṅgā (see Ganges) and the Ocean, who had immense strength and was able to conquer the gods and the three worlds. Brahmā (see Brahmā) had given him the gift of being able to raise the dead. He defeated the great Viṣṇu (see Viṣṇu) in battle and perhaps would have killed him had the god's wife, Lakṣmī (see Lakṣmī), not intervened. He is said to have attempted to seduce Śiva's (see Śiva) wife, Pārvatī (see Pārvatī). Jalandhara was finally defeated in single combat with Śiva, who used a flaming disc to decapitate him and then instructed the goddesses to become ogresses and to drink the demon's blood before he could raise himself from death.

Japan (origin of)—See Izanagi and Izanami.

Japanese Afterlife—The pre-Buddhist or Shinto (see Shinto entries) version of afterlife (see Afterlife) is both complex and somewhat inconsistent. In the *Kojiki* (see *Kojiki*) we are told that Izanagi (see Izanagi and Izanami) visits his wife Izanami in *Yomi no kuni* (see Yomi), a place of darkness and impurity inhabited by furies. The passage to it is blocked by a boulder, and the putrefied Izanami reigns there as queen in a palace. There is no indication of judgment in this afterlife setting, but gloom decidedly prevails. In other stories *Yomi* is less gloomy, and there is a tradition that the dead live in the sky or on top of mountains (where they are often buried). During the annual rites of the Buddhist-originated (see Japanese

Buddhism) *Bon* festival, the dead ancestors are said to return to visit their families (see Pure Land and see Jigoku).

Japanese Buddhas—In the esoteric sects of Buddhism (see Japanese Buddhism, Buddhism) such as the Shingon (see Shingon sect), the deities of Shinto (see Shinto entries), the *kami* (see *Kami*), are manifestations of the Absolute Buddha, the Dainichi Nyorai (see Dainichi). The theory behind this concept is called *honji suijaku.* The process by which Shinto deities were assimilated into Buddhism as *bodhisattvas* (see *Bodhisattva*), or *bosatsu,* that is, future Buddhas *(nyorai),* and then as avatars *(gongen)* or temporary manifestations on earth of Buddhas, was gradual until by the Middle Ages, Shinto *kami* became, in effect, Buddhist *kami* (see individual *bosatsu* and *nyorai,* for example, Shaka, Amida, Miroku, Yakushi, Kannon, Jizo).

Japanese Buddhism—Buddhism (see Buddhism) in Japan takes several forms but is particularly marked by a tendency toward the esoteric. The religion was introduced into Japan during the fifth and sixth centuries CE in connection with the gradual influx of Sino-Korean philosophy and imagery and the adaptation of the Chinese script. When Buddhism was officially introduced to the Japanese court in the sixth century, there was strong reaction against it on the part of the conservative guardians of the ancient Shinto (see Shinto entries) tradition and its divinities, or *kami* (see *Kami*). It was the powerful Soga clan that supported Buddhism and attached it to the state. Under the regent Prince Shotoku in the late sixth and early seventh centuries there was a bringing together of Buddhism and the indigenous Shinto religion that would color Japanese Buddhism from then on. In the eighth century—the Nara period—the religion flourished, especially in the capital, Nara, where many monasteries were established. The ninth century was marked by the development of the characteristic esoteric tradition that stressed enlightenment. The leaders in this movement were the Tendai (see Tendai Sect) and Shingon sects (see Shingon Sect). The Shingon sect especially stressed the esoteric, believing that the true Buddhist could achieve union with the absolute (see Japanese

Buddhas, *Bodhisattva*). Influenced by Tantrism from India (see Tantrism), the esoteric sects gained in popularity with the Japanese people because of the emphasis they put on the accessibility of the nature of Buddha. They also gained in popularity by their willingness to assimilate the old Shinto *kami* into their systems. In the tenth century, the cult of the Buddha Amitābha or Amida Buddha (see Amida Buddha) gained in popularity. The Tendai sect especially preached the idea that Enlightenment through the teachings of the Buddha Sākyamuni (see Gautama Buddha) was no longer possible. To achieve Enlightenment the devout person would have to be reborn in the Pure Land (see Pure Land), or *Gokuraku-jodo,* the land where the Buddha Amida preached. It was the monk Honen and his disciple Shinran who in the twelfth and thirteenth centuries developed this doctrine. In reaction to Amidism the Zen (see Zen Buddhism) sect arose. Its first master was the thirteenth-century monk Dogen. Dogen advocated the practice of ecstatic meditation and a return to the original principles of the Buddha Sākyamuni. Some sects of Zen Buddhism consider him their founder.

Japanese Cosmogony—See Izanagi and Izanami.

Japanese Mythology—See Shinto Mythology, Japanese Buddhas, Japanese Buddhism, *Kami.*

Japanese Shamanism—In pre-Buddhist animistic (see Animism, Shinto entries) Japan, shamans (see Shamanism) had the responsibility of organizing religious ceremonies and performing cures for the various clans. With the coming of Buddhism (see Buddhism, Japanese Buddhism) with its magical formulae, or *mantras* (see *Mantras*), shamans participated in more secular activities as well. Furthermore, *shido-so,* monks unattached to temples, wandered the countryside practicing magic, exorcising demons, and telling the future to paying customers. Some Buddhist shamanic figures such as one Ozuno from Mount Katsragi, became the source of legends. Ozuno walked on water, flew through the skies each evening on a multicolored cloud, and kept company with spirits.

Japanese Sun Cult—The Yamato tribes—the people of the first emperor (see Jimmu Tenno)—were members of a sun cult in which the primary deity was the sun goddess Amaterasu (see Amaterasu). Amaterasu remains an important aspect of the emperor cult. It is said that she is the ancestor of the emperors. Her sanctuary is at Ise, near Nagoya (see Shinto entries, *Kami*).

Jātaka Tales—*Jātaka* literature is composed of some 550 myths and legends that have developed over the centuries about former existences of the Buddha (see Gautama Buddha, *Bodhisattva*). Some of the tales are clearly Buddhist (see Buddhism) in origin, some are taken from earlier folklore. There are animal tales with morals attached, much as in the tradition of Aesop or the later La Fontaine in Europe. Most important, however, the *jātaka* literature serves to illustrate the law of *karman* (see *Karman*), according to which events can be explained by past occurences. Thus the Bodhisattva develops into the being he has created by his past actions. In a tale that relates to the story contained in the *Rāmāyaṇa* (see *Rāmāyaṇa*) of the bridge made between India and Lanka by the monkey king Hanumān (see Hamumān), the Boddhisattva, who in a previous life was a monkey king, saved his monkey followers from archers by making a bridge, of which his own body was a segment, across the Ganges (see Ganges). Unfortunately, the monkey who would be the future Buddha's jealous cousin Devadatta deliberately fell on the king, breaking his back. The monkey king took no revenge but died a beautiful death at Banāras (see Banāras), all the while advising the local king on proper governing. The moral of the tale is centered in the compassion that will become one of the primary attributes of the future Buddha.

Javanese Mythology—With the establishment of Islam (see Islam) in Indonesia, the indigenous myths of Java and other areas have been retained as folktales rather than as vehicles for religious truth. The first part of one of these tales, that of the hero Jaka Tarub, is reminiscent of the Indian story of Kṛṣṇa (see Kṛṣṇa) and the *Gopis* (see *Gopis*).

One evening Jaka Tarub comes across several beautiful maidens or *bidadari* (angel-like heavenly spirits) swimming in a pond. As the spirits' winged clothes are on the bank of the pool, Jaka Tarub steals one set of them, making it impossible for the spirit Nawangwulan to fly away. Jaka Tarub and Nawangwulan marry and produce a daughter named Nawangsih. Nawangwulan feeds her family by magic, placing one grain of rice in the pot each day that produces more than ample food, but she does so only on the condition that her husband not look into the pot. Of course, when she is away one day he does look into the pot and the magic is immediately dispelled, making it necessary for the family to use rice supplies like everyone else. Disappointed in her husband, the *bidadari* finds her winged garment and flies off to the other world.

Jayadeva—See Govinda.

Jigoku—A name for Hell as opposed to *gokuraku* (paradise) in Japanese Pure Land Buddhism (see Pure Land Buddhism, Japanese Afterlife).

Jimmu Tenno—According to the *Kojiki* (see *Kojiki*) and the *Nihongi* (see *Nihongi*), the primary sources for Japanese mythology, Jimmu Tenno was the first in the long line of Yamato emperors of Japan. His mother is said to have descended from the god of the sea and from the sun goddess Amaterasu (See Amaterasu). His wife, the first empress Ahira-tsu-hime, was of the family of the storm god Susanowo (see Susanowo). Jimmu Tenno led his people from the place where Amaterasu's grandson Ninigi (see Ninigi) had first come to earth to Yamato, which he made his capital. He lived to be well over 120 years old.

Jīva—The true "life" or "soul" for the Hindu (see Hinduism) and the Jain (see Jainism), the *jīva,* ideally, achieves freedom from deterministic *karman* (see *Karman*)—the person's past actions—so that it can be liberated rather than tied to another material incarnation.

Jizo—Jizo-bosatsu or Bodhisattva (see *Bodhisattva*) Kṣitigarbha, has gradually become a popular figure in Japanese Buddhist (see Japanese Buddhism) mythology. Jizo is of the earth and of the lower world. He is traditionally the advocate for the dead in their judgment in Hell (see Jigoku). His fame owes much to his development by the esoteric Tendai (see Tendai Sect) and Shingon (see Shingon Sect) sects of Japanese Buddhism. Jizo's solemn vow is to stay in the world to alleviate the suffering of humanity rather than to achieve Enlightenment and Nirvāna (see Nirvāna) for himself (see Emma).

Jodo—see Pure Land Buddhism.

Journey to the West (Xiyouji)—See Xuanzang, see Monkey.

K

Ka'bah—Literally the "cube," it is located in the Saudi Arabian city of Mecca and is called the "House of Allah." As the primary Islamic (see Islam) shrine, it is faced by Islamic worshippers worldwide during the five daily ritual prayers and is the pilgrimage *(Hajj)* goal of all Muslims at least once during a given lifetime. The myths surrounding the Ka'bah suggest that its corner stone—the "Black Stone"—fell from Heaven or was brought to Mecca by angels. The stone is traditionally kissed by Muslims on their pilgrimage as it was said to have been kissed by the Prophet Muhammad.

Kālakācāryakathā—This is a series of twelfth-century CE stories about the famous first-century BCE Śvetāmbara Jain (see Jainism) teacher named Kālaka—the "black teacher." As the stories are not only in Sanskrit but the vernacular Prākit, it has been suggested that they are in reality about the deeds of several Jain teachers who supposedly righted wrongs, one going so far as to confront the god Indra (see Indra) himself.

Kālī—One of several forms of the great Indian Goddess or Devī (see Devī, Pārvatī, Durgā, Śakti), Kālī is the black goddess of destruction, the logical wife for Śiva (see Śiva) in his aspect of great Destroyer in the dance of existence (see Dance of Śiva). But whereas Śiva's dance is in the cosmic realm, Kālī's is in this world.

Kālī's name is the feminine form of the word *kāla,* meaning Time, that which relates to the ever-devouring principle that dominates the animate world. Her name is also related to the Vedic (see Vedic entries) name for one of the tongues of the sacrificial fire. Kālī might be said to be the embodiment of the Hindu (see Hinduism, Hindu Mythology) belief: that the world exists only by way of sacrifice. Essential to this belief is the idea that the consumption of aspects of life is the source of prosperity. It should be noted in this connection that "Prosperity" is the meaning of Lakṣmī (see Lakṣmī), the wife of Viṣṇu (see Viṣṇu), the Preserver. In the popular depiction of Kālī, who has wild eyes, bloody fangs, and human heads as a necklace around her neck, she is standing on an apparently dead Śiva, who nevertheless has an erection. The combination of Śiva's virility, the destructive nature of the Kālī figure, and the fact that the goddess carries a bowl overflowing with the abundance of life, would seem to suggest the necessity of death for fertility and the constant creation of life. It may be said that Kālī's rampages also represent the spiritual necessity of killing weaknesses of the spirit without mercy in order to discover the true self. Kālī is particularly popular in Bengal.

Kāliya—Kāliya, the black serpent king who lived in the Yamunā River, was the incarnation of the demon Kālanemi who had been killed by the Hindu (see Hindu Mythology) god Viṣṇu (see Viṣṇu). It was appropriate that as Kālanemi's incarnation Kāliya should be killed by Viṣṇu's incarnation, or avatar (see Avatars of Viṣṇu), Kṛṣṇa (see Kṛṣṇa). It is also significant that before Kṛṣṇa's confrontation with Kāliya, the serpent has insulted Viṣṇu by taking an offering away from Garuḍa, the bird especially associated with the god. The *Bhāgavata Purāṇa* (see *Purāṇas*) tells the story of how Kṛṣṇa freed the waters polluted by Kāliya's poison, as Indra (see Indra) had once freed the waters by slaying the demon Vṛtra (see Vṛtra, Indra and Vṛtra). In this myth, the young Kṛṣṇa proves his worthiness, like so many heroes before him and after him, by vanquishing the "dragon." To purify the waters, Kṛṣṇa jumps from a tree into the Yamunā causing a tremendous splash that attracts the demon. After a great wrestling match the Kāliya is so exhausted that Kṛṣṇa dances on his head, symbolizing Viṣṇu's sleep on Ananta (see Ananta), the serpent of eternity. When the serpent's wives beg Kṛṣṇa to spare their master and Kāliya himself bows down before the Lord, Kṛṣṇa agrees to spare Kāliya's life but banishes him and his family to the depths of the ocean, where all evil things are ultimately sent. The river is thus purified for the people and the cows so loved by Kṛṣṇa.

Kāma—Kāma means "desire" in Sanskrit and thus Kāma is the Indian god of love. A well-known myth of the *Sāura Purāṇa* (see *Purāṇas*) tells how Kāma awakened the great Śiva (see Śiva) from his meditation to call attention to the amorous Pārvatī (see Pārvatī). Śiva, as the ascetic yogi, becomes so angry that he destroys the god of love with the fire of his third eye. But when Pārvatī points out that without Kāma there can be no love between men and women, Śiva, as the god of the *liṅga* (see *Liṅga*), relents and allows Kāma to circulate in the world.

Kāmadhenu—Kāmadhenu is the general name applied to the cow so sacred to Hindus (see Hinduism). The cow stands for prosperity—as does Lakṣmī (see Lakṣmī), the wife of Viṣṇu (see Viṣṇu). Kāmadhenu is especially associated with *brahmans* (see *Brahmans*) and their "wealth," because she is the producer of the milk and the clarified butter, the offerings traditionally placed on the sacrificial fire. Cows are protected as *brahmans* are; the two cannot be separated. To destroy a cow would be to defy the cosmic order and to deny the need for the gifts of rain, plants, and animals that sacrifice brings to earth. In short, order can only be maintained by means of proper sacrifice, both at the cosmic and worldly level. The cow is distinctly of the world, as she is associated with earth, and it is by her that the essential offerings are given (see Churning of the Ocean of Milk).

Kāmamma Katha—The Telugu people of southern India sing this epic of the young widow Kāmamma, a relative of the river goddess Gaṅgā (see Ganges), who wishes to perform *satī* (see *Satī*)—

self-immolation on the funeral pyre—to honor her dead husband and to raise herself beyond her caste. By means of a miraculous projection of herself into the dream of a resisting British official she convinces the authorities to allow her to do as she wills, and her friends congregate to watch her burn. Hers is a sacrifice that results in a deification.

Kami—Shinto (see Shinto entries) deities in Japan are known as *kami*. Shinto is literally "the way of the *kami*." For the Japanese Buddhist (see Japanese Buddhism) the Shinto *kami* are sometimes earthly representations of buddhas (see Japanese Buddhas). In the esoteric traditions of the Shingon sect (see Shingon sect) the *kami*—like everything else in the universe—were outward representations of the Buddha Dainichi (see Dainichi). But the concept of *kami* involved more than divinities *per se* in the pre-Buddhist Japanese culture. That culture was animistic (see Animism); that is, everything in the world was seen as "animated" by a vitality that came from the spirit realm, so that all beautiful things could be worshipped as *kami*.

Kaṃsa—In Hindu mythology (see Hinduism entries), the evil King Kaṃsa, cousin or brother of Kṛṣṇa's (see Kṛṣṇa) mother Devakī (see Devakī), reminds us of King Herod in the Christian story or of Kronos in Greek mythology. Hearing from a prophecy that his sister's eighth child will kill him, he decrees that each of her children must be killed upon delivery. Viṣṇu (see Viṣṇu), however, foils his plans by substituting embryos of demons in Devakī's womb and arranging for the baby Kṛṣṇa, his own incarnation (see Avatars of Viṣṇu), to be exchanged with another at birth. Kaṃsa is later killed by the adult Kṛṣṇa.

Kan Pudei—Kan Pudei is the hero of a Central Asian (see Central Asian Mythology) Altaic (see Altaic Mythology) tale of a boy who longs to avenge the murder of his father and eventually convinces his mother to allow him to do so.

Kannon—Kannon or Kanzeon-bosatsu, the Japanese version of the Bodhisattva (see *Bodhisattva*) Avalokiteśvara (see Avalokiteśvara), is perhaps the most admired of the Japanese Mahāyāna

Buddhist (see Mahāyāna Buddhism) *bodhisattvas*. Like the Chinese counterpart Guanyin (see Guanyin), Kannon, who is sometimes male, sometimes female, is compassionate. People of many sects of Buddhism (see Japanese Buddhism) in Japan make special offerings and prayers to Kannon for help with their everyday lives. One tradition holds that Kannon can take thirty-three forms. Thus for some thousand years people have been making pilgrimages to the thirty-three Kannon shrines in Kyoto and Nara.

Kanyakā Amavāri Katha—Like *Kāmamma Katha* (see *Kāmamma Katha*), this is a medieval epic of southern India. It is the story of Kanyakā, a woman and subsequent goddess of the *kōmaṭi* or commercial caste. Kanyakā introduced cross-cousin marrying to her people so that their women would be unattractive and therefore not be bothered by men. This was because she had been persecuted by a lustful king who had demanded her hand in marriage and vowed to win it by war if necessary. Rather than marry the king, Kanyakā leads a group of the leading *kōmaṭis* to death on a funeral pyre. As she has decreed before her death, the lustful king dies upon entering her city.

Karman—For Hindus (see Hinduism) and Jains (see Jainism), *karman* (*karma* is the nominative Sanskrit form) originally referred to proper ritual actions, but the term has come to denote past actions that will affect what happens to a person in various hells or paradises after death and in the individual's particular rebirth or reincarnation. Literally, what one is now is the result of what one did in the past and what one is now contains seeds for the future. According to the Law of Karman, life is a series of deaths and rebirths determined by one's past actions. To achieve true liberation from the cycle of life (see *Saṃsāra*), one must theoretically achieve total nonaction, total negation of *karman*.

Buddhists (see Buddhism) also consider that a person's situation is determined by his or her *karman*, and that good *karman* can in some ways eliminate the results of bad *karman*.

Karṇa—Karṇa is a hero (see Hero Quest) in the Indian epic the *Mahābhārata* (see *Mahābhārata*) who is allied with the enemies of the Pāṇḍavas (see Pāṇḍavas). Until late in the epic he is not aware that he is the half brother of three of the Pāṇḍava brothers, as he is the son of their mother, Kuntī (see Kuntī), and the Sun (see Sūrya). Karṇa was the firstborn of Kuntī while she was still a virgin (see Virgin Birth). By invoking a spell taught her by the sage Durvāsa, Kuntī became impregnated by the "light of the Universe." Karṇa's life is marked by several aspects of the archetypal hero's biography, such as a miraculous conception and an abandonment in a basket in a river. In a sense, his role in the epic is that of dark shadow to Arjuna (see Arjuna), the true hero. It will be Karṇa's fate to be sacrificed in a climactic battle with Arjuna. It is a death that is a reminder of the necessity of sacrificial destruction for redemption in the Hindu (see Hinduism) world view, a world view of which the *Mahābhārata* is a kind of narrative map.

Kārttikeya—The brother of Gaṇeśa (see Gaṇeśa) and the son of Śiva (see Śiva) and Pārvatī (see Pārvatī), Kārttikeya—also known as Skanda—is essentially an opposite to his brother, as Śiva the ascetic is an opposite to Pārvatī, the Mountain Mother goddess. As Śiva and Pārvatī form a whole, so do Gaṇeśa and Kārttikeya. A popular myth about the two brothers has to do with the desire of their parents that they marry. As marriage is a question of the achievement of *śakti* (see *Śakti*), or true inner energy personified by the wife, it is important to the parents to decide which of their sons should achieve this power first. A test is arranged by which the brothers are to enter a race around the earth. Kārttikeya takes the command literally and circles the earth itself. Gaṇeśa wins, however, by simply circling his parents seven times, following a Vedic (see Vedic entries) formula, or *mantra* (see *Mantra*) for the honoring of parents and symbolizing by this act that Śiva and Pārvatī in union *are* the world (see Murugan).

Kāṭamarāju Kathi—This medieval epic of southern India exists in a written version attributed to the fifteenth-century poet Śrīnātha. The epic is concerned with a cattle-herding caste claiming descendancy from Lord Kṛṣṇa (see Kṛṣṇa). A cattleman hero, Kāṭamarāju, makes an agreement with a king regarding grazing rights. An argument develops and leads to a war between the cattlemen and the king's army. One of the cattlemen becomes afraid and deserts his comrades in battle. He is derided by his wife and mother for his cowardice and returns to battle only to be killed. When he is brought home for the ritual cremation, his wife proves her devotion by joining him on the pyre.

Kauravas—The Kauravas are the one hundred sons of the blind Dhṛtarāṣṭra who challenge their cousins the Pāṇḍavas (see Pāṇḍavas) for control of the Bharata kingdom in the *Mahābhārata* (see *Mahābhārata*). Their leader is the jealous Duryodhana who in his immoral actions takes on his father's blindness in the form of spiritual blindness opposed to moral duty or *dharma* (see *Dharma*).

Kay Husroy—According to Zoroastrian (see Zoroastrianism) tradition, Kay Husroy is a hero king who joins the struggle against the forces of evil and reigns with Saoshyant (see Saoshyant).

Kersāspa—Kersāspa or Sam Kersasp, is the hero king who defeats the evil King Dahaka in the great Zoroastrian (see Zoroastrianism) struggle between good and evil (see Thraētaona).

Kesar Saga—See *Gesar Saga.*

Khvarenah—In the ancient Mazdian-Zoroastrian (see Mazdaism, see Zoroastrianism) tradition of Iran, the supreme god Ahura Mazda (see Ahura Mazda) creates the *khvarenah,* which is at once holiness and fortune. Mythologically, the concept is a deity of sorts, which is associated with both water and fire. *Khvarenah* is essentially *charisma,* that which is the source of the power of Iranian heroes, kings, and the nation itself.

Kishimo—This Japanese Buddhist (see Japanese Buddhism) deity, originally known as Mother Hārītī (Karitei-mo), the Mother of Demons, fed on the children of Rajagriba during the days of the Buddha Sākyamuni (see Gautama Buddha). The people asked for the Buddha's help against the demonness and the Buddha hid Mother Hārītī's youngest child under his alms bowl. When the demonness, in despair over the loss of her child, asked for the Buddha's help he pointed out to her the similarity of her pain to that of the parents whose children she had devoured. So Mother Hārītī was converted and became the guardian of children. A Kishimo-jin cult developed in China in the seventh century CE and later in Japan under the Shingon (see Shingon Sect) and Nichiren sects. Babies are taken to shrines of the goddess to ensure their health and protection.

Kojiki—The *Kojiki* ("Record of Ancient Matters") is a product of the commands of the Japanese emperor Temmu in the seventh century CE. The object was to collect and record ancient myths and legends of Japan. We are told that the storyteller Heida no Are recited the legends to the scribe O no Yasumaro. The selection of stories and the way they were written down were influenced by the political and social mores and priorities of the time. With the *Nihongi* (see *Nihongi*), the *Kojiki*, published in 712, is the major source for present knowledge of Shinto mythology (see Shinto entries).

Kongiue Dongnan Fei—This is a Chinese folk ballad from the beginning of the third century CE during the Han dynasty. It is a *Romeo and Juliet*–like tale of star-crossed lovers faced with the conventional marriage plans of their elders. The lovers are separated. The woman drowns herself, causing the man to hang himself, and the now understanding families bury the young lovers in the same grave.

Kordabbu—This epic of the Tulu-speaking people of southern India tells the story of the magical and apparently virgin-born (see Virgin Birth) hero (see hero Quest) Kordabbu, who, although of a low caste, is raised by an upper caste family after he is orphaned. Kordabbu is a trickster and a miracle maker whom the king finds threatening. The king tricks the hero into entering a well, where he is trapped until he is freed by the magic of a young woman named Tani, who then becomes his "sister" to preserve her virtue. The two travel about performing magical acts and are much revered.

Korean Mythology—The indigenous pre-Buddhist (see Buddhism), pre-Confucian (see Confucianism), pre-Daoist (see Daoism), and pre-Christian religion of the Korean peninsula seems to have been shamanistic (see Shamanism) in nature. At the center of the religious rituals were women called *mudang,* who communicated with deities and ancestors and told fortunes. They were also knowledgeable about the afterlife. The religion of the *mudang* was polytheistic and somewhat animistic (see *Animism*). There were several Mountain Gods, an Earth God, and figures called Dragon King God, Good Luck God, Kitchen God, Childbirth God, and even Smallpox God. And there were—and often still are—gods for nearly every part of the house: toilet gods, house beam gods, chimney gods, and so forth. There are ancient myths of creation and heroes that resemble those in Chinese mythology (see Chinese entries), as in the case of the hero Čumong, known as the "good archer," as was the Chinese Yi (see Yi). A creation story tells us that after a crack appeared in chaos so that the sky and earth could be separated, an archer shot down one of two suns and one of two moons before humans were made from earth. The archer here may have been Čumong. If so, he is even more directly connected with the Chinese Yi, who shot down nine of ten original suns.

Čumong has many characteristics of the archetypal hero (see Hero Quest). First, in some versions he is conceived miraculously (see Virgin Birth). His mother-to-be was Ryuhwa, sometimes seen as a daughter of the god of the waters, sometimes as maiden daughter of a king. One day the sun or the "son of the sky" shines on her, causing her to become pregnant and to deliver an egg. Horrified, the king tries to dispose of the egg by abandoning it, as Moses and Siegfried (Sigurd) and many other heroes were abandoned. But like other abandoned heroes the child is protected by animals who refuse to eat the egg. Eventually, under Ryuhwa's renewed care, a beautiful boy breaks out of it. This is Čumong, the archer.

When followers of the King plotted to kill the hero, as followers of kings so often do, Čumong was saved by the power of his father, the "Emperor of Heaven" and his mother, daughter of the god of the waters. Čumong went on the traditional hero journey of adventures, achieving, in his case, the shamanic (see Shamanism) powers symbolized by the mastery of the drum, the ability to cause water to dry up with his whip, and the power to conquer evil kings.

As a shamanic figure or as the son of the sun and a descendant of the waters, Čumong could move freely between the various worlds. He could fly into the heavens or travel under the sea. Čumong fathered a son and left behind a sign that the son had to find—in the manner of Theseus and King Arthur, for example—before he could be recognized as the crown prince. Eventually the son, Yuri, found a piece of a broken sword belonging to his father and was duly recognized. The stories of Čumong are found in many texts, especially the *Wei che*.

Kotan Utunnai—The indigenous Ainu (see Ainu Mythology) people of Japan sing this epic of the hero Poiyaunpe, born on the mainland and raised in a place called Kotan Utunnai by a woman of the Okhotsk sea-oriented culture. As he grows up, the boy hears rumblings of the spirits of his mainland culture mingling with the rumblings of the spirits of his personal being and he asks his adopted mother about his origins. She reveals that his parents had been killed in a struggle with her own people. Horrified, the boy asks for his father's clothes and sword, puts them on, and flies up the smoke hole. Once away he goes on the traditional hero adventure quest (see Hero Quest), followed by his adopted mother. Together the pair kill monsters, gods and goddeses of pestilence, and defeat wicked chiefs including, with the help of a brother the hero has rescued, one called Shipish-un-kur, whose shamaness (see Shamanism) sister, Shipish-un-mat, Poiyaunpe abducts. Together, the hero and the shamaness ravish various lands. At one point the hero almost dies but is miraculously saved by his companion. After many other adventures, the duo return to Poiyanaupe's native land.

Kṛṣṇa—Lord Kṛṣṇa (Krishna), the "Dark One," is perhaps the most important avatar (see Avatars of Viṣṇu) of the god Viṣṇu (see Viṣṇu), or Hari. The mythology of Kṛṣṇa is among the richest in Hinduism (see Hinduism). There are various versions of each part of the man-god's history as recorded in the *Mahābhārata* (see *Mahābhārata*), particularly in the section called the *Bhagavadgītā* (see *Bhagavadgītā*), in the *Harivaṃśa,* and the *Viṣṇu* and *Bhāgavata Purāṇas* (see *Purāṇas*). At times, as, for instance, in the running narrative of the *Mahābhārata*, Kṛṣṇa seems to be more the ideal warrior king than an avatar, but at other times, as when he miraculously saves Draupadī (see Draupadī) from shame during the famous attempt on the part of the Kauravas (see Kauravas) to disrobe her and as when he lectures the hero Arjuna (see Arjuna) in the *Bhagavadgītā,* he is very much the god, the container within himself of the whole universe. What follows is one composite version of the myth of Kṛṣṇa.

Both Kṛṣṇa and his older brother Balarāma (see Balarāma) are miraculously conceived in Devakī (see Devakī) through the agency of Viṣṇu with the help of the Goddess (see Devī) as Māyā (see Māyā) or "holy illusion or illusion". Devakī's husband and Balarāma's and Kṛṣṇa's surrogate father is Vasudeva (see Vasudeva). The wicked King Kaṃsa (see Kaṃsa), fearing a prophecy of his own murder at the hands of a child of his cousin Devakī, commands that her children be killed at birth. To save Balarāma, the Goddess removes the embryo from Devakī and places it in Vasudeva's other wife, Rohiṇī. Kṛṣṇa is born to Devakī, but at birth, to protect him from King Kaṃsa, he is exchanged with a child of Yaśodā, the wife of the cowherd Nanda (see Nanda). This child, a girl born at the same time as Kṛṣṇa, is an incarnation of the Goddess, who, when she is murdered by Kaṃsa, thus serves as the necessary Hindu "sacrifice" (see *Māyā*) for the birth of something positive, in this case the greatest of the avatars of Viṣṇu. Both Balarāma and Kṛṣṇa are "adopted" for their protection by Nanda and are raised along the river Yamunā among the cowherds.

As a very young child, Kṛṣṇa performs miraculous feats and defeats demons (see *Asuras*). On one occasion when his adopted mother looks into his mouth she is astounded to see the whole universe there. Kṛṣṇa is especially dear to the women cowherds, the *gopīs* (see *Gopīs*). Always something of a trickster, Kṛṣṇa teases them. In one story he steals their clothes while they are bathing in the river and convinces them to leave the water with their hands held together over their heads, signifying worship and supplication. The *gopīs* here embody deliverance that comes from the worship of Lord Kṛṣṇa. One of the *gopīs,* Rādhā, becomes his lover, a prime symbol of Kṛṣṇa devotion. The erotic delight in Kṛṣṇa as a representation of total devotion and joy is contained in the *Gītāgovinda* (see *Gītāgovinda*), which some have compared to the Hebrew *Song of Songs.*

In adulthood Kṛṣṇa returns to his homeland of Mathurā and kills Kaṃsa. He also becomes involved in the war between the Pāṇḍavas (see Pāṇḍavas) and Kauravas depicted in the *Mahābhārata,* serving as the hero Arjuna's charioteer and mentor. His lesson as expressed to Arjuna is in the *Bhagavadgītā* segment of the epic. Arjuna declares his reluctance to carry on a war of needless slaughter of friends and relatives, but Kṛṣṇa reminds him that as a warrior his only proper commitment is to *dharma* (see *Dharma*), proper action or duty according to his warrior caste. To worry about the effects of action based on *dharma* would be wrong. Kṛṣṇa-Viṣṇu goes on to reveal to Arjuna the proper means of achieving oneness with Brahman (see Brahman).

Just after the war, Kṛṣṇa dies, as he had predicted he would, when, in a position of meditation, he is struck in the heel by a hunter's arrow. He ascends in death to the heavens and is greeted by the gods.

Kshatra—Also known as Shatevar, meaning "Power," this is one of the Zoroastrian (see Zoroastrianism) Amesa Spentas (see Amesa Spentas). He is a war god of sorts who uses his power in the interest of peace, religion, and the poor. He is assisted by the powers of the heavens—the Sky, the Sun, and Mithra (see Mithra).

Kunda—One of several Indian Buddhist (see Buddhism) mother goddesses of compassion and knowledge, Kunda has sixteen arms or sometimes only four. Her symbols are all powerful weapons such as the discus and the thunderbolt, although her many hands also hold prayer beads, ambrosia, and the lotus flower. She can be merciful to the good and hard on the wicked.

Kung Kung—See Gonggong.

K'ung Fu-tzu—See Confucius.

Kuntī—In the Indian epic the *Mahābhārata* (see *Mahābhārata*),

Kuntī is a wife of Pāṇḍu, who because of a curse cannot have sexual relations with his two wives. Kuntī becomes the mother of the three main Pāṇḍava (see Pāṇḍavas) brothers—the heroes of the epic—by the gods Dharma (see Dharma), Vāyu (see Vāyu), and Indra (see Indra). Because of a promise inadvertently made by Kuntī, the Pāṇḍava brothers must share one wife, Draupadī (see Draupadī). Kuntī is also the mother, by the sun god, of the anti-hero Karṇa (see Karṇa) before she became the mother of the Pāṇḍavas. It might be said, then, that the gods use Kuntī as a kind of catalytic vessel for many of the events of the epic. It is perhaps for this reason that she is also called Pṛthā, which associates her with the primal vessel, Pṛthivi (see Pṛthivi) or Earth.

L

Lac Long Quang and Au Co—See Vietnamese Mythology.

Lakṣmī—A form of the Goddess (see Devī) as the wife of the cosmic Hindu preserver god Viṣṇu (see Viṣṇu), Lakṣmī, or Śrī (see Śrī), stands for prosperity and good fortune in this world. In short, she is the worldly reflection of Viṣṇu's power, literally, the world that emerges from the god. Lakṣmī is Viṣṇu's *śakti* (see *Śakti*), the energy without which he cannot be active or material. Thus, when Viṣṇu sleeps on the serpent Śeṣa (see Ananta) during the cosmic night before the creation of the world, Śrī is at his feet as Bhu (Earth), ready to be united with him when he awakens. By extension, the wives of the great Viṣṇu avatars (see Avatars of Viṣṇu), such as Rāma's (see Rāma) Sītā (see Sītā), are incarnations of Lakṣmī. She is also incarnate in Draupadī (see Draupadī), the wife of the Pāṇḍavas (see Pāṇḍavas) in the *Mahābhārata* (see *Mahābhārata*). Prosperity in India is associated with gold, so when a bride brings gold in some form to her marriage, she comes to the marriage as Lakṣmī. To preserve Lakṣmī—prosperity—proper sacrificial rituals must be performed, because, as in the cosmos, prosperity on earth depends on sacrificial destruction.

Lalitavistara—One of several biographies of Gautama, the Buddha Sākyamuni (see Gautama Buddha), the *Lalitavistara* is an ancient and continually evolving Sanskrit text that is concerned with the early years of the Buddha.

Lamism—See Tibetan Buddhism.

Lao Origin myth—See Nithan Khun Borom.

Laozi—Laozi (Lao-tzu) is the quasihistorical central figure of the Chinese philosophy and religion known as Daoism (see Daoism). The *Daodejing (Tao-te ching)*—sometimes simply called the *Laozi* or *Lao-tsu*—has been traditionally attributed to him. Known from the mid third century BCE, this book, with the earlier Zhuangzi *(Chuang-tzu)* (see Zhuangzi) contains the basis of Daoist philosophy. By the end of the first century BCE, Laozi had become a deity to many of his followers.

One of the most famous legends about Laozi describes his supposed meeting with Confucius (see Confucius), who had come to consult the sage about ritual practices. Apparently Laozi was more interested in advocating Daoist principles, and Confucius was left so impressed that he compared his "teacher" to a dragon.

Over the centuries, Laozi's life took on elements of the mythological hero's biography (see Hero Quest). He was said to have been conceived by a shooting star and to have been born from his mother's side (see Virgin Birth). Some say that Laozi lived for two hundred years before disappearing into the west and becoming the Buddha (see Buddha). Those who have deified him say he could change shapes at will, and that his abode is Heaven's center. Clearly, there are indigenous Chinese as well as Buddhist (see Buddhism) and even Hindu (see Hinduism) influences on this biography.

Laws of Manu—The Indian *Mānava-dharmaśāstra* or *Manusmṛti*, that is, the *Laws of Manu,* composed between 200 BCE and 200 CE, is, as indicated in one of its titles, human-based *smṛti* (see *Smṛti*) rather than "revealed" *śruti* (see *Śruti*) literature, but the *Laws,* like all *smṛti,* are necessarily closely related to the *śruti* Vedic (see Vedic entries) revelations. The *Laws* are the first metrical *smṛti,* treatises on *dharma* (see *Dharma*) or the proper righteous way of orderly life for Hindus, depending on caste and status—the worldly laws derived from the cosmic ones of the *Vedas* (see *Vedas*). Their authorship is attributed to the mythical Manu Svāyaṁbhuva, the first of the *Manu,* or fathers of humanity (see Manu). The *Laws* provide us with certain mythical constructs as well. There is, for example, an elaboration on the Vedic creation myths: that Brahman (see Brahman)—that which is "self-existent," the Absolute—created the chaos and the seed out of which he was born. During his year in the primal egg of his own making, Brahman created existence by way of his own thoughts.

Līlā—Inside of the sleeping Hindu (see Hinduism entries) god Viṣṇu (see Viṣṇu), the Goddess (see Devī, Lakṣmī) is the world contained within him waiting to be created. In creation she is Māyā (see Māyā) or the illusion of reality. That is to say, she becomes Lila or "divine play," divine illusion in the created world.

Liṅga—The *Liṅga* is the sacred phallus and principal symbol of the Hindu (see Hinduism entries) god Śiva (see Śiva). Some scholars have suggested that the phallic worship aspect of Śiva indicates that he existed as a fertility god in the pre-Aryan (see Aryan) Indus Valley (see Indus Valley Mythology) culture, especially as the *liṅga* is nearly always presented in connection with the *yoni* (see *Yoni*), or vulva of the Goddess (see Devī, *Liṅga* Myths). In a sense, the *liṅga* united with the *yoni* symbolizes creation. This sense is supported by the fact that the *liṅga-yoni* often sits on an octagonal form representing Viṣṇu's (see Viṣṇu) jurisdiction over the cardinal directions and a square base representing Brahmā (see Brahmā) and the four *Vedas* (see *Vedas*). Thus the *liṅga-yoni* as a total structure contains the Goddess and the *trimūrti* (Śiva-Viṣṇu-Brahmā) of Hinduism.

Liṅga Myths—Sacrifice is at the center of Hinduism (see Hinduism entries); it is the price paid for prosperity or *śrī* (see Śrī, see Lakṣmī). Traditionally, near the sacrificial altar, standing as a kind of guard over it, is the *yūpa* or sacrificial column to which the sacrificial victim was once tied. The *yūpa* is at once a pillar of the universe and a representation of the *liṅga* (see *Liṅga*), or phallus, of the god Śiva (see Śiva). The myths related to *liṅga* worship are found in the *Purāṇas* (see *Purāṇas*) and usually involve the gods of the *trimūrti*—Śiva, Viṣṇu (see Viṣṇu), and Brahmā (see Brahmā). These myths, like the *liṅga,* are particularly important to the *bhakti* (see *Bhakti*), or special devotion, associated with Śiva, whose phallus is the appropriate symbol of the destruction and regeneration that is the essence of creation. Śiva's *liṅga* is often unified with the *yoni* (see *Yoni*) or vulva of the Goddess (see Devī).

The following myth occurs in the *Śiva Purāṇa.* At the beginning of an age, Śiva as destructive fire, Brahmā as creative water, and Viṣṇu as mediating wind, arose from the primal waters. Viṣṇu and Brahmā bowed to the greater Śiva and called on him to create. Śiva agreed but dove back into the waters. Viṣṇu then asked Brahmā to create and he gave Brahmā creative energy *(śakti)* (see *Śakti*) so that he could do so. Brahmā created. Then Śiva returned and was furious that Brahmā had not waited for him before creating the world. In a rage, he burned up all that had been created. Impressed by this power, Brahmā pleased Śiva by bowing to him. To reward Brahmā for his devotion, Śiva asked him what he wished for, and the creator god asked to have his creation restored and Śiva's creative energy transferred to the sun. Brahmā promised to worship the Śiva *linga,* that which denotes past, present, and future. Śiva broke off his *liṅga* and flung it to the earth, where it reached down into Hell and then up into Heaven. Viṣṇu tried to find its source below and Brahmā tried to find its tip on high; both were unsuccessful because the *liṅga* of Śiva is without end. At this point, a voice from above cried out: "Worship the *liṅga* of Śiva and be granted all that can be granted." So it was that Viṣṇu and Brahmā and all the gods worshipped the *liṅga,* the source of all destruction and creation.

Liṅgal—Liṅgal is the culture hero of the Gond (see Gond Mythology) tribe and several other groups in Central India. As always, the mythologies of the indigenous peoples of India are a mixture of Hinduism (see Hinduism entries) and perhaps earlier religious traditions (see Dravidians, see Indus Valley Mythology). The story is told of how the mother of the Gond gods deserted her progeny, who were taken in by Mahādeo and Pārvatī (see Pārvatī). These Gond god guests demanded alcohol and meat and were imprisoned until Liṅgal and a goddess freed them. Liṅgal was a holy musician, who gave the gond gods—really the first humans—homes and taught them proper social arrangements, including the clan system and rituals. On the way to their new homeland the gods were saved from a rushing river by a monkey, or in some related versions of the story, by a tortoise.

Loka—See Three Worlds.

Lord Lo—*Pra Lo* is a Siamese tragic romance in verse composed in the seventeenth century from a much older work.

Lotus of the Good Law—In 804 CE a Japanese Buddhist (see Japanese Buddhism) monk, Saicho (Dengyo-daishi) visited China and came back with a doctrine learned from Chinese monks on Mount Tendai. This was the beginning of the Tendai sect (see Tendai Sect), a Mahāyāna (see Mahāyāna Buddhism) sect, which, like the Chinese Tendai monks, based its beliefs on the *Hoke-kyo* or *Lotus of the Good Law,* or *Lotus Sutra.* This was a text that stressed the existence of the Buddha nature and the drive for Enlightenment even in inanimate nature. The Tendai sect brought together various strands of Japanese Buddhism including the worship of Amida Buddha (see Amida Buddha). By the twelfth century a Zen monk named Nichiren reacted against what he saw as the corruption of the *Lotus* by the Tendai sect and another esoteric group, the Shingon sect (see Shingon Sect), and by Amidism in general. He called for a return to the *Lotus* and to the teachings of the true Buddha, the Buddha Sākyamuni (see Gautama Buddha). But eventually the book itself became an object of worship, and Nichren's call for a return of focus away from peripheral matters to the Buddha Sākyamuni was thus undermined.

Luofuxing—*The Song of Luofu* is a Chinese ballad of the first century CE about the beautiful young wife of the house of Ch'in.

M

Magic Crossbow—See Vietnamese Mythology.

Mahābhārata—The great Sanskrit Hindu (see Hinduism entries) epic, the *Mahābhārata* is perhaps the world's longest literary work. It is eight times as long as the *Iliad* and *Odyssey* combined. Not considered "revealed" text or *śruti* (see *Śruti*), the epic is a traditional, or *smṛti* (see *Smṛti*), but it is the source for many of the most popular and complex myths and legends of Hinduism and India. Perhaps most important, it is considered a reliable source for questions having to do with proper actions and social arrangements (see *Dharma*) and the relations between the human and divine worlds. *Mahābhārata* means "Great *(mahā)* Story of the Bharatas," the Bharatas being the legendary first Indians and, by extension, Hindus. "The Epic," as it is sometimes called, continues to be performed and read all over India. There are even comic book versions widely sold.

The legendary author of the *Mahābhārata* is Vyāsa (see Vyāsa), a particularly powerful sage (See *Ṛṣi*) otherwise known as Kṛṣṇa (see Kṛṣṇa) Dvaipayāna—the "island-born Kṛṣṇa," and thus perhaps an avatar of Viṣṇu (see Viṣṇu, Avatars of Viṣṇu). The epic was dictated by Vyāsa to the elephant-headed god Gaṇeśa (see Gaṇeśa), who used one of his tusks as a pen. The work is sometimes called the "Veda of Kṛṣṇa," suggesting a religious connection between

Vyāsa and the Kṛṣṇa-Viṣṇu figure who is so central to the epic, particularly to the highly philosophical section we know as the *Bhagavadgītā* (see *Bhagavadgītā*). Vyāsa is also said to have brought the *Vedas* themselves to humanity. There is a tradition that holds Vyāsa as the begetter of the Bharatas, the ancestors of both the Pāṇḍavas (see Pāṇḍavas) and Kauravas (see Kauravas), the warring parties in the *Mahābhārata*. In fact, the authorship of the epic was collective and gradual. Much of what was transcribed by *brahmans* (see *Brahmans*) in the fifth century BCE was based on earlier material, reaching back to ancient tribal warfare, and additions were made to the text as late as 500 CE. The central issue of the epic is the war between the Pāṇḍavas and the Kauravas, which, according to tradition, took place on the sacrificial field of Kurukṣetra in ancient times.

The stories of the *Mahābhārata* are clearly representative of cosmic religious issues. It seems fair to suggest that the *Mahabarata* as *smṛti* is an example of particular sectarian devotion or *bhakti* (see *Bhakti*) in connection with Kṛṣṇa-Viṣṇu, specifically, as well as a reexamination of older Vedic (see Vedic entries) ideas of *dharma* and Brahmanic (see Brahmanism) sacrifice. The work contains eighteen books *(parvans)* and is supplemented by the *Harivaṃśa*, a geneology of Hari (Viṣṇu).

The epic begins with the establishment of the need for sacrifice in order that true prosperity (see *Śrī*) might be restored. The goddess Earth is oppressed by demons and evil. Viṣṇu and several other gods descend to assist the Goddess. Viṣṇu is Kṛṣṇa, friend and cousin to the Pāṇḍava brothers, who are fathered by gods for whom they become earthly vehicles or *avatars*. The Pāṇḍava king, Yudhiṣṭhira (see Yudhiṣṭhira), is fathered by Dharma, who embodies that proper order and duty that needs to be reestablished in the world. His brothers Arjuna (see Arjuna) and Bhīma, whose mother Kuntī (see Kuntī) is also the mother of Yudhiṣṭhira, are fathered by the gods Indra (see Indra) and Vāyu (see Vāyu), representing warriors. The less famous brothers, the twins Nakula and Sahadeva, whose mother is Mādrī, are fathered by the twin physician gods called the Aśvins (see Aśvins), who in this case represent social welfare. Together, the Pāṇḍavas, supported by Kṛṣṇa, stand for proper action and social arrangement or *dharma.* The Pāṇḍavas share one wife, Draupadī (see Draupadī), an incarnation of Śrī/Lakṣmī (see Lakṣmī), the wife of Viṣṇu. Opposed to the Pāṇḍavas are their hundred Kaurava cousins, led by the arrogant Duryodhana, who embodies cosmic discord, in alliance with Karṇa (see Karṇa), the son of the sun god Sūrya by Kuntī. Together the Kauravas represent *adharma,* or the opposite of *dharma.* The stage is thus set for a war that will be the cleansing sacrifice between ages (yugas) and a lightening of Earth's burden.

When, after political struggles and a decision to divide the kingdom, Yudhiṣṭhira lays claim to universal kingship, Duryodhana challenges him to a game of dice. In this famous game, Yudhiṣṭhira loses everything, including the joint Pāṇḍava wife Draupadī. He thus gambles away prosperity, as Draupadī is an incarnation of Śrī/Lakṣmī. The Kauravas attempt to disrobe Draupadī in order to insult and humiliate her and her husbands but are prevented from doing so by the powers of Kṛṣṇa. After losing another gambling match, however, the Pāṇḍavas are exiled for thirteen years. The religious significance of the exile is that it stands for the period of preparation *(dīkṣa)* for a sacrifice.

The ensuing war between the Pāṇḍavas and Kauravas is prepared by Kṛṣṇa who, as the *avatar* of Viṣṇu (see Avatars of Viṣṇu), knows it must take place in order that Śrī (Prosperity) can be restored to Earth. Early in the great battle, Arjuna begins to doubt the value of the inevitable carnage and has to be convinced by the divine revelations of Kṛṣṇa—his charioteer—of the necessity of the sacrifice in the interest of *dharma.* These revelations form the *Bhagavadgītā.* The war is the war to end wars, resulting in the victory of the Pāṇḍavas but the death of almost everyone. It is the universal sacrifice that will bring to an end the age *(yuga)* that precedes our own *kaliyuga.* Viṣṇu has thus achieved the original goal of coming to the rescue of Earth.

Mahajati—The *Mahajati* (the Great *Jātata*) is a Siamese (Thai) epic written down in the fifteenth century. It is based on certain of the *Jātaka Tales* (see *Jātaka Tales*) of the Buddha (see Gautama Buddha).

Mahāśakti—In order to relate to the physical world, the Hindu gods must give forth the power of manifestation that is called *śakti* (see *Śakti*), which usually takes the mythological form of Śiva's (see Śiva) wife or "great *Śakti (mahāśakti)*". This form, in turn, can take many manifestations such as Kālī or Mahākālī (see Kālī) or Pārvatī (see Pārvatī). As *mahā* means great, Viṣṇu's wife can be called Mahālakṣmī (see Lakṣmī) and Brahmā's wife Mahāsarasvatī (see Sarasvatī). *Mahāśakti* is also a term used to refer to the totality of the divine mother, the *śakti* of the Absolute, Brahman (see Brahman).

Mahāvaṃsa—This fifth-century CE Pali (see Pali) text contains many Buddhist (see Buddhism) myths of (Sri Lanka) (Ceylon) based on earlier texts and oral traditions.

Mahāvastu—This is the second century BCE legendary biography of the Buddha (see Gautama Buddha).

Mahāvīra—Vardhamāna Mahāvīra, sometimes called the Jina ("Victor"), was born in Bihar, India in the sixth century BCE. He was a contemporary of the Buddha (see Gautama Buddha) and was the founder or prophet of Jainism (See Jainism).

Mahāyāna Buddhism—The "Great *(Mahā)* Vehicle *(yāna)*" Buddhism (see Buddhism) or Mahāyāna Buddhism is the reformed Buddhism that replaces the Nirvāna (see Nirvāna), monastic, and Gautama Buddha (see Gautama Buddha)-oriented Hīnayāna (*hīna* = lesser, *yāna* = vehicle) or Theravāda ("Doctrine of the Elders") Buddhism (see Hīnayāna Buddhism, Theravāda Buddhism). Its emphases are on *bodhisattvas* (see *Bodhisattva*), an all-encompassing and pervasive "Buddha Nature," and the ability of lay people to achieve spiritual release.

Maitreya—In Buddhist (see Buddhism, see Mahāyāna Buddhism) mythology, Maitreya, "the Friendly," is the Buddha of the future, the eighth Buddha who is still the *Bodhisattva* (see *Bodhisattva*) living in the heavenly paradise or Tuṣita (see Miroku, Japanese Buddhism).

Manasā Devī—Manasā is a popular snake and childbirth goddess of the Bengali section of India (see Manasa-Mangals, Devi).

Manasa-Mangals—These are poems on the subject of the Bengali snake goddess Manasā (see Manasā Devī, Devī). Developed from the oral tradition, the poems were transcribed in the late sixteenth century. In some of the poems Manasā appears as the offspring of the god Dharma (see *Dharma*), who mates with her. Regretting his sin, Dharma convinces Śiva (see Śiva) to marry the girl, who, after throwing herself on a funeral pyre takes new form as Śiva's wife Pārvatī (see Pārvatī). It should be noted, in this connection, that the word *manasā* means "spiritual" and that it is also the name of a holy mountain, and that Pārvatī is the "Mountain Mother" or the "Daughter of the Mountain." Sometimes Manasā is Śiva's daughter. Often she is a jealous goddess who threatens people if they do not worship her.

Maṇḍala—*Maṇḍala* is Sanskrit for "circle", and is used in various ways by peoples in many parts of the world—especially Asia—as a representation of sacred wholeness or significance. The snake biting its own tail (Ouroboros) can be a *maṇḍala* (see Dayak Myths). Tibetan Buddhists (see Tibetan Buddhism) and North American relatives of central Asian cultures—for example, the Navajo Indians—use *maṇḍalas* in sand paintings, as part of curing or initiatory ceremonies. The *maṇḍala* in such cases is a representation of creation itself, an appropriate setting for the recreation of the person who is ill or not yet initiated into the "real" world of knowledge. In the same sense a *maṇḍala* can be a kind of labyrinth through which the initiate or pilgrim must pass in order to achieve union with the "center," which is the supreme deity. *Maṇḍalas* do not have to be circles. Vedic (see Vedic entries) altars of various geometrical designs were arranged so that the various deities could have appropriate seats for rituals. Square *maṇḍalas* are used in Buddhist (see Buddhism) and Hindu (see Hinduism) Tantric (see Tantrism) traditions and by the Jains (see

Jainism). Temples can be arranged architecturally as *maṇḍalas* to suggest the pilgrimage to the center in various communal liturgies. *Maṇḍalas* are, in a sense, dwelling places of the Absolute, and they are always sources of or containers of spiritual or divine power in a given ritual. For the Buddhist, the *maṇḍala* can be a potent symbol of liberation, with various gods surrounding the sacred center of Enlightenment. In esoteric Japanese Buddhism (see Shingon sect, Japanese Buddhism), the Womb World *Maṇḍala* and the Diamond World *Maṇḍala* are central symbols of the process of Enlightenment—elaborate designs containing deities surrounding the central figure of the cosmic Vairocana (see Vairocana), a Buddha much revered by the Shingon sect.

Mandara—See Churning of the Ocean.

Mangi—See Siberian Underworld.

Mani—Mani was the third-century CE Persian prophet of Manichaeism (see Manichaeism).

Manichaeism—A religious system from Iran based on the teachings of Zoroastrianism (see Zoroastrianism) with some elements of Gnosticism, Buddhism (see Buddhism), Christianity, and Hinduism (see Hinduism), Manichaeism was the creation of the prophet Mani (see Mani) in the third century CE. It is a system that stresses the dualistic nature of the universe. There is a principle of Good, which is purely spiritual, and a principal of Evil, which is material. These principles are represented by the Father of Light and the Prince of Darkness. The first humans are drawn into evil and are only eventually freed by messenger-prophets of the Father.

Manimekhalaï—A Tamil verse epic of the second century CE, the *Manimekhalaï* is attributed to Shattan. The heroine of the epic is Manimekhalâ, who, with her mother Mâdhavi, has determined to enter the monastic life rather than continue the life of dancer-prostitute in Indra's (see Indra) honor. The goddess of the Ocean, also named Manimekhalâ, comes to protect the heroine from the advances of a Chola prince. The goddess explains that the prince is a reincarnation of her husband from a former life. After many complications involving the prince and a magic bowl with which Manimekhalâ feeds the hungry, the heroine becomes a Buddhist (see Buddhism) nun and achieves release from the cycles of life (see *Saṃsāra*, *Nirvāna*).

Maṅkaṇaka—Born of the mind of his sage father Kaśyapa, the Indian sage (see *Ṛṣi*) Maṅkaṇaka had immense ascetic powers. Once when bathing with several beautiful nymphs, however, he had an orgasm. He collected his "seed" in a bowl and the seed gave birth to the seven Marut sages or storm gods who hold up the universe. One day, according to the *Vāmana Purāṇa* (see *Purāṇas*), plant sap, the symbol of life, sprang from a wound on Maṅkaṇaka's hand, and this caused him to dance for joy. His dancing was so full of energy that the universe itself began to dance. It was then that the gods called on the god Śiva (see Śiva), who is also Nāṭarāja—the "Lord of the Dance"(see Dance of Śiva)—whose performance is the dance of life and death, destruction, and regeneration. Śiva appeared to the sage as a *brahman* (see *Brahmans*) and caused ashes of death to emanate from the blood of his thumb. Maṅkaṇaka immediately recognized the god and his superior power and bowed down before him, begging that he might keep his ascetic power. Śiva agreed and increased the sage's gifts.

Mantra—A *mantra* is a sacred formulaic phrase, verse, or sound, used in religious rituals, especially in those of India.

Manu—Each age *(manvantara)*—lasting 4,320,000 years—in the Hindu (see Hinduism entries) scheme of things has a demiurge called Manu, who is the progenitor of the human race (thus "human" = *manava*). The first Manu was Svāyaṁbhuva, who produced the "Laws of Manu" (see *Laws of Manu*). The Manu of our age is Satyavrata or Vāivasvata, son of the sun (Vivasvat), who is best known for the flood story (see Fish and the Flood). Satyavrata Manu was given the *Vedas* (see *Vedas*) so that he might teach the human race *dharma* (see Dharma).

Manusmṛti—See *Laws of Manu*.

Marichi—Marichi is one of a pantheon of Buddhist (see Buddhism) goddesses. Her Hindu (see Hinduism entries) form is Uṣas (see

Uṣas) and she is associated with the dawn. She has an eye in the middle of her forehead, three frightening faces, and ten arms. In Japan (see Japanese Buddhism), she is Marishi-ten, who was popular among the *samurai,* who placed her image on their helmets as protection. She is also depicted as riding on a boar, and one of her faces is that of a boar. The esoteric Nichiren sect sees Marishi-ten (or Marichi) as a male figure.

Mārkaṇḍeya—In the Indian epic the *Mahābhārata* (see *Mahābhārata*), the story is told of the sage Mārkaṇḍeya, who, floating on the cosmic ocean after the dissolution of the universe, took refuge inside of the mouth of a sleeping boy under a banyan tree. The boy was Viṣṇu (see Viṣṇu) and the sage discovered within the god's mouth the entire universe. Thus Viṣṇu absorbs and contains the universe. The same message is contained in a *Bhāgavata Purāṇa* (see *Purāṇas*) myth, in which the adopted mother of Viṣṇu's *avatar* (see Avatars of Viṣṇu), Kṛṣṇa (see Kṛṣṇa), sees the universe in her son's mouth.

Matsya—Matsya is the fish *avatar* (see Avatars of Viṣṇu) of the Hindu (see Hinduism entries) god Viṣṇu (see Viṣṇu, Fish and the Flood).

Māyā—Māyā is at once a concept and a name reflecting that concept. Its root is *mā,* meaning the mother goddess and to measure out or create, and *māyā* is the transformation of the god's thought into the material form often represented mythologically by his wife—his particular goddess or *śakti* (see *Śakti*), his creative energy—or as the all-encompassing Goddess (see Devī) as Mahādevī or Mahāśakti. It is the principle of māyā that can explain the movement from the intangible and indivisible Self that is Brahman (see Brahman) to the differentiated and tangible reality that is the world. Among some Buddhist (see Buddhism) schools *māyā* is the source of the "illusion" that we think of as the "real." It should be noted that Queen Māyā or Mahāmāyā is the mother of Gautama Buddha (see Gautama Buddha), the vehicle of his incarnation and of his transformation to worldly form. Māyā is also Māyādevī, the personification of delusion. In the *Bhāgavata Purāṇa* (see *Purāṇas*), she is the girl who is exchanged for Kṛṣṇa (see Kṛṣṇa), thus the illusion of reality exchanged for divine reality.

Maya—In the battle between the Hindu (see Hinduism entries) gods and demons described in the epic the *Mahābhārata* (see *Mahābhārata*), Maya is the evil architect of the three cities of the demons—one of gold, one of silver, one of black iron—representing Heaven, Sky, and Earth. The cities are destroyed by the god Śiva (see Śiva) with the help of a chariot made by the gods' architect, Tvaṣṭṛ (see Tvaṣṭṛ). The chariot is made of all of the elements of the primeval creation. The myth is a kind of preface to the sacrificial destruction of the world that inevitably ends each age.

Mazdaism—Mazdaism is a term sometimes used to indicate the ancient Iranian religion that became Zoroastrianism (see Zoroastrianism) under the influence of Zarathustra (see Zoroaster). It takes its name from the supreme god of Zoroastrianism, the Ahura Mazda (see Ahura Mazda).

Meru—The Olympus of the Hindu (see Hinduism entries) gods and goddesses, Mount Meru, or sometimes Sumeru or Mandara (see Mandara) is, according to the *Mahābhārata* (see *Mahābhārata*), a golden mass of intense energy. Brahmā's golden city is at its summit. It is the *axis mundi* (see Mountain Mythology) for both Hindus and Buddhists. For Pure Land (see Pure Land) Buddhists, it is the place of the Buddha fields.

Miroku—The Japanese Buddhist (see Japanese Buddhism) version of the great future Buddha, the Bodhisattva (see *Bodhisattva*) Maitreya (see Maitreya), is Miroku-bosatsu or, in his future form, Miroku Nyorai. Miroku was a popular figure among early Japanese Buddhists but was somewhat displaced by the Pure Land Buddhist (see Pure Land Buddhism) emphasis on Amida Buddha (see Amida Buddha) and the possibility of the salvation of the individual in the Pure Land (see Pure Land) of the West.

Mithra—An ancient Indo-Iranian god, corresponding originally to the Vedic (see Vedic entries) Mitra (see Mitra), Mithra was repudiated along with other ancient gods by the prophet Zarathustra (see Zoroaster) in favor of the one Wise Lord, Ahura Mazda (see Ahura

Mazda). In this context, he was demoted to a position as judge of the dead. But the cult of Mithra remained strong and gained popularity in the first centuries CE in the Roman world as well as in Iran. Historically, Mithra is a rival to Ahura Mazda for the central place in pre-Islamic Iranian religion. His name is derived from the concept of proper arrangements or contracts. He represents loyalty, true friendship, and truth. Mithra is also a war god, a promulgator of the faith and of the Iranian "nation." He is also a solar god. Many extraordinary myths are associated with Mithra in both his Iranian and assimilated Roman form: the magical cave in which the sun god lives when he is not driving his chariot pulled by white horses across the sky, his birth from a rock (see Virgin Birth, Hero Quest), and his ritual slaying of the primal bull, the symbol of disorder. This slaying reminds us more of the Vedic Indra (see Indra), the slayer of the primal demon Vṛtra (see Vṛtra, Indra and Vṛtra), than it does of the Vedic Mitra (see Mithraism).

Mithraism—In the early centuries of the Common Era, a strong Mithra (see Mithra) cult developed in the Roman Empire. The cult was particularly important for soldiers, as it involved the ritual sacrifice of an ox and a bath of blood that would bring strength and loyalty.

Mitra—The Indian Vedic (see Vedic entries) god Mitra (the "friend"), one of the Ādityas (see Ādityas) is the realized aspect of his twin brother Varuṇa (see Varuṇa), the all-encompassing infinity. He represents perfection, good judgment, proper laws, and harmony. Mitra, according to one sage, is Varuṇa "perfectly illumined." In classical Hinduism (see Hinduism entries) he becomes a sage himself rather than the powerful god he once was (see Mithra).

Modi—See Chu-tzu.

Mokṣa—Mokṣa—its feminine Sanskrit form is *mukti*—is the Hindu (see Hinduism) term for the much-desired release from the endless cycle of transmigration or rebirth called *saṃsāra* (see *Saṃsāra*, *Karman*). *Mokṣa* is central to Brahmānic (see Brahmanism) Hindu thought as well as to Buddhism (see Buddhism) and Jainism (see Jainism).

Momotaro—A Japanese legend tells how the hero Momotaro was born of a peach (see Virgin Birth, Hero Quest) and was adopted by a childless couple. Momotaro means "peach child." To reward his adopted parents and friends for their generosity, Momotaro, at age 15, with the help of a dog, a pheasant, and a monkey, defeated a band of horned demons *(oni)* who had been oppressing the people.

Monju—The Japanese (see Japanese Buddhism) version of the Mahāyāna (see Mahāyāna Buddhism) Bodhisattva (see *Bodhisattva*) Mañjuśrī, Monju sits on a lion and holds a book and a sword. The book symbolizes his position as a source of wisdom and the sword refers to his war against those who oppose wisdom, or Enlightenment.

Monkey—Monkey or the monkey king Sun Wukong was said to have accompanied the famous Chinese Buddhist (see Chinese Buddhism) monk Xuanzang (see Xuanzang) on his trip to India in search of the sacred *sūtras* (see *Sūtra*). Monkey was a trickster of sorts, who was born from a stone egg (see Virgin Birth) that had been in the world since the creation. He was made king of the monkeys and reigned for three hundred years until he decided to go in search of immortality. Xuanzang taught him the path to immortality and gave Monkey the name Sun Wukong, meaning "enlightened monkey." From the monkey, Sun also learned how to change forms and to fly. In China he defeated a monster and stole a magic weapon from the Dragon King (see Chinese Deities, Chinese Emperors), with which he beat the emissaries from Hell who refused to believe in his immortality. He also crossed his name off of the list of the dead. When Yama (see Yama), the king of the Underworld (see Underworld), and the Dragon King complained of Monkey's arrogance, it was decided by the great Jade Emperor himself that Monkey should be taken to Heaven where he could be controlled. But in Heaven, Monkey committed one arrogant sin after another. He even drank Laozi's (see Laozi) elixir of immortality. After several attempts to destroy him, the Jade Emperor asked for Buddha's help and eventually Monkey was imprisoned. It was 500 years later that Guanyin (see Guanyin) had him released on the condition that he accompany Xuanzang on his journey to India. Monkey, Xuanzang, and their companion, the worldly Pigsy, received the sacred sūtras from the Buddha (see Gautama Buddha) himself. After a final trial set by the Buddha, the three companions were allowed into Heaven and Monkey became the god of Victory.

In general, monkeys are important figures in the mythologies of Asia (see, for example, Hanumān, Jātaka Tales, Momotaro).

Moon Myths—As in most parts of the world, the moon has significant roles in the mythologies of Asia. In the Chinese creation myth (see Chinese Cosmogony) the eyes of the primal cosmic man are the sun and the moon. When the sun eye is open there is daytime, when the moon eye is open there is night. There is also a Chinese myth about the ten suns and twelve moons, the former inhabited by crows, one of the latter by a hart and a toad. The moons stand for the annual lunar cycles. The moons have a mother, Changyi, who regularly bathes her children in a sacred lake in the west. The famous archer Yi (see Yi), who destroys nine of the ten suns to save the world, takes possession of the drink of immortality, which is then stolen from him by his wife Henge who, having run to the moon, becomes the lunar toad. In this connection, it is of interest to note that in Indian mythology, where *soma* (see Soma) is the ambrosial source of immortality for the gods or the means of communication with them, the moon is also its storage place and is sometimes personified as the god Soma. A Daoist (see Daoism) tradition in China holds that the source of immortality, or at least long life, is the cinnamon tree in the moon, a tree that no amount of chopping can fell. Finally, in China, the moon and the sun are representative of the perfect *yin* and the perfect *yang* in the well-known *yinyang* symbol (see Yinyang).

A similar *yinyang* association of the sun, the moon, and other elements occurs in the Indonesian Moluccas, where the wholeness or unity of the Absolute divinity is based on the coming together of the opposite but complementary Father Sun and Mother Moon.

But as in the Chinese *yinyang* system, there is maleness in the moon and femaleness in the sun as well. Thus the moon is female in its waning and male in its waxing.

In Korea, as in China, there is a mythological archer who shoots down unwanted heavenly bodies—in this case, one sun and one moon (see Korean Mythology).

As in most of the world, Asian moons are usually predominantly female, but in Vedic (see Vedic entries) India the moon is male when personified. There are myths in which this male moon marries the daughter of the sun. In Cambodia, there are stories of marriages between lunar and solar deities. The Khmer believed that the moon protects humans by at least dimly lighting up the night world by riding a silver chariot each night across the sky.

Mountain Mythology—In ancient China mountains were seen as divinities who had the power to send needed rain (see Chinese Deities). They were also places to which the dead were sent. Certain mountains were purely mythical. Kunlun was such a mountain and was the dwelling place of the heavenly Emperor and 100 gods. Some texts say that Kunlun is ruled by a being that is half human and half tiger. Sometimes Kunlun is seen as a kind of platonic symbol of the various levels of holiness leading to knowledge of the Supreme Ruler. For some, as the home of Xi Wang Mu, the Queen of the West, Kunlun is a place of immortality.

In India, Śiva's (see Śiva) wife P ārvatī (see Pārvatī) is the daughter of the Mountain, which itself holds up the sky and makes life possible. The Mountain is also the retreat of Śiva in his aspect as the ultimate *yogi*.

In the Japanese mythology (see Shinto Mythology) of mountains, the influence of China is evident. Mountains contain divinity or *kami* (see *Kami,* Yama no kami, Shinto mythology) and are sources of necessary water. They are also places of burial and the *loci* for festivals of the dead, such as one called *bon.*

In Central Asia, Tibet, Korea, and other places in Asia, it was thought that the primal being or first king arrived on earth by landing on the summit of a mythical mountain. Mountains are the gateway to heaven (see Meru).

Mulua Satene—See Hainuwele.

Murugan—Ancient Dravidian in origin (see Dravidians), Murugan or Murukan is an important god among the Tamils (see Tamil Mythology) of southern India. Sometimes he seems to be a version of the war god Skanda (see Kārttikeya), the six-headed son of Śiva (see Śiva). His roots are more likely to be found in fertility worship, however. He is clearly associated with love and youthfulness, as he rides, handsome and young looking, on his peacock, in the company of young women. His exploits as Skanda are described in the *Mahābhārata* (see *Mahābhārata*) and the *Rāmāyaṇa* (see *Rāmāyaṇa*).

N

Nāga—Nāgas (or the feminine *Nāginīs*) are serpent figures who play a role in both Hindu and Buddhist mythology. Their source seems to lie in the pre-Aryan fertility cults of India. The nāgas reside within the earth in an aquatic underworld. They are personifications of terrestrial waters as well as door and gate guardians. They are beings of great power who protect the underworld and bestow fertility and wealth on the areas of the world with which they are individually associated, be that area a field, a place of worship, or even a whole country. If a nāga is properly worshipped prosperity can be the result. If ignored or slighted, the nāga can bring about disaster. When the Buddha achieves enlightenment he is said to have been protected by cobra hood of the *nāgaraja* Mucilinda, symbolizing the fact that the nāgas are placing their natural powers in the service of the Buddha. Between the dissolution of one age and the beginning of another, Viṣṇu sleeps on what is left of the old world, the remainder of the cosmic sacrifice represented by the serpent or nāga Śeṣa or Ananta (see Ananta). Viṣṇu and his avatar Kṛṣṇa (see Kṛṣṇa, Avatars of Viṣṇu) are both conquerors of serpents, indicating their power over the waters and over the potential chaos represented by the serpent principle.

Nanda—The foster father of the Hindu Lord Kṛṣṇa (see Kṛṣṇa).

Nārāyaṇa—Nārāyaṇa is a name sometimes used for the Hindu (see

Hindu entries) god Viṣṇu (see Viṣṇu). The *Viṣṇu Purāṇa* (see *Viṣṇu Purāṇa*, see *Purāṇas*) tells us that Viṣṇu, who is identified with Brahmā-Prajāpati (see Brahmā, Prajāpati) and by implication with the idea of Brahman (see Brahman) as the creator of the universe, is "the supreme Nārāyaṇa . . . the lord of all . . . without a beginning," who is the "source of all . . . the beginning and the end of the universe." Viṣṇu is called Nārāyaṇa because the waters are called *Nārā* and the waters are the offspring of the Man *(nara),* who is presumably the primal male Puruṣa (see Puruṣa) who joined with Prakṛti (see Prakṛti), or "Nature", became the universe, and made the waters his dwelling place. Viṣṇu is known as the "son of the Waters" or the "son of Man" because in the form of his *avatar* (see *Avatar,* see *Avatars* of Viṣṇu) the Boar (see Boar), his body composed of the *Vedas* (see *Vedas*), he raised the Earth (see Pṛthivi) with his great horn, rescuing her from the demonic chaotic waters and re-creating the world that had been destroyed as the cosmic sacrifice at the end of the previous creation. During the time between the worlds, Viṣṇu as Nārāyaṇa sleeps on the sacrificial remnants of the old world that floats on the waters in the form of the serpent Ananata (see Ananta) or Śeṣa—the "infinite" (see *Nāga*). Viṣṇu's eventual awakening is a symbol of the spiritual awakening that comes to the one who meditates sufficiently on Viṣṇu-Nārāyaṇa (see Puranic Cosmogony).

Nārada—Nārada is a *ṛṣi* (see *Ṛṣi*), or sage, with great ascetic powers. He is a creation of the Hindu (see Hindu entries) god Brahmā (see Brahmā). Like the other *ṛsis,* he is a messenger between humans and deities. But Nārada is a notorious troublemaker. It is he who tells Kaṃsa (see Kaṃsa) that he will be killed by Devakī's (see Devakī) eighth child, causing the threat to Kṛṣṇa's (see Kṛṣṇa, Vālmīki) life.

Narasiṃha—The man-lion Narasiṃha is the forth *avatar* (see *Avatars* of Viṣṇu) of the Hindu god Viṣṇu (see Viṣṇu). In this "descent" to the world, Viṣṇu comes to support a fusion of *bhakti* (see *Bhakti*), specifically, devotion to Viṣṇu, and *dharma* (see

Dharma), or the orthodox Brahmanic (see Brahmanism) social order that *bhakti* sometimes appears to challenge. The association of Narasiṃha with Viṣṇu is made visually clear by the depictions of the man-lion with Viṣṇu's wife Lakṣmī (see Lakṣmī, Śrī), or "Prosperity," on his knee. The myth of the man-lion *avatar* is contained, with variations, in both the *Viṣṇu Purāṇa* (see *Purāṇas, Viṣṇu Purāṇa*) and the *Bhāgavata Purāṇa*. In the myth, Hiraṇya, (Hiraṇyakaśipu) the king of the *asuras* (see *Asuras*) is pitted against his son, a *bhakta,* or yogic devotee of Viṣṇu. Hiraṇya hopes to overthrow Indra (see Indra) as king of the gods and to usurp even the position of Brahmā (see Brahmā). His son Prahlāda (see Prahlāda), however, is a good *asura,* who combines within himself the values of *bhakti* and *dharma,* signifying the fact that true *dharma* can only exist, as far as Viṣṇu is concerned, in conjunction with *Viṣṇu-bhakti*. To make this clear, Viṣṇu descends as the man-lion. Meanwhile, as Hiraṇya has been unsuccessful in his attempt to turn his son away from the god, he ties him up and throws him into the sea. Instead of dying, however, Prahlāda drifts into mystical union with the object of his *bhakti,* and Narasiṃha kills Hiraṇya.

Nat—*Nats* are spirits who dwell in the mountains of Burma, especially on the sacred Mount Poppa (see Mountain Mythology). But *nats* can also live in all aspects of nature, in people's houses and even in people. Some *nats* are troublemakers—rather like poltergeists—while some are protectors—like guardian angels. *Nats* once lived in the world as humans, many of whom were wrongly killed by evil kings. Included in the official list of thirty-seven *Nats,* for instance, are a famous blacksmith and his sister who were burned alive because a king was jealous of what he saw as the blacksmith's mysterious power (see Neak-tā, Phi).

Neak-tā—In Cambodia, the *neak-tā* are earth spirits who watch over people, places, and things, as long as they are paid proper respect. A *neak-tā* can take the name of particular places or objects with which it is associated. It seems that, like the *Nats* (see *Nat*) of Burma, the *neak-tā* may be incarnations of people, sometimes dead children, who lived long ago. Some *neak-tā* are directly associated with Hindu (see Hindu entries) deities such as Gaṇeśa (see Gaṇeśa) and Durgā (see Durgā). Khmer Buddhists (see Buddhism) include them in their prayers (see Phi).

Nihongi—Like the slightly earlier *Kojiki* (see *Kojiki*), the *Nihongi* ("Chronicles of Japan"), published in 720 CE, records the mythological "history" of Japan (see Shinto Mythology, Shinto entries). The myths of the *Nihongi* are particularly influenced by Chinese thought, which was popular in Japan at the time, and several variants of particular myths are often given, some of them making use of actual Chinese myths.

Ninigi—The first ruler of the Japanese islands and the grandson of the sun goddess Amaterasu (see *Amaterasu*).

Nirvāna—*Nirvāna* is a Buddhist (see Buddhism) reworking of the Hindu (see Hinduism) ideal of *mokṣa* (see *Mokṣa*), or "liberation," from the cycles of death and regeneration called *saṃsāra* (see *Saṃsāra*). It has become commonplace in the West to associate *nirvāna* with some sort of afterlife (see Afterlife), but, in fact, it is more an ideal or a state. Gautama Buddha (see Gautama Buddha) achieved *nirvāna* under the Bodhi tree (see Bodhi Tree). Nirvāna is essentially Enlightenment, but spiritual enlightenment or release in this world from the agony of the human condition. By overcoming the illusory powers of human desires, the individual can achieve *nirvāna,* which means, literally, "no wind" or "extinction" of the sense of self that is, in any case, illusion or delusion. For different sects of Buddhism, the paths to *nirvāna* are different. For some it can be achieved through discipline and asceticism in this life. For others it is synonymous with immortality. For those who see *saṃsāra* as life itself, *nirvāna* is sometimes "the farther shore" or almost a physical afterlife. For most Mahāyāna Buddhists (see Mahāyāna Buddhism) Enlightenment is a way of living in this world, a state of mind. Thus the tradition of *bodhisattvas* (see *Bodhisattvas*) developed, in which the nearly enlightened individual remains in this world to help others move toward *nirvāna*. In this connection, there are several understandings of *nirvāna*. There are Buddhists who see enlightenment as instantaneous; some who see it as a process taking eons, through various deaths and rebirths; and some who see it as something to be achieved gradually in this life. Among more esoteric Buddhists—especially in Tibet (see Tibetan Buddhism) and Japan (see Japanese Buddhism, Japanese Afterlife), ritual acts can relate the practitioner directly to the reality of the Buddha's Enlightenment, so that the act of worship becomes a sacramental participation in the actual Buddha nature, perhaps a type of temporary mystical union. The Japanese followers of Amida Buddha (see Amida Buddha) speak of the Pure Land (see Pure Land) paradise—in reality a state of being—into which the believer must be reborn before Enlightenment can be achieved. Such enlightenment can result in the individual's returning to this life as a teaching *bodhisattva*.

Nithan Khun Borom—This is a narrative that describes the origins of the Lao people. According to the story, an argument among the gods led to a life-destroying great Flood (see Flood) that left only three giant gourds on the earth. When the gods (the *khun*) heard noises in the gourds, they broke them open and released animals of all kinds and a great number of people: the black Kha and the light-skinned Tai Lao. The *khun* tried to teach the people proper social arrangements, but they were unruly, so the chief god, Phaya Then, who was also Indra (see Indra), sent help in the person of his son Khun Borom, also called *Parama* (the Lord). Khun Borom landed in a rice paddy and began to organize the world. When a giant plant began to grow and cut off light from the world, an old man and woman who had come to the earth with Khun Borom volunteered to cut down the plant but lost their lives in the process. These are the Lao ancestors, the Pu Ngoe Nga Ngoe (also called Pu Thao Yoe or Pu Yoe Ya Yoe) and the Me Ya Ngam, who still participate in masked form in Laotian festivals.

Khun Borom had seven sons and divided the territory into seven areas that included parts of China, Vietnam, Thailand, Burma, and all of Laos (Lan Xang).

Northern Caucasus Mythology—Before the rise of Islam, the people of the Caucasus—the Cherkess, the Abkhaz, the Ubyhk, the Georgians, and others—worshipped a Supreme Being. For many of these groups god was divided into two aspects, one benevolent, one judgmental. The first was associated with the sky, the second with storms and with lightning, which was considered to be sacred. The Cherkess and the Abkhaz have a blacksmith god linked to a sacred forge; he ensures fertility among women. There were also hunting gods, grain gods, and culture heroes.

Nügua—Nügua (Nu-kua or Nüwa), is the great Mother Goddess of Chinese mythology (see Chinese Deities). The sister-wife of the August emperor-god Fuxi (see Fuxi, see Chinese Emperors), she was a serpent figure, capable of changing shapes at will, who is said to have created the first humans out of yellow soil and mud, the yellow soil forming aristocrats, the mud the lower orders. It was Nügua who defeated the Black Dragon, Gonggong (see Gonggong) and repaired the sky after he had removed one of its support pillars.

O

Ohrmazd—See Ahura Mazda.

Okuninushi—This *kami* (see *Kami*), or Shinto (see Shinto entries) spirit-god, was the son of the sun goddess Amaterasu's (see Amaterasu) brother Susanowo (see Susanowo). He ruled Izumo (see Izumo Cycle) until the arrival of Amaterasu's grandson Ninigi (see Ninigi), who became the ruler of what would become the islands of Japan.

Oṃ—The Vedic (see Vedic entries) *Upaniṣads* (see *Upaniṣads*) tell us that the syllable *oṃ (auṃ)* is the "primary sound . . . the one indestructible thing or syllable *(akṣara)*." Recited as a *mantra* (see *Mantra*), for example, at the beginning and end of prayers—something approximating the Christian *amen* but much more important—it is a sound that expresses the divine. The *Katha Upaniṣad* says that meditation on *oṃ* can bring one to union with the Absolute—that is, with *Brahman* (see Brahman). In a sense, *Oṃ* is *Brahman* and the cosmos itself. In keeping with this idea, the *Māṇḍūkya Upaniṣad* breaks the syllable into its connected components, *a*, *u*, and *m*. It relates *a* to being awake, *u* to dreaming, *m* to a sleep without dream, and the whole *auṃ,* or *oṃ,* to the *turīya* state—that which is Brahman. The same *Upaniṣad* speaks of the use of the *oṃ* in meditation, the sacred syllable being the bow; the *ātman* (see *Ātman*), or Self, being the arrow; and Brahman being the target. Eventually the *oṃ,* as the sound of the contraction of *a, u,* and *m* was related to the *trimūrti* of Brahmā (see Brahmā), *a* as creating; Viṣṇu (see Viṣṇu), *u* as sustaining; and Śiva (see Śiva), *m* as dissolving.

P

P'an-ku—See Pangu.

Pābūjī Epic—This is an epic of Rajasthan in northern India. The hero is Pābūjī, who is the son of a king and a nymph. His mother dies but returns to earth as a beautiful mare who is given to her son by an incarnation of the goddess (see Devi). Pābūjī is eventually killed in a war with a rival prince, but his son, who was removed from his mother's womb before she ascended the funeral pyre (see *Satī*), lives to avenge his death.

Pahlavi Texts—The Zoroastrian (see Zoroastrianism) sacred book, the *Avesta* (see *Avesta*), was translated into the Middle Iranian or Pahlavi (Parthian) language from the no-longer-understood older Avestan language beginning in about 250 CE. These translations are known as the Pahlavi texts.

Pāli—A form of Indian non-Sanskrit (see Sanskrit) or vernacular Prākrit, Pāli was the language of the original southern Indian Buddhist (see Buddhism) scriptures. The term Pāli text or Pāli canon refers to these ancient works of Hīnayāna (see Hīnayāna Buddhism) and Theravāda Buddhism (see Theravāda Buddhism, Tripiṭaka).

Palnāḍu Epic—This Telugu epic of southern India tells the histories of various heroes of Palnāḍu. Much of it involves a *Mahābhārata* (see *Mahābhārata*)-like war between two related families.

Pañcatantra—Also known as the *Fables of Bidpai*, the *Pañcatantra* ("five books") is the *Grimm's Fairy Tales* and *Aesop's Fables* of India, a collection of Sanskrit tales written down between about 100 BCE and 500 CE, attributed to Viṣṇuśaram. The stories are meant both to teach moral lessons and to entertain.

Pañcarātra—The name for an early sect devoted to the Hindu (see Hinduism entries) god Viṣṇu (see Viṣṇu), the *Pañcarātra* is best known for texts known as the *Saṃhitās*. The *Saṃhitās* are concerned, among other things, with Creation in stages, the highest of which is pure, emanating from Vāsudeva (see Vāsudeva), the union of Viṣṇu and his *śakti* (see *Śakti*) as Lakṣmī (see Lakṣmī). It is the *śakti* who gives form or realization to Viṣṇu's qualities in creation.

Pāṇḍavas—The five Pāṇḍava brothers are the heroes of the Indian epic the *Mahābhārata* (see *Mahābhārata*) who fight the great battle against their cousins the Kauravas (see Kauravas). All five brothers are married to Draupadī (see Draupadī). Although Pāṇḍu (see Pāṇḍu) is officially the father of the Pāṇḍavas, their parentage is said to be the result of the unions between mortal women and gods. Pāṇḍu's wife Kuntī (see Kuntī) is the mother of the most important of the five brothers. She produces the Pāṇḍava leader Yudhiṣṭhira (see Yudhiṣṭhira) by Dharma (see *Dharma*), the *Bhagavadgītā* (see *Bhagavadgītā*) hero Arjuna (see Arjuna) by Indra (see Indra), and the great warrior Bhīma by Vāyu (see Vāyu). The fathers of these heroes are personifications of characteristics associated with their sons. Yudhiṣṭhira, as king, is driven by a sense of *dharma* or ideal social order; Arjuna, the spiritual "king" especially close to Kṛṣṇa (see Kṛṣṇa), is represented by the ancient king of the gods; Bhīma is above all a warrior as is his father, the wind. The lesser Pāṇḍavas, Nakula and Sahadeva, are the offspring of Pāṇḍu's second wife Mādrī and the Twin Gods called the Aśvins (see Aśvins), the physicians of the gods.

Pangu—Pangu the giant was the first living creature in the Chinese creation myth (See Chinese Cosmogony).

Paṇis—The Indian philosopher Aurobindo (see Aurobindo Ghose) considered the myth of the Paṇis to be the most significant of Hindu (see Hinduism entries) myths, one that reveals the true mystery of the *Vedas* (see *Vedas*). The Paṇis ("misers") were an Indian race of demons, sometimes considered to represent the cattle-raiding indigenous Dravidians (see Dravidians), who fought the invading Aryans (see Aryans) for riches. The *Bṛhaddevatā* and the ancient *Rg Veda* (see *Ṛg Veda*) contain the story of how the Paṇis stole Indra's (see Indra) cows. Indra sent the female dog Saramā (intuition) to bring them back, but the Paṇis seduced her with the milk of the cows, and when she returned to Indra, she denied that she had found his animals. Indra became so angry that he kicked Samarā, who vomited up the milk. Indra followed her back to the Paṇis, killed them, and took back his cows. In Sanskrit the word *go* can mean "cow" or refer to illumination. When Indra retrieves the cows, guided by Saramā (intuition), he frees true illumination.

Parade of Ants—The Hindu (see Hinduism entries) *Brahmavāivarta Purāṇa* (see *Purāṇas*) contains a story that reveals a post Vedic (see Vedic entries) view of the ancient king of the gods, Indra (see Indra), now surpassed in importance by other gods. According to the story, Indra commanded the great divine architect Viśvakarman (see Viśvakarman) to build him an appropriately splendid palace. As Viśvakarman worked, Indra kept demanding more and more until, in despair, the architect approached the creator Brahmā (see Brahmā) to complain, and Brahmā approached the still higher power, Viṣṇu (see Viṣṇu). Viṣṇu agreed that something must be done to dampen Indra's delusory pride. One morning a *brahman* (see *Brahmans*) boy appeared before the king of gods and blessed him. Indra asked him why he had come. The boy replied that he had heard of Indra's great palace and wondered how long it would take to complete. He pointed out that no other Indra had ever succeeded in building such a place. Surprised, Indra asked how many Indras there could possibly have been. The boy then spoke to Indra as to a child, revealing himself as an ancient being who knew both Brahmā and Viṣṇu and who had witnessed many endings and creations of the universe. When twenty-eight Indras have come and gone, said the boy, only one day and night of Brahmā has passed. At this point, a parade of ants four yards wide appeared in an endless column. Each ant, said the boy, was at one time an Indra; those Indras who pursue vain desires will become as ants (see *Karman*). Indra learned his lesson and achieved humility.

Paraśurāma—See Avatars of Viṣṇu.

Parsis—Zoroastrians (see Zoroastrianism) in western India are called Parsis ("Persians"). According to Parsi tradition contained in the *Quissa of Sanjan* (Sanjan's Story), a four-hundred line Persian verse narrative of 1600 written by the Parsi priest Bahman, the Parsis fled Muslim persecution in Iran, spent one hundred years hiding in the mountains, and then sailed to India. Parsis are known especially for the central place of fire in their worship. A continuous fire burns in the *agiari* or fire temple and *mantras* (see *Mantras*), or magical formulae, are offered up to the fire as prayers to the divine presence. Also important are *dakhmas,* or "towers of silence," where the bodies of the dead are placed to be consumed by vultures.

Pārvatī—Perhaps the most popular form of the great Hindu (see Hinduism entries) Goddess, or Devī (see Devī), Pārvatī, "Daughter of the Mountain," is one of several aspects of the Goddess as Śiva's (see Śiva) wife (see Satī, Umā, Durgā, Kālī). Pārvatī is depicted as a beautiful woman who characteristically sits in an embrace with her husband, signifying her position as his *śakti* (see *Śakti*) or energizing power. Pārvatī is the mother of Gaṇapati, also known as Gaṇeśa (see Gaṇeśa).

Phi—The *phi* are spirits in Thailand and Laos who are known for their magical power and for their effect on everyday life. They resemble the *nats* (see *Nats*) of Burma. The *phi* are, above all, associated with the land and the soil and are a link between Buddhism (see Buddhism) and pre-Buddhist animism (see Animism). There is a hierarchy of *phi* and a cult associated with them (see Neak-tā).

Prahlāda—An *asura* (see *Asuras*) devotee of Viṣṇu (see Viṣṇu), who would become lord of the Underworld (see Underworld) after Viṣṇu in the form of Narasiṃha (see Narasiṃha, see Avatars of

Viṣṇu), the man-lion, killed his father, the wicked *asura* king Hiraṇyakaśipu (Hiraṇya), brother of another demon, Hiraṇyāksa.

Prajāpati—Prajāpati is the "lord of creatures," the primal being associated with creation in the Indian (see Hinduism entries) *Brāhmaṇas* (see *Brāhmaṇas*). But by the time of the epic the *Mahābhārata* (see *Mahābhārata*), he has lost his position as the primal soul or first god and has become simply a god whose job is to create. From the time of the *Upaniṣads* (see *Upaniṣads*) on, he is frequently the same being as Brahmā (see Brahmā) the creator god in the Hindu *trimūrti* that is Brahmā, Viṣṇu (see Viṣṇu), and Śiva (see Śiva). There are several myths about the process by which Prajāpati created the world. The *Aitareya Brāhmaṇa* contains a story of incest that echoes the *Ṛg Veda* creation myth (see *Ṛg Veda*, Vedic Cosmogony). Prajāpati came to his daughter, the sky or dawn, as a stag, she becoming a doe, and had intercourse with her. But the gods disapproved, and Rudra (see Rudra), who later is Śiva, pierced him with an arrow. Prajāpati's seed flowed forth and became a lake protected by Agni (see Agni), or Fire, out of which came many things, including Bṛhaspati (see Bṛhaspati), the lord of sacred speech—sometimes Indra (see Indra)—necessary for proper sacrifices and *mantras* (see *Mantra*). In the *Kauṣitāki Brāhmaṇa,* it is Prajāpati's sons who are seduced by his daughter. From their spilled seed, captured by Prajāpati in a golden bowl, emerges the thousand-eyed Bhava or "Existence," a version of the old Vedic (see Vedic entries) primal man or Puruṣa (see Puruṣa). In still another myth—in the *Śatapatha Brāhmaṇa*—Prajāpati masturbates and spills his seed into Agni. The seed becomes the sacred milk of clarified butter used in sacrifices. By producing progeny and making proper sacrifice, Prajāpati, setting a standard for humans, saved himself and existence from the death that is Agni.

Prakṛti—The Vedic (see Vedic entries) *Prakṛti* (Nature), in India is the active female element with which the primal male or Puruṣa (see Puruṣa) must unite in order to become real as the universe. As such, Prakṛti is the forerunner of the later *śakti* (see *Śakti*, Vedic Cosmogony).

Primal Bull—See Gayomart and see Mithra.

Pṛthā—See Kunti.

Pṛthivi—Pṛthivi is the Vedic (see Vedic entries) goddess associated with the Earth. It is likely that she was originally a goddess of the Indus Valley culture (see Indus Valley Mythology, Prakrti Kunti).

Pu Ngoe Nga Ngoe—the first mythic couple of Laos (see Ancestor Cults and Nithan Khun Borom).

Purāṇas—The *Purāṇas* are a body of Vedic Hindu (see Vedic entries, Hinduism entries) texts containing myths, legends, and ritual instructions. Of the many works designated as *purāṇas* ("ancient narratives"), only eighteen—the *Mahāpurāṇas* ("Great Purāṇas")—are official. Even they, composed early in the common era, are *smṛti* (see *Smṛti*), or remembered texts, rather than *śruti* (see *Śruti*), the revealed word. The *Purāṇas* are often attributed to the sage Vyāsa (see Vyāsa), also said to be the author of the *Mahābhārata* (see *Mahābhārata*). If a single theme dominates the *Purāṇas* it is that of *bhakti* (see *bhakti*) or proper devotion (see Puranic cosmogony).

Puranic Cosmogony—In the *Purāṇas* (see *Purāṇas*) of Vedism (see Vedic entries), two essential creation myths are developed from the myths of the sacred revealed, or *śruti* (see *Śruti*) tradition. In the first creation the primal man, or Puruṣa (see Puruṣa), is also designated as Ātman (see Ātman) or Brahman (see Brahman) or *Mahāyogin* (Great Yogi). But unlike the original Puruṣa, who as sacrificial victim becomes the universe, this creator uses *yoga* (see *Yoga*) to complete the process by which Existence comes about through the release of the active female aspect of Nature or *Prakṛti* (see *Prakṛti*). In the other myth the Purusa Nārāyaṇa (see Nārāyaṇa), a form of Viṣṇu (see Viṣṇu), who has been asleep on the primeval waters, awakens during the period between two *kalpas* (ages) and becomes the creator Brahmā (see Brahmā) then Vāyu (the Wind) then the Cosmic Boar (see Boar, Avatars of Viṣṇu), who serves as the sacrificial diver who brings up earth from the depths (see Earth-Diver Creation). The Puranic cosmogony also contains stories of the dissolution of existence in the cosmic fire that emerges from the breath of Rudra (see Rudra), or Śiva (see

Śiva). Wind and floods complete the work (see Vedic Cosmogony, *Upaniṣad* Cosmogony).

Pure Land—A pure land or "Buddha land" in Mahāyāna Buddhism (see Mahāyāna Buddhism) is the land of Buddhas and *bodhisattvas* (see *Bodhisattvas*). Ordinary humans live in impure lands tainted by passions. The Mahāyāna Buddhists say that the Buddha Sākyamuni (see Gautama Buddha) has his own land and that other Buddhas have their own. The best known is Sukhāvatī (see Pure Land), the home of Buddha Amitābha, or Amida Buddha (see Amida Buddha), and the source for the name Pure Land Buddhism (see Pure Land Buddhism) so important in Japan (see Japanese Buddhism). Amida's Pure Land can be said to be a physical representation of Enlightenment. For some Buddhists, in fact, "Pure Land" is exclusively of the mind. For others it has a more literal quality, as in the Japanese and Chinese Tuṣita, or Heaven, of the *Bodhisattva* Maitreya (see Maitreya).

Pure Land Buddhism—The Pure Land Sect of Buddhism (see Buddhism, see Mahāyāna Buddhism), called Jōdoshu in Japan (see Japanese Buddhism), was founded by a monk named Honen in the twelfth century CE and was based on the Chinese version called Jingtu. It stresses salvation through Amida Buddha (see Amida Buddha) and the possibility of rebirth in Sukhāvatī, the Pure Land (see Pure Land) where Amida Buddha reigns. At the center of Pure Land worship is meditation and repeating the name of Amida Buddha.

Puruṣa—The Sanskrit for "person" or "man," Purusa in the so-called Puruṣa Hymn of the ancient Indian sacred text, the *Ṛg Veda* (see *Ṛg Veda*), is the "first (or primal) man," who is the universe past, present, and future, and is the object of the first sacrifice of Existence. His mouth became Brahman (see Brahman) and the moon came from his consciousness. Eventually Puruṣa became synonymous with the Absolute—the universal "self"—Brahman or Ātman (see Ātman). Puruṣa entered Existence, knew himself and exclaimed, "I am." Eventually Puruṣa as "Consciousness" became associated in the ancient philosophical tradition of Sankhya (Sāṃkhya) with the idea of Prakṛti (see Prakṛti), or

"Nature," the creative energy necessary for the realization of materiality (see also *Śakti)*. With the development of Vedic Hindu mythology in the *Brāhmaṇas* (see *Brāhmaṇas*), *Upaniṣads* (see *Upaniṣads*), and *Purāṇas* (see *Purāṇas*), the idea of Puruṣa is somewhat superseded by Brahman, Ātman, and figures such as Prajāpati (see Prajāpati), Brahmā (see Brahmā), and Viṣṇu (see Viṣṇu, Vedic Cosmogony, Puranic Cosmogony, *Upaniṣad* Cosmogony).

Q

Qat—Qat, or Quat, is the Melanesian spirit who created living beings. After he carved the first three men and three women from a tree, he hid them among some trees for three days and then literally enlivened them by dancing for them to a drum beat. Humans would have been immortal had the spirit Marawa not also fabricated human beings and then buried them for three days. When he dug them up they were already dead; so death came into the world. It was Qat who brought about night and day and a regular passing of time so that agriculture became possible.

Queen Maya—Mahā (Great) Māyā is the mother of Gautama Buddha (see Gautama Buddha, see Māyā).

Qur'an—The *Qur'an (Koran)* is the sacred scripture of Islam (see Islam). Its contents were sent down from Allah to the Prophet Muhammad between 610 and 632 CE, and the book was compiled in Arabic after the Prophet's death. As the "word of God," the *Qur'an* is the basis for the proper way of life in all parts of the Muslim world, including Asia.

R

Rādhā—In the twelfth century *Gītāgovinda,* "The Song of the Cowherd" by the Bengali poet Jayadeva (see Govinda) Radha, a married *gopī* (see Gopis), or cowherd, fell madly in love with the younger Kṛṣṇa (see Kṛṣṇa) and eventually won his love. The beautifully erotic love bouts and the obvious allegory of the longing of the human soul for absolute union with Kṛṣṇa-Viṣṇu (see Viṣṇu, see Avatars of Viṣṇu) leads to a comparison with the Hebrew *Song of Songs*.

Rāma—Rāma or Rama-candra ("charming one") is one of the greatest of the avatars (see Avatar) of the Hindu (see Hinduism entries) god Viṣṇu (see Viṣṇu, Avatars of Viṣṇu). The son of King Daśaratha of Ayodhyā, Rāma is forced, because of his stepmother's misbehavior, to give up his throne and go into exile. Rāma's wife is Sītā (see Sītā). Their story is the principal tale of the epic, the *Rāmāyaṇa* (see *Rāmāyaṇa*).

Rāmāyaṇa—Traditionally attributed to the sage Vālmīki (see Vālmīki), the *Rāmāyaṇa* is one of the two greatest Sanskrit epics of India, the other being the much longer *Mahābhārata* (see *Mahābhārata*). Popular in India and much of southeast Asia, especially in the Indonesian Hindu island of Bali, the *Rāmāyaṇa* is a compilation of material dating between 500 BCE and 200 CE. It stands as a record of Hindu virtues and values. Rāma (see Rāma), the seventh avatar of Viṣṇu (see Viṣṇu, Avatars of Viṣṇu), is the epic's hero who represents the perfect prince, an embodiment of *dharma* (see *Dharma*). His wife Sītā (see Sītā), as the incarnation of Viṣṇu's wife Śrī (see Śrī) or Lakṣmī (see Lakṣmī), is the perfect wife who represents Prosperity. Rāma's faithful brother, Lakṣmaṇa, is the perfect brother.

The plot of the *Rāmāyaṇa,* like that of the *Mahābhārata,* is highly symbolic—even allegorical—with each event representing some aspect of the Hindu spiritual journey. Rāma and Sītā, for example, stand as *dharma* and Prosperity symbolizing faithfulness and the sacred sacrifice against the demonic defiler of the sacrifice, Rāvaṇa (see Rāvaṇa). Rāma and Sītā's exile in the forest is an ascetic preparation for the sacrifice and the defeat of the anti-*dharma* or *adharmic* forces represented by Rāvaṇa.

Rāma and his three brothers grow up in the court of their father, King Daśaratha. Rāma and his brother Lakṣmaṇa are "borrowed" by the sage Viśvāmitra, to fight against the evil sacrifice-defiling *rākṣasa,* followers of the demon Rāvaṇa. Only Rāma, he says, can defeat them. As an avatar of Viṣṇu, Rāma is indeed the proper defender of the faith, and he succeeds in defeating the *rākṣasa.* Rāma and his brother then travel on to Mithilā, where Rāma wins King Janaka's earth-born daughter Sītā by succeeding in bending the great bow of the god Śiva (see Śiva). On his way home, Rāma succeeds in still another trial by accepting Paraśurāma's (see Paraśurāma) challenge to bend the bow of Viṣṇu, a task he accomplishes. Upon his return home, Rāma's father decides to appoint him heir to the throne, but an intrigue of his stepmother forces the king to honor an old oath and to exile his son to the forest for a number of years. Sītā insists on accompanying her husband to the "punishment forest." Eventually the evil Rāvaṇa abducts Sītā from the forest and takes her to his fortress in Laṅkā. Now begins the essential aspect of the epic, Rāma's quest for Sītā, mirroring Viṣṇu's need of his Śrī or *śakti* (see *Śakti*), or energy source.

Rāma is helped in his quest by the monkey god Hanumān (see Hanumān) and his monkey army. With magic, the monkey troops are able to build a bridge to Laṅkā, and during a terrible battle, Rāma is able to kill Rāvaṇa and rescue Sītā. By killing the king of the sacrifice-defiling *rākṣasa,* Rāma fulfills the purpose for which he has been sent as Viṣṇu's avatar to earth.

Since Sītā has been possibly defiled by having been abducted by Rāvaṇa, Rāma allows a trial by fire in which the innocent Sītā climbs upon the funeral pyre but is miraculously refused by the fire god Agni (see Agni, *Satī*). Rāma can now receive her again as his wife. Later his doubts about Sītā revive, and he exiles her to the forest where she gives birth to twin sons and stays with the sage Vālmīki, who composes the *Rāmāyaṇa* and recites it to Rāma and Sītā's sons. Sītā returns to Rāma and asks her mother the Earth to take her back as proof of her undying innocence. Immediately Pṛthivi (see Pṛthivi) rises on her throne, takes her daughter on her lap and the earth swallows them. Rāma reigns for another one thousand years.

Rāvaṇa—Rāvaṇa is the multiarmed, multiheaded *rāksasa* (demon) who holds Sītā (see Sītā) prisoner in the Hindu epic the *Rāmāyaṇa* (see *Rāmāyaṇa*). It is said that the god Śiva (see Śiva) imprisoned him under his mighty leg for ten thousand years as punishment for his having attempted to move the Mountain of Heaven to Laṅkā.

Ṛg Veda—The *Ṛg Veda* (after *ṛks* meaning *mantra*) is the oldest of the collections *(saṃhitās)* of Indo-Aryan (see Aryans) *mantras* (see *Mantras*) and hymns, dating from about 2000–1700 BCE. These are hymns "revealed" directly to seers (see *ṛṣis*) by a higher power. In short, the *Ṛg Veda,* like other Vedic (see Vedic entries) literature, is what is called *śruti* (see *Śruti*) or the most sacred sort of Hindu (see Hinduism entries) text. There are ten books or *maṇḍalas* (see *Maṇḍala*) in the *Ṛg Veda,* each attributed to a privileged family of seer-sages. These books are the primary source for our knowledge of the most ancient Indian mythology, forming the basis for the development of Hinduism. Mythology within the *Ṛg Veda* develops from the most ancient period dominated by Varuṇa (see Varuṇa), the fire god Agni (see Agni), and the cult of *soma* (see Soma), to the phase centered on the warrior gods led by Indra (see

Indra), to the later phase out of which comes Hinduism, one in which both non-Aryan Indus Valley-Dravidian (see Indus Valley Mythology, Dravidians) gods such as Rudra-Śiva (see Rudra, Śiva), the Goddess (see Devī), and popular Aryan figures such as Viṣṇu (see Viṣṇu) become increasingly important. The *Ṛg Veda* is perhaps best known for its creation myth (see Vedic Cosmogony).

Ṛg Veda Creation—See Vedic Cosmogony.

Ritual Theater—Ritual theater has long been a means by which mythology has been transmitted in Asia. It is particularly important for illiterate audiences but has also remained popular—especially in parts of India and in Java and Bali in Indonesia—among the educated. There are ritual temple plays in parts of India to celebrate the life of Draupadī (Draupadī), for example, and any number of dramatic versions of the *Mahābhārata* (see *Mahābhārata*) and the *Rāmāyaṇa* (see *Rāmāyaṇa*) can be found there, as well as in Java and Bali. Perhaps the most elaborate ritual drama is the Balinese one based on the *Rāmāyaṇa,* where masked versions of the demon Rāvaṇa (see Rāvaṇa) and a chorus of Hanumān's (see Hanumān) monkeys play significant roles in Rāma's quest (see Rāma) for Sītā (see Sītā).

Ṛṣi—A Ṛṣi is an Indian seer or hearer and revealer of divine knowledge such as that contained in the *Vedas* (see *Vedas*) and other sacred "revealed" Hindu (see Hinduism entries) texts (see *Śruti*). *Veda* means "knowledge" and the *ṛṣis* were, therefore, transmitters of divine knowledge revealed to them in visions.

Rudra—Rudra is the early Indian form of the later Hindu god Śiva (see Śiva). Rudra means "one who roars." Some scholars see Rudra as originally a non-Aryan (see Aryans) fertility god of the Indus Valley (see Indus Valley Mythology), a god whose symbol was the bull and who is sometimes depicted in the posture of a yogi. All of these aspects suggest a link to the later Śiva. In the *Ṛg Veda* (see *Ṛg Veda*), Rudra—whose wife's name, Pṛśni, means "water bag"—is a bringer of life-giving rain and other boons. As a fertility god he is represented by the phallus, or *liṅga* (see *Liṅga*), which will take on increased importance in the śiva cult.

Like Śiva, he is a destroyer, whose arrows are feared by all, and sometimes he seems to deny the ancient Vedic (see Vedic entries) sacrifice. Not surprisingly, he is closely associated with the god of death, Yama (see Yama); with the god of Fire, Agni (see Agni); and with the magical drink, *soma* (see *Soma*). "Rudra" is essentially synonymous with Bhava, Śarva, Ugra, Mahādeva, and, of course, Śiva. Some of these names are attached to the Rudras, followers of Rudra who represent various aspects of the god, such as fear, howler, thunderbolt, and arrows. Rudras are sometimes called Maruts, who are also sometimes storm gods who can bring havoc.

S

Sacred Cow—See Kāmadhenu.

Sacrifice—Sacrifice is a universal religious act, one closely associated with the mythologies of particular traditions. Sacrifices are often offered to divinities in the name of society by priestly castes. The offerings themselves may be symbolic or literal, vegetable or animal. Scapegoats of various kinds may be used to substitute for living offerings that a given group is unable or unwilling to give up. For example, Abraham was instructed to offer Isaac as a sacrifice and did so, but an animal became a substitute for Isaac; the Christians say that Christ died as an offering for humanity. Sacrifices are often accomplished at sacred times of the year in sacred places. In Asian myth and religion sacrifice plays important roles. Japanese emperors offered sacrifices to the dead and to nature divinities (see Kami, Shinto entries). The Chinese Emperor, representing his people, made winter solstice sacrifices to the gods and to the dead. Sacrifice is important in the bear cults of the Ainu (see Ainu Mythology) and to the indigenous religions of Indonesia (see Hainuwele). It is central to the fire rituals of the Zoroastrians (see Zoroastrianism, *Avesta*). In the Hindu (see Hinduism) tradition of India sacrifice can be said to be the central issue. In the Sāṇkhya tradition, life emerges from the sacrifice of the primal male or Puruṣa (see Puruṣa), and the continuance of existence depends on the proper practice of ritual sacrifice (see Hindu Mythology, Agni, Dakṣa, Devī, Kālī, etc.). For the Hindu, life and the world itself represent a sacrifice—that which must continually be destroyed and re-created through the eons of history.

Sādhana—See Tantrism.

Śaiva—A Hindu (see Hinduism entries) worshipper of Śiva (see Śiva) as the supreme god (see *Bhakti*).

Śaivism—The aspect of Hinduism (see Hinduism entries) that is based on the worship of the god Śiva (see Śiva, Śaiva), Śaivism contains many sects and is found in all parts of India.

Śakaṭ Kathā—A *kathā* is a narrative performed as part of a Hindu (see Hinduism entries) ritual. The *Śakaṭ Kathā* is an instructive myth told in Northern India on the occasion of a festival honoring the elephant-headed Gaṇeśa (see Gaṇeśa). It stresses the importance of proper fasting and proper ritual practice.

Śakta—A Hindu (see Hinduism entries) worshipper of the Goddess (see Devī) as ultimate power (see *Śakti*).

Śakti—The Sanskrit word for "power" or "energy," *śakti* is the energizing material power of a given Hindu (see Hinduism entries) god, a power that is personified as his wife. Often depicted in a state of sexual union, the god and his *śakti* together represent the Absolute, the god being nonactivated Eternity, the goddess being activated Time. The Goddess, or Devī (see Devī), *is śakti* or the "Universal Power." As Prakṛti (see Prakṛti) she is the *śakti* or female energy by which the original Puruṣa or primal man becomes creation (see Puruṣa). As Lakṣmī (see Lakṣmī) she is the manifestation of the divine energy associated with Viṣṇu (see Viṣṇu). Śiva's *śakti* takes many forms that includes Umā (see Umā), Durgā (see Durgā), the terrifying Kālī (see Kālī), and the motherly Pārvatī (see Pārvatī). By extension, Sītā (see Sītā) is Rāma's (see Rāma, Avatars of Viṣṇu) *śakti* (see the *Rāmāyaṇa*) and Draupadī (see Draupadī) is the *śakti* of the Pāṇḍavas (see Pāṇḍavas) in the *Mahābhārata* (see *Mahābhārata*). And by further extension, the Hindu wife is a manifestation of her husband's *śakti*. Thus, *śakti* is present in all women.

Śāktism—With the worship of Śiva (see Śiva, see Śaivism), and Viṣṇu (see Viṣṇu, Vaiṣṇava), Saktism—worship of the Goddess (see Devī) or Śakti (see *Śakti*) as the supreme deity or as the consort of Viṣṇu or especially Śiva—is at the center of Hinduism (see Hinduism entries), in particular the branch of Hinduism called Tantrism (see Tantrism). Śaktism has roots in the pre-Aryan (see Aryans) Indus Valley civilization (see Indus Valley Mythology). In Tantric imagery there is the tradition of the union of Śiva and Śakti as the Absolute.

Sāma Veda—The *Sāma Veda* is one of the four *Vedas* (see *Vedas*, see Vedic entries) or sacred *śruti* (see *Śruti*) texts of Hinduism (see Hinduism entries).

Samguk Sagi and Samguk Yusa—Collections of Korean myths (see Korean Mythology) and legends of prehistoric times, these two books were compiled by Buddhist (see Buddhism) monks. They contain epic tales of the founding of the Korean nation, sun and moon myths, and various hero stories.

Saṃsāra—For the Hindu (see Hinduism entries) *saṃsāra* is the never-ending cycle of life or of rebirths, which seems real to those who do not understand eternal truth. To the enlightened one, *saṃsāra* is illusion, the material of artifice or *māyā* (see *Māyā*). In a sense, the union of the god and his *śakti* (see *Śakti,* Śaktism) represent the Absolute—the union of Eternity and Time or *Nirvāna* (see Nirvāna) and *saṃsāra*. For Buddhists (see Buddhism), it is the teachings of the Buddha (see Gautama Buddha) that provide the desired release from *saṃsāra*. Through Enlightenment the impurity of this world becomes the utter release, or the void that is *nirvān*a.

Sanskrit—*Sanskrit* (or *Sanscrit*) is a word derived from *saṁskṛta,* meaning "perfectly formed." It is the ancient language of India, the oldest of Indo-European languages, and the one used in sacred Hindu writings from the *Vedas* (see *Vedas*) on. According to Hindu myth, language and speech were discovered by Sarasvatī, the wife of the creator god Brahma. As the creator's *śakti* (see *Śakti*) it was appropriate that she should articulate creation (see Sarasvatī).

Sanyāsamma Katha—This epic story of southern India is one of many narratives culminating in the *satī* (see *Satī*) or ritual self-immolation of a wronged virgin-widow who then is deified. The heroine of this story is the saintly Sanyāsamma.

Saoshyant—Saoshyant or Saoshyans or Sōšyant is a Zoroastrian (see Zoroastrianism) term for "savior." According to Zoroastrian tradition, three great Saoshyants will come after Zarathustra (see Zoroaster), himself a Saoshyant (see Zoroastrian Apocalypse). All later Saoshyants will come from the seed of Zarathustra that are saved in Lake Kansaoya and guarded by spirits until the savior's virgin mother (see Virgin Birth) is impregnated while bathing there. The last and greatest of the post-Zarathustra Saoshyants is to be Astvatereta—sometimes simply called Saoshyant—who will finally destroy the forces of evil aligned against those of the good in Zoroastrian theology.

Sarasvatī—Sarasvatī means "flowing," thus this Vedic (see Vedic entries) goddess appears in the *Ṛg Veda* (see *Ṛg Veda*) as a sacred river and as Vāc, a personification of speech. She is a goddess of learning and the arts. As the wife and *śakti* (see *śakti*) of the creator god Brahmā (see Brahmā), Sarasvatī is appropriately the inventor of the sacred language, Sanskrit (see Sanskrit), the "flow" by means of which eternal creation is articulated in Time. But with the dying out of the Brahmā cult Sarasvatī was sometimes seen as a wife of another creator, Viṣṇu (see Viṣṇu), and sometimes in the ancient texts she is associated as an aspect of sacrificial fire with the fire god Agni (see Agni).

Satī—*Satī* or *suttee* is the Hindu (see Hinduism entries) custom in which wives are immolated on the funeral pyres of their husbands. Satī ("good woman") is also a name of the great Goddess (see Devī), who as the daughter of Brahmā's son Dakṣa (see Dakṣa) and a consort of Śiva (see Śiva), is an embodiment of the perfect Hindu wife. The *Devībhāgavata Purāṇa* (see *Purāṇas*) tells how Satī used the "fire of her yoga" (see *Yoga*) to reveal the *dharma* (see *Dharma*) of the practice of *satī* (*suttee*). Satī was burned in the world-destroying fire of Śiva. Śiva took her out of the fire and

Viṣṇu dismembered her with his arrows. Where each limb fell a devotional area for Śiva was established.

Sāvitrī—Sāvitrī, "Daughter of the Sun," celebrated in India as the ideal wife (see also Satī), is a version of the wife and *śakti* (see *śakti*, Sarasvatī) of the Hindu (see Hinduism entries) creator god Brahmā (see Brahmā). While Sarasvatī is the founder of language and Sanskrit, Sāvitrī is the birth-giver of and sometimes, as Gāyatrī, a personification of the *Vedas* (see *Vedas*). Brahmā felt great desire for Sāvitrī and placed his seed in her where it remained for a hundred years before producing the *Vedas* and many other aspects of creation, such as Memory, the Kali Age, and day and night. As Sāvitrī, the goddess saves her husband Satyavān from the clutches of Yāma (see Yāma), the god of Death (see Descent to the Underworld).

Secret History of the Mongols—The *Manghal un Niuca Tobca'an* or *Secret History of the Mongols* is an extensive narrative compiled in the thirteenth century to reveal the history of the Mongols (see Turko-Mongol Mythology) and their attempt to achieve unity from mythical times to the time of Genghis Khan. From the time of the mythical giant Qutula, known for his enormous strength, the Mongol leaders saw themselves as descendants of the Sky, Tangri or Tengri (see Tengri). The narrative in question tells the story of the brutal battles for supremacy over their neighbors, battles justified by the belief in divine Mongol origins.

Śeṣa—See Ananta.

Seven Gods of Fortune—In the esoteric Tendai sect (see Tendai Sect) of Japanese Buddhism (see Japanese Buddhism), there developed a composite representation of good fortune made up of the god Daikoku-ten (see Daikoku), an ancient Shinto *kami* (see *kami*) called Ebisu, and the gods Benzai-ten (see Benzai) and Bishamon (see Bishamon). Joined in the sixteenth century by three deities of good fortune of Chinese origin—Hotei, Fukurokuju, and Jurogin—the seven deities became the Seven Gods of Fortune, or Happiness, and since then have represented good luck, especially to people in business.

Seven Wise Men—An Indo-Iranian series of tales, the *Seven Wise Men* tells of the son of a king who is taught by a wise man called Sindbad (*not* Sindbad the sailor). As the prince must learn to control his emotions, he is ordered by his tutor to be silent for a week. During that time, his stepmother attempts to seduce him. She tells the king a false tale for each day of the week about how the prince supposedly tried to seduce her, but each tale is refuted by one of seven sages. After the week is over the prince tells his father the truth and is exonerated.

Shāh-Nāmah—The *Shāh-Nāmah* or *Book of Kings* is an epic containing the legendary and actual early history of Persia (Iran). Collected in the main in about 1000 CE by the poet Firdausi, it is a compilation of his own work as well as later added material and ancient histories and tales composed long before his time. In some sixty thousand couplets, the epic covers the period between the rule of the invading Aryan (see Aryans) Keyumars to the historical emergence of Islam (see Islam) in 651. Popular segments include the story of the rule of the evil tyrant Zahhak and his defeat at the hands of the dragon king hero Feridun, the coming of Zoroaster (Zardosht or Zarathustra, see Zoroaster), and the tale of the giant hero Rostam, who, defending the Shah Key Kavus, unwittingly kills his own son, Sohrab. It is this story of Rostam that was used by Matthew Arnold in his poem "Sohrab and Rustam" in 1853.

Shaka—This is a Japanese name for the Buddha Sākyamuni or Gautama Buddha (See Buddha Sākyamuni).

Shakti—See *Śakti*.

Shamanism—Shamanism is a religious phenomenon involving the disciplines and the practices of *shamans*. Although existing in various forms in various parts of the world, *shamanism* in its purest form is native to Siberia and Central Asia (see Central Asian Mythology, Siberian Shamanism) and to the indigenous peoples of North and South America who seem likely to have Central Asian origins. Shamans have also existed in the context of Shinto (see Shinto entries) in Japan (see Japanese Shamanism), their duties relating primarily to village rituals. In Indo-China (see Indo-

Chinese Mythology), shamans are concerned with curing. Korean shamans (see Korean Mythology) communicated with the spirit world. Shamans are, in a sense, religious magicians, who have power over fire and who are capable of achieving trance states in seances in which their souls vacate their bodies to go on curing missions to the spirit worlds above or below the earth. The shaman's primary purpose everywhere is to cure. The successful shaman controls the spirits with whom he works, and he can communicate with the dead. Thus it is that he often wears bones signifying the skeletal remains of the dead. His is a mystical vocation in that he works from an otherworldly state of ecstasy. In many cases a shaman realizes his vocation because of dreams and non-voluntary trances. Sometimes a shaman is trained as an apprentice by a master shaman. In any case, the shaman must learn to control and use certain ritualistic paraphernalia—especially the drum, the vehicle on which he travels to the other worlds—and he must memorize the necessary ritual forms and songs. Some shamans undergo an initiation period during which they seem to die. According to these shamans they are dismembered before being given new flesh and blood. Shamans are most often male, but there are female shamans as well in many cultures.

Shang-ti—See *Ti*.

Shijing—The *Shijing (Book of Odes)* is a series of collections of Chinese poetry dating from as early as 1100 BCE and complied in about 600 BCE. Tradition has it that Confucius (see Confucius) collected some of the poems. The collection reflects the Chou dynasty sense of the relationship between humans and gods (see Chinese entries). The poems were set to music and sung in praise of gods and ancestors and were accompanied by particular rituals.

Shingon Sect—The Shingon sect or Shingonshu of Japanese Mahāyāna (see Mahāyāna Buddhism) Buddhism (see Japanese Buddhism) is the only sect today that keeps alive the esoteric or *Mikkyō* tradition centered on Dainichi Nyorai (see Dainichi), or the Buddha Mahāvairocana, the cosmic illuminator, who, as the perfect expression of the ultimate truth of pure "emptiness," is the creator. The *Mikkyō* tradition is opposed to the *Kengyō* tradition based on the understandings of Sākyamuni Buddha (see Gautama Buddha). Shingon comes via the Chinese *Zhenyan*, meaning "true saying" from the Sanskrit term, *mantra* (see *Mantra*). *Zhenyan* was a form of Tantric Buddhism (see Tantrism, Vajrayāna). The monk Kūkai (774–835) founded the Shingon sect during the Heian period. He had been introduced to the esoteric rituals and texts of Zhenyan by the Chinese monk Huiguo. At the center of Shingon are two Tantric *sūtras* (see *Sūtras*), the *Mahāvairocana* and the *Sarvatathāgatatattvasaṃgraha.* An essential aspect of these *sūtras* and of Shingon is the idea that the illumination of the Dainichi Nyorai exists in everyone. All beings are, therefore, capable of Enlightenment, not just a perfect few (see Bodhisattva). The union of the illuminator and the illumined is expressed in two complicated diagrams or sacred *maṇḍalas* (see *Maṇḍala*) taught to Kūkai.

Shinto—Shinto, meaning the "kami way" (see kami), is a term applied to the ancient pre-Buddhist (see Buddhism) religion of Japan to differentiate it from *Butsudo,* the "Buddha way" (see Japanese Buddhism). Shinto is a polytheistic system that expresses in some profound way the Japanese world view. There are Shinto prayers and Shinto rituals, but the doctrine is minimal. Some might call Shinto a way of life rather than a religion *per se*. The mythic basis of Shinto is the belief in *kami*. Originally the word *kami* was used to describe any mysterious or sacred reality, anything that seemed to possess numinosity. However, everything is potentially *kami* and, thus, worthy of reverence. Because of the concept of *kam*i, Shinto at once affects the way tea is served, the way a package is wrapped, the way a war is fought, and the way an emperor is crowned. Gradually the *kami* concept took on concrete forms—deities who lived in natural objects or phenomena, ancestor divinities, and abstract concept divinities. Shinto shrines and rituals were at first local and agricultural in nature, but eventually they became associated with larger entities, including clans and the nation itself. The gods of Shinto are directly related to the imperial family and thus to the Japanese state (see Shinto Mythology). It could be argued that all Japanese are practitioners of Shinto, even if they happen to be Buddhist or Christian. By the eighth century, Shinto and Buddhism achieved a kind of marriage, with Shinto and Buddhist deities becoming merged and/or deities of one religion revered in the temples of the other (see Japanese Buddhas).

Shinto Mythology—Early Shinto (see Shinto) envisioned a standard northern Asian cosmology made up of an upper world or Heaven (Takamanohara) for the gods, a middle world (Nakatsukuni) for humans, and an underworld (Yomi) for the dead. Yet simultaneously, Shinto understood the universe as the world with an adjacent eternal paradise (Tokoyo) across the sea. Under the influence of Chinese culture there was a drive to compile and standardize Shinto myths that had formerly belonged to regional and family groups. This drive for standardization coincided with the political drive for national unification and began to take concrete form during the reign of the Emperor Temmu (672–687). The culmination of the movement for mythological unity came with the creation of the two primary sacred books of Shinto, the *Kojiki* (see *Kojiki*) and the *Nihongi* (see *Nihongi*), early in the eighth century. It is in these books and other early eighth-century texts (for example, the *Fudoki* and the *Sendai kujihongi*) that the purest form of Shinto mythology is found. They contain the stories and descriptions of the Shinto deities or spirits called *kamis* (see *Kamis*), as opposed to the amalgamation of Buddhist (see Japanese Buddhism, Japanese Buddhas) and Shinto deities that became popular with the advent of Buddhism in Japan. Perhaps the most important of the anthropomorphic Shinto deities is the sun goddess Amaterasu (see Amaterasu), the patroness and ancestor of the Japanese emperors. It was her relatives and descendants who founded the Japanese nation. In the beginning, when Earth and Heaven separated, *kamis* appeared, including Izanagi and his wife Izanami (see Izanagi and Izanami), who created the natural world and various clans before their tragic separation and enmity. Their most important offspring were Amaterasu, the moon god Tsukiyomi no

Mikoto, and the underworld god Susanowo (see Susanowo). It was Susanowo's offspring Okuninushi no Kami (see Okuninushi) who ruled Japan until the coming of Ninigi no Mikoto (see Ninigi), the grandson of Amaterasu (see Izumo Cycle). But it was Ninigi's grandson Jimmu Tenno (see Jimmu Tenno) who reigned as the first emperor.

Shoten—Shoten, or Binayākya, or Daisho-kangiten, is esoteric Japanese Buddhism's (see Japanese Buddhism) version of the Indian elephant-headed god Gaṇeśa or Vināyaka (see Gaṇeśa). As in India he came to be thought of as the son of Śiva (see Śiva), or Daijizaiten in Japan. The cult of Shoten was brought to Japan from China and Tantric Buddhism (see Vajrayāna) by the founder of the Shingon sect (see Shingon Sect) early in the ninth century and was also taken up by the Tendai sect (see Tendai Sect). Shoten is depicted as a double figure: a powerful male god in an embrace with a gentle goddess or *bodhisattva* (see *Bodhisattva*). The connection between this dual image and the embracing Śiva and his *śakti* (see *Śakti)* is obvious. In both cases the embrace has symbolic importance, conveying wholeness. The Japanese esoteric Buddhist figure also signifies the union of the individual with the Buddha (see Japanese Buddhas, see Gautama Buddha). With Enlightenment the two images become one.

Shun—One of the ancient Chinese emperors (see Chinese Emperors) who form a part of Chinese mythology as well as history (see Chinese Deities, Chinese Mythology), Shun was the successor of Yao (see Yao), considered by the Chinese to be the ancestor of the Han emperors. It was Yao who named the pious Shun the heir to his throne. Shun is a model of Confucian (see Confucius) values. The myths and legends surrounding Shun are many. It is said that a blind peasant named Gu Sou dreamed of a phoenix who carried rice to him and said he would become his child and that soon after, the peasant's wife gave birth to Shun. Shun was remarkable for having two pupils in each eye, which led to his being called Chong Hua as well as Shun. When Shun's mother died and the father remarried, this time to a woman with her own children, Shun's life became one of great suffering. Longing for his mother, the boy left home and lived in a small hut. There he sang of his lost mother and so moved the people that they gave him land and good fishing spots. Eventually he prospered and was adopted by the Emperor Yao, who gave the former peasant his two daughters as wives. With the help of heavenly magic and his loyal wives, Shun was able to overcome his family's attempts to murder him. The Emperor now devised a series of tests for the man who had been recommended as his successor. Helped by his loyal wives, Shun succeeded in all of the tests and was named Yao's heir. After a reign in which evil was expelled from the kingdom and goodness established, Shun died and was buried in the Jiuyi Mountains.

Siberians—The Siberian (see Siberian entries) peoples are made up of several groups possessing similar pantheons and myths. Before the arrival of the Russians, Siberia was home to the Samoyeds, the Tungus, Ostiaks, and Voguls of the Finno-Ugrian race; the Altaic, Yakut, Tuvin, Buryat, and Khakass peoples of the Turko-Mongol race; and Palco-Siberian peoples including the Chuckchi, the Gilyaks, the Koryak, and the Yukaghir (See Central Asian Mythology).

Siberian Creation—Among some Siberians (see Siberians, Siberian entries), an earth-diver creation (see Earth-Diver Creation) prevails (see Central Asian Creation, Altaic Mythology). For most, the egg-like universe is made up of three earths: upper, middle, and lower. An axis tree with an earth goddess at its roots in the lower earth rises up through the navel of the middle earth to the pole star. The Sun and the Moon sit at the top of the tree and the souls of the unborn live in its branches. The Sun is worshipped as a sustainer of life, the Moon brings the unborn to human mothers. The Turko-Mongols (see Turko-Mongol Mythology) and Finno-Ugrians, in particular, see creation as a work of a spirit (for example, Num or Ulgan) and a competing devil-like figure (for example, Nga or Erlik).

Siberian Earth Deities—The first of the Siberian (see Siberian entries) earth deities seems to have been an Earth Mother, such as the one who sits at the roots of the great axis tree. The ancient Mongols (see Turko-Mongol Mythology) called her Atugan. For some peoples the Great Goddess is the wife or sister of the supreme Sky God (see Siberian Sky Gods) who sometimes is said to have assisted in the creation process. Most important, the Great Mother figure is associated with the Earth and Nature. For some peoples there are several Earth Mothers—each responsible for an aspect of life. The Yakuts, for instance, have the goddess Itchita, who protects health; Ynakhsyt, who protects cattle; and Ajysyt, who is connected with children and childbirth. The ancient Turks worshipped Umay, or Umai (see Umai), a childbirth goddess who was of primary importance and whose name means "source." The Tungus worshipped a similar goddess. The earth was also full of lesser deities or earth spirits, avatars (see *Avatars*) of the Great Mother with whom shamans (see Shamanism) communicated and who were associated with particular places and functions.

Siberian Shamanism—In Siberian myth (see Siberian entries) and religion, shamanism (see Shamanism) is an ever-present reality. Not only does the shaman concern himself with individual cures and with the placating of spirits who have entered a body to cause disease, but he is also responsible for ceremonies by which spirits can be appeased for the benefit of the whole community (see Siberian Spirits). Siberian shamans perform important rites before hunts, for example, and other rites to end droughts. In short, the shaman is the important mediator between the spirit world and the human world. It is said that shamans are able to travel in various forms—often as animals—into the spirit world to retrieve souls. The shamanic travel takes place during a trance or seance. As the shaman undergoes trials in the other world, his assistant describes his adventures to the people in attendance. Usually Siberian shamans are "called" to their profession by shaman ancestors in the underworld rather than appointed by the tribe. It is said by some that the shaman's soul enters the world in the form of his special animal—his totem—given him by the Earth Mother at the root of the world tree (see Siberian Creation, Siberian Underworld).

Siberian Sky Gods—The supreme being for most Siberians (see

Siberian entries) is the Sky, a creator who tends not to interfere in his creation, but whose presence assures harmony and order in the universe. His contact with humans is by way of messengers and shamans. The Tungus call this god Buga. Others call him Es or Turum, or Num (see Tengri). The Sky usually has an evil brother or companion who competes with him as a creator and who can cause difficulties for humans (see Siberian Creation). Associated with the supreme deity are lesser sky gods such as the Sun and Moon, who are sometimes husband and wife, sometimes brother and sister. Often it is the Moon who is male (see Siberian Spirits).

Siberian Spirits—The Siberian (see Siberian entries) mythological world is dominated by master-spirits. Any given people's territory—its water, its mountains, its animals, its particular places—is ruled by master-spirits who are necessarily enemies of people of other territories. If a person dies, he goes to live with the master-spirit of the element responsible for his death. Often the master-spirits take on animal shapes, usually human. Certain master-spirits seem to be ubiquitous. The master-spirit of fire is one such figure, sometimes taking the form of an old woman who watches the fire. Each home has a Mother Fire that is much valued. Among some groups, the fire, as Grandmother Fire, is fed pieces of food as the protector of the herds. Animals are associated with the master-spirit of the woods, who is the guardian of the hunt. The master-spirit of water is usually an ancient man who watches over the fish and lives in the waters. The Tungus have territorial master-spirits known as Territory Mothers (Dunne Enin). There are also master-spirits of the lower world who are shaman (see Shamanism) ancestors (see Siberian Shamans). The Buryats have spirits called *tengri* (see Tengri), fifty-four good ones in the west where the god Eseg Malan is king and fifty-five bad ones in the east where the god of the dead, Erlik, reigns.

Siberian Underworld—The Siberian (see Siberian entries) Underworld (see Underworld) lies somewhere below the domain of the Great Mother Goddess and is a place ruled by a male king who commands the spirits of the Underworld and judges its inhabitants.

However, it must be noted that the period of death below the earth is for many Siberians a period of gestation leading to rebirth. For some Tungus Siberians, the corporal soul or *been* takes the river to the Underworld while the individual's clan soul, the *omi,* eventually returns to the earth, enters a tent smoke-hole and into the womb of a woman, producing a new clan member. Some Tungus say that the soul of an individual is attached to the master-spirit (see Siberian Spirits) Seveki in the upper world and that when evil spirits cut the string, the individual dies. Still others say that the *been* soul goes to the Underworld ruled by the chief ancestor Mangi or Xargi, the ancestor of shamans (see Siberian Shamanism), and the bear brother of the creator. Mangi then searches for the *omi* soul, which has taken the shadow form called *xanjan.* When he finds it, the soul turns into a bird and returns to Earth to enter another being.

Siddhārtha—Siddhārtha in Sanskrit (see Sanskrit) or Siddhatta in Pāli (see Pāli) is the personal name of Gautama Buddha, the Buddha Sākyamuni (see Gautama Buddha). The name suggests the idea of the *siddha,* one who has achieved perfection, namely Enlightenment.

Sikhism—Sikhism is the religion of people who call themselves Sikhs, that is, "learners." The primary teacher is the one god, the ultimate *gurū,* Sat Gurū. Below God are several human *gurūs,* beginning with the fifteenth-century northern Indian Gurū Nānak and including the famous sixteenth-century teacher Gobind Siṅgh. The Sikh holy book is the *Ādi Granth,* considered itself to be the *gurū* successor of Gobind Singh. Gurū Nānak chose to move away from the conflict between Hinduism (see Hinduism) and Islam (see Islam) by worshipping the *Nām,* the *mantra* (see *Mantra*), or formula, connoting God's true name. Nānak believed that, with God's help and self-discipline rather than traditional rituals, *saṃsāra* (see *Saṃsāra*), the endless cycle of existence, could be overcome and release achieved. The path to release involves many stages. Gradually the evil passions can be defeated and God's will achieved.

Sindbad the Sailor—The tales of Sindbad the sailor are a part of the collection of Indian, Persian, and Arabic folktales known as *The*

Thousand and One Nights or *Arabian Nights*. The Sindbad tales originate in the eighth and ninth centuries CE and may have been influenced by Greek tales of Odysseus. In the tales, the old sailor Sindbad tells of his seven voyages to different parts of the world. On the first voyage, Sindbad and his companions land on an island that turns out to be a whale. After the whale is awakened by the fire the travelers build on his back, he dives into the depths. Eventually Sindbad is rescued and finds favor with a king. On the second voyage, Sindbad is marooned on an island, but with the help of a giant bird, he is able to collect many diamonds before returning home. The third voyage involves confrontations with a race of wicked dwarfs and a Cyclops-like giant who reminds us of Homer's Polyphemus. The giant eats several sailors before Sindbad is rescued. During the fourth voyage Sindbad is shipwrecked in a land of cannibals, but he avoids insanity by not eating the food. In the kingdom to which he escapes he is given a wife who soon dies. The custom of the country demands that he be buried with his wife but he manages to escape from the tombs, carrying with him the treasures buried with the dead. A monster, who turns out to be the mythical Old Man of the Sea, captures the shipwrecked Sindbad on the fifth voyage and demands a ride on the sailor's back. Sindbad gets the monster drunk and kills him. Sindbad's ship sinks on the sixth voyage. The survivors are washed up on the island of Sri Lanka, where they find jewels. After his companions die, Sindbad collects the jewels and leaves for a distant land on a raft. He presents the king of that land with the jewels and is given a ship to return to his home, which is Baghdad. The final voyage is the most complex. Sindbad escapes his ship as it is being swallowed by a whale. He manages to get to an island and to build a raft. After floating down a river, he is rescued and taken to a man who gives him his daughter as a wife. When the islanders grow wings, Sindbad hopes to fly home on one of them. The winged men, including the one on which he is flying, however, turn out to be agents of the Devil, and when flying high in the sky Sindbad praises Allah, he is dropped onto a mountain top. He returns to find his wife and then sails with her for home, having been away for twenty-seven years.

Śiśupāla—A character in the Hindu (see Hinduism entries) *Purāṇas* (see Purāṇas) and the epic the *Mahābhārata* (see *Mahābhārata*), Śiśupāla is the evil relative of the Viṣṇu (see Viṣṇu) avatar (see Avatars of Viṣṇu) Kṛṣṇa (see Kṛṣṇa). It was said that the extra eye and extra two arms with which he was born would disappear when he first saw his future killer. The disappearance took place when as a child he was placed on Kṛṣṇa's lap. The child's mother begged for mercy and Kṛṣṇa agreed to do nothing until he had been offended by Śiśupāla one hundred times. The one-hundredth offense took place when the Pāṇḍava (see Pāṇḍavas) king Yudhiṣṭhira (see Yudhiṣṭhira) honored Kṛṣṇa at his coronation and Śiśupāla objected. Kṛṣṇa flung his discus at his enemy cousin, cutting off his head.

Sītā—The wife of the Viṣṇu (see Viṣṇu) avatar (see Avatars of Viṣṇu) Rāma (see Rāma) in the Hindu (see Hinduism entries) epic, the *Rāmāyaṇa* (see *Rāmāyaṇa*), Sītā is an incarnation of Viṣṇu's wife Lakṣmī (see Lakṣmī) and is the daughter of the ancient Vedic (see Vedic entries) Earth Goddess Pṛthivi (see Pṛthivi). Sītā's father, Janaka (the "begetter"), was plowing a field when Sītā emerged from a furrow in the sacred earth.

Śiva—In the trinity or *trimūrti* of Hinduism (see Hinduism entries), Śiva, meaning "auspicious one," stands as the "destroyer" with Viṣṇu (see Viṣṇu) the preserver and Brahmā (see Brahmā) the creator. For Śaivas (see Śaiva), practitioners of Śiva devotion (see *Bhakti,* Śaivism), he is the principle manifestation of ultimate divinity (see Brahman). In practice, he stands with Viṣṇu and the Goddess (see Devī, Śakti, Vaiṣṇavism, Śaktism) as one of the three principle deities of Hinduism. It seems likely that Śiva, like the Goddess, has roots in the ancient pre-Aryan (see Aryans) culture of the Indus Valley (see Indus Valley Mythology). An Indus Valley seal from the city of Harappā depicts a three-faced figure sitting cross-legged in a yogi style, suggesting the great yogi-ascetic that the god was to become in later Hinduism. In the *Vedas* (see *Vedas*),

Śiva is known more as Rudra (see Rudra). It was not until the second century BCE that the god came into his own as the equal and sometimes the superior of Viṣṇu and the other gods. In the epic poem the *Mahābhārata* (see *Mahābhārata*), he is even worshipped by his fellow gods. Śiva's role as god of destruction is intricately involved with his role as the god of generation. The implication is that without death there can be no life. The process of the universe is one of destruction and generation, death and renewal. It is not surprising, therefore, that Śiva is often depicted in union with his *Śakti,* or consort—his materializing power—or that he is worshipped by way of the *liṅga* (see *Liṅga, Liṅga* Myths), or sacred phallus, often planted in the *yoni* (see *Yoni*), or female sexual organ, which can represent the Goddess or Śakti. Śiva is worshipped in many guises. He is Nāṭarāja (see Nāṭarāja), the Lord of the Dance (see Dance of Śiva), he whose dance is the process of the Universe itself. He is the ultimate *gurū,* the model for the yogi-ascetic. He brings *mokṣa* (see *Mokṣa*), or release, to those who trust in him. There are literally thousands of myths associated with this important manifestation of Hindu godhead. Many of the myths are associated with the various forms of his consort, the Goddess. These include the terrifying goddesses Kālī (see Kali) and Durgā (see Durga), as well as the beneficent daughter of the Mountain, Pārvatī (see Pārvatī), the mother of the great elephant-headed god Gaṇeśa (see Gaṇeśa). (For myths of Śiva see also Agni, Aṇṇamār, Banāras, Brahman, Dakṣa, Descent of the Ganges, Durvāsas, Hari-hara, Indra and Vṛtra, Jaladhara, Kārttikeya, Mahāśakti, Manasa-Mangals, Maṅkaṇaka, Māyā, Mountain Mythology, Murugan, Prajāpati, Puranic Cosmogony, Satī, Shoten.)

Skanda—See Kārttikeya.

Sky Gods—See Siberian Sky Gods.

Smṛti—See *Śruti.*

Soma—The word *soma* is derived from the Sanskrit root meaning "to press." Recent scholarship suggests that the sometimes hallucinatory and psychedelic drink called *soma,* personified and worshipped as the god Soma in the ancient Indian *Vedas* (see *Vedas*), was in fact pressed from a type of mushroom called *soma*. The *Sāma Veda* (see *Sāma Veda*) is a collection of ritual hymns dedicated to the god Soma as a source of imaginative power. Soma is much praised in the *Ṛg Veda* (see *Ṛg Veda*), in which is told the myth of the discovery of the *soma* plant in Heaven. It was an eagle who plucked some of the plant from the heights and planted it on earthly mountains, where it was gathered by Vedic (see Vedic entries) priests. The priests pressed the plant, extracting the sacred essence, which they then filtered through wool and mixed with clarified butter. They used the resulting liquid in rituals. If consumed, it would bring remarkable insights. If placed in the ritual fire as a sacrifice, it would rise up to the gods in the smoke and become their ambrosia of immortality and the source of their power. In the Persian Avestan tradition (see *Avestas*), we find a similar drink of immortality called *haoma* (see *Haoma*). Soma is also a name given to the Moon, where it is said that the gods store *soma*.

Song-sen-gam-po—Sometimes known as Songstan Gambo, Song-sen-gam-po is a legendary historical hero celebrated in countless folktales of the kingdom of Ladakh. He is said to have been responsible, by way of marriage to princesses from Nepal and China, for making Tibet—and by example Ladakh—officially Buddhist (see Buddhism).

Southeast Asian Flood—See *Nithan Khun Borom*.

Southeast Asian Mythology—Mainland Southeast Asia, made up of countries now called Vietnam, Cambodia, Laos, Thailand, and Burma, and populated by Austroasiatic or Austronesian peoples, lies between two cultural giants, China and India. Southeast Asia mythologies are both indigenous and deeply influenced by the mythologies of these neighboring cultures. Characters of Indian epics and other mythological works become characters in local myths and are changed to meet the needs and concerns of the adapters. It is as if certain Brahmanic (see Brahmanism) gods and traditions were pasted upon the creation and origin myths indigenous to Southeast Asia (see Nithan Khun Borom). From China came the Buddhist (see Buddhism) influence and eventual dominance (see Angkor). Spirits play an important role in the ancient indigenous Southeast Asian mythology, controlling many aspects of daily life (see Nat, Phi, Neak-tā). Moon myths and rituals are important here, as they are in China and India. In Cambodia, for instance, there is the tradition of the Moon Goddess, who is somehow associated with the Hindu (see Hinduism entries) female serpent Nāgī (see *Nāga*), who was married to the Brahman (see *Brahmans*) Kaundinya, and who marries the originator of the Khmer dynasty, who was himself the Sun god. There is also the story of the Moon as Lord Braḥ Chan, who marries the mortal maiden Bimān Chan. When Bimān Chan asks her husband to take her further and further into the heavens, the wind blows her head off, and the head falls into a Buddhist monastery. When the head is restored to the body, the woman marries a mortal descendant of the sun, Suryavaṅ. Earth goddesses, too, are important in Southeast Asia, as they are in India. The goddess Dharaṇī owes much to the Vedic-Hindu (see Vedic entries) stories of Sītā (see Sītā) and Aditi (see Aditi). But here the earth goddess works with the Buddha (see Gautama Buddha) to achieve Enlightenment. Many of the ancient Hindu gods survive in the Buddhist context. In Cambodia, Śiva (see Śiva) is Braḥ Iśvara and the yoni-liṅga/Śiva-Śakti (see *Yoni,* see *Liṅga,* see *Śakti*) symbol of regeneration and wholeness is found in traditional candlesticks used in Buddhist marriage ceremonies. The Temple of Angkor Wat is dedicated to the Hindu god Viṣṇu (see Viṣṇu).

Spendamart—See Armaïti.

Śrī—*Śrī* means "prosperity" in Sanskrit and, for Hindus, is an honorific title (see Hinduism entries). Thus, the name of a famous *gurū* or philosopher might be preceded by the term. *Śrī* is also a late Vedic (see Vedic entries) goddess—a personification of the idea of "prosperity." The male gods were jealous of her and took over her powers. Śrī is also another name for Viṣṇu's consort Lakṣmī (see Lakṣmī), who also represents prosperity.

Śruti—Literally "that which is heard," *śruti* is revelation, or the highest form of sacred text, for Hindus (see Hinduism entries). The *Vedas* (see *Vedas*) are *śruti*, while other important texts are merely *smṛti*—still sacred but only "remembered" and therefore corrupted by the human element rather than transmitted directly from the divine source. The *Mahābhārata* (see *Mahābhārata*), for instance, is *smṛti*.

Stone and the Banana—In the central Celebes of Indonesia (see Indonesian entries), the people of Poso tell how the Creator used to send things down to the first people by a rope from his nearby sky home. Once he sent down a stone, and the people rejected it as useless. The creator pulled up the stone and lowered a banana instead, and the people rushed to take it. Then the voice of the creator called down and scolded the people for their foolishness. Had they accepted the stone, he said, they would have achieved its solidity and immortality, but having chosen the banana, they had chosen its mortality and had introduced death into the world.

Sun—The Sun plays an important role in Asian mythology, especially in Japanese Shinto (see Shinto entries) mythology, where the dominant deity is the sun goddess Amaterasu (see Amaterasu). The Chinese yellow emperor, Huangdi (see Huangdi) is sometimes associated with the Sun, and in India one of the primary Ādityas (see Aditi and the Ādityas), who are the Vedic (see Vedic entries) ruling forces of the Universe and themselves associated with the sun, is the Sun himself, the god Sūrya (see Sūrya). The *svastika* (see *svastika*) is a Hindu (see Hinduism entries) symbol of the sun.

Sun Wukong—See Monkey.

Sūrya—Sometimes called Savitar or Savitṛ, which means "he who nourishes," Sūrya, the Vedic (see Vedic entries) god of the Sun (see Sun), is one of the *Ādityas* (see Aditi and the *Adityas*) or main gods of the *Vedas* (see *Vedas*). He rules over the phenomenon of life and, as the Sun, is the great illuminator and source of life. Many of his qualities and aspects were later taken on by the god Viṣṇu (see Viṣṇu).

Susanowo—The "Impetuous Male," brother of the Japanese Sun (see Sun) Goddess Amaterasu (see Amaterasu), Susanowo was ruler of the oceans and the source of rain, thunder, and lightning. Because of unruly behavior when drunk, he was banned from Heaven.

Sūtras—Sūtras are the collections of the teachings of the Buddha Sākyamuni (see Gautama Buddha) important to Hīnayāna Buddhism (see Hīnayāna Buddhism). Mahāyāna Buddhism (see Mahāyāna Buddhism) has also made significant use of *sūtras,* as in the famous *Lotus Sūtra* (see *Lotus of the Good Law,* Tendai Sect). In Hinduism (see Hinduism), *Sūtras* are essentially guides to proper ritual action.

Svastika—In Hinduism (see Hinduism) what later became familiar as the hated Nazi Swastika—the cross with ends bent at right angles—is a symbol of wholeness, the word literally meaning "wellness." It also refers to the Sun (see Sun) as the ultimate source of renewal. For Buddhists (see Buddhism), the svastika represents *dharma* (see *Dharma*), or cosmic order.

T

Taihao—Taihao (see Taiyi) is the name of an ancient Chinese god who in later Han texts became confused with the god-emperor (see Chinese Emperors, Chinese Deities) Fuxi (see Fuxi).

Taiyi—In Chinese, Tai is the "supreme being," and in religious Daoism (see Daoism) he is the ultimate god or the god within (see Taiyidao, Chinese Deities, Di, Tiandi, Tian).

Taiji—Taiji (see Taiyi) is the Chinese concept of ultimate reality, that which in the *Yijing* (see *Yijing*) is the source of all being, including the *Yinyang* (see *Yinyang*) and the consequent four ways of combining Heaven and Earth, and eventually the five elements of creation. All of this is represented in the self-defense and meditative exercise movements known as *Taijiquan*.

Taiqing—For Daoists (see Daoism), *Taiqing* (see Taiyi) is the place of ultimate purity, a heaven under the rule of Daodetianzun, who is often seen as the Daoist founder Laozi or Lao-tsu (see Laozi).

Taiyidao—Taiyidao is a form of Daoism (see Daoism) developed by the twelfth-century sage Hsiao Pao-chen. The term means "the path of the Supreme Being" (see *Taiyi*).

Tales of Yamato—Many tales are told in the *Kojiki* (see *Kojiki*) and elsewhere of the hero Yamato-takeru, son of the Japanese Emperor Keikō. These tales often have supernatural aspects. Yamato is a knight in search of adventures that will identify him as a hero. In various wars he defeats the "barbarians." He even defeats a god who confronts him as a white deer. But when he fights the white boar, in reality the god of the evil breath, he is overcome. After his death he becomes a white bird and flies off into the unknown (see Shinto Mythology).

Tamil Mythology—The Tamil people, who live mostly in the southern part of India called Tamil Nadu, possess a religious and mythological tradition that is a particularly interesting mix of ancient pre-Hindu (see Hinduism entries) Dravidian–Indus Valley (see Dravidians, Indus Valley Mythology) elements and Vedic (see Vedic entries) and orthodox Hindu aspects of the Sanskritic (see Sanskrit) tradition. In the Neolithic period, the Tamils were a herding, nature-oriented culture with a nature-based mythology of deities of the land. Muragan or Murakan (see Murugan) was a major god of the hunt who battled evil forces and Ventan was a god responsible for rain and general well-being. A tradition of ecstatic worship involving sexuality and intoxication apparently existed among the early Tamils. In sacred places a *liṅga*-like (see *Liṅga*) pillar called a *kantu* represented the god concerned—perhaps more often than not Murugan, who, like the Greek Dionysos or Hindu Kṛṣṇa (see Kṛṣṇa), was often accompanied by a following of beautiful young women. With the arrival in the South of Jains (see Jainism), Buddhists (see Buddhism), and Hindu *brahmans* (see *Brahmans*) in the third century BCE, the myths and religious practices of the Tamils became somewhat staid. By the eighth century the land of the Tamils had become the setting for a particularly powerful form of Hinduism marked by devotional (see *Bhakti*) poetry written by poet-saint followers especially of Śiva (see Śiva) called Nāyaṉārs and of Viṣṇu (see Viṣṇu) called Āḻvārs. Among the most famous of the Āḻvārs was Nammāḻvār, who lived in the late ninth and early tenth centuries, wrote especially about Viṣṇu's avatar (see Avatars of Viṣṇu) Kṛṣṇa, and espoused the beliefs of Vedānta (see Vedānta). The most notable of the Nāyanārs was the ninth century Māṇikāvacakar, who stressed the ecstatic aspect of the worship of Śiva. The poet saints took stories from the

Sanskrit texts and gave them Tamil settings and a peculiarly Tamil sense of the closeness that could be achieved between the given deity and the worshipper. The late eighth and early ninth century was also the period of Śaṅkara, who preached Advaita Vedānta (see Advaita, Advaita Vedānta) Hinduism that stresses the absoluteness of Brahman (see Brahman). Also important to the mythology and religion of the Tamils is the person of the Goddess (see Devī, Kālī), who from ancient times had been a popular deity and who by the tenth century had regained a position of equality with Śiva and Viṣṇu, a position she holds to this day. Other popular deities who retain positions of importance with Śiva, Viṣṇu, and the Goddess are Śiva's sons Murugan and Gaṇeśa (see Gaṇeśa). The twelfth century saw a flowering of Tamil literature in the Tamil version of the epic the *Rāmāyaṇa* (see *Rāmāyaṇa*) by the poet Kampaṉ. Since the sixteenth century, a tradition of stories about the childhoods of the gods has been a significant aspect of Tamil mythology. Finally, it can be said that Tamil mythology is among the richest and most complex narrative traditions in India (see *Aṇṇaṇmār, Catakaṇṭarā-vaṇaṉ, Manimekhalaï*).

Tantra—Tantra, a Tantric (see Tantrism) text, is almost always associated with the Hindu (see Hinduism entries) god Śiva (see Śiva, Śaiva) in connection with his *śakti* (see *Śakti*), the Goddess (see Devī), as a unified absolute. In certain Tantras and *Śakta Upaniṣads* (see Śaktism, *Upaniṣads*), it is the Goddess who is the primary object of worship as the personified Śakti. The word Tantra is also applied to texts, such as the *Lakṣmī Tantra* (see Lakṣmī) of the *Pañcarātra* (see *Pañcarātra*) devoted to Viṣṇu (see Vaiṣṇavas, Viṣṇu). Usually, however, Tantras are dialogues between Śiva and the Goddess.

Tantric Buddhism—See Vajrayāna.

Tantrism—With its roots in pre-Aryan (see Aryans), pre-Hindu (see Hinduism entries) India, Tantrism stands as an alternative of sorts to the orthodox Hinduism of the Vedic (see Vedic entries) tradition. It emphasizes the feminine aspect of a bipolar absolute and makes use of a spiritual practice known as *sādhana*, which can lead to a unification of the two poles and liberation or *mokṣa* (see *Mokṣa*) in our corrupt Kaliyuga or Kali age. The body is of great importance in *sadhana* as liberation may be achieved through bodily perfection. Thus, *yoga* (see *Yoga*) is as important as more traditional worship. Mantra *Yoga* involves meditation on sounds, Kuṇḍalinī *Yoga* brings together the Śiva (see Śiva) and Śakti (see Śakti) within ourselves. Important to Tantric *Yoga* is the series of bodily energy points called *cakras,* which are connected by channels called *nāḍīs*. The sacred texts of Tantrism are *tantras* (see Tantra), which are important to worshippers of Viṣṇu (see Vaisnavism) and especially to those of Śiva (see Śaivism) and most especially to those of Śakti (see Śaktism). A form of Buddhist Tantrism exists (see Vajrayāna).

Tao—See Daoism.

Tao te ching—See Daoism.

Taoism—See Daoism.

Tārā—The "Mother of Buddhas" in Tibet (see Tibetan entries), Tārā is a major *bodhisattva* (see *Bodhisattva*) and deity there. Tradition has it that Tibetans are descended from Tārā and Avalokiteśvara (see Avalokiteśvara), or Chenrezi, Tārā having taken the form of a rock-ogress and the god that of a monkey. Another myth says that Tārā was born of Avalokiteśvara's tears as he looked back at the world he was leaving for Nirvāna (see Nirvāna). In Hinduism (see Hinduism entries), Tārā is associated with the Goddess (see Devī), as Pārvatī (see Pārvatī), Kālī (see Kālī), and other forms. There is a Tantric (see Tantrism) aspect to Tārā, especially as the Śakti (see *Śakti*) in union with Avalokiteśvara. In Tibetan Buddhism Tārā takes many forms and has many functions, associated colors, and *mantras* (see mantra).

Tathāgata—Tathāgata, perhaps meaning "discoveror of truth," is a name Gautama Buddha (see Gautama Buddha) is said to have given himself.

Tendai Sect—Known as Tendai Shū or Hokkeshū, meaning "Lotus School" (see *Lotus of the Good Law*), the Tendai sect is an esoteric sect of Buddhism (see Japanese Buddhism, Mahāyāna Buddhism) brought to Japan in the ninth century CE by the monk Saicho from China, where it had been founded in the sixth century by Zhiyi. Zhiyi had interpreted the Indian Buddhist *sūtras* and arranged them according to the stages of the Buddha's career and the development of his thought. When Saicho founded his temple on Mount Hei near Kyōto, he integrated elements of the esoteric form of the Shingon school (see Shingon sect) into his form of Tendai, and later, elements of Shinto were assimilated. It was Tendai's all-inclusive synthesis of various forms of Buddhism that led to the founding in the twelfth century of various new sects by monks who had been trained at the Tendai Temple. The monk Honen founded the Jōdo or Pure Land school (see Pure Land Buddhism); Shinran founded *Jōdo Shinshū* or True Pure Land sect; Eisai and Dogen founded Zen (see Zen Buddhism) sects; and Nicheren founded the school named after himself (see Seven Gods of Good Fortune, Amida Buddha, Japanese Buddhas).

Tengri—Tengri was the Sky God of the Turko-Mongols (see Turko-Mongol Mythology). *Tengri* are also spirit figures among certain Siberian (see Siberian entries) groups (see Siberian Spirits).

Tengu—The *tengu* are Japanese (see Shinto Mythology) mountain demons who, like tricksters and shamans, can change shapes, have supernatural powers, and can even fly. They appear among people unexpectedly and have the power to enchant or bewitch. In the medieval period, *tengu* were sometimes thought to be proud monks—particularly the shaman-like (see Shamanism, Japanese Shamanism) mountain ascetics known as *yamabushi* (see Yamabushi)—turned into animals. The *tengu* are depicted with wings, bird-like beaks or long noses, sometimes red faces, and the clothing of monks, especially those of the *yamabushi*. In one story, it is said that the *yamabushi* Unkei attended a meeting of *tengu* on Mount Atago, where the demons were deciding the fate of the world. This tale suggests an actual connection between these ascetic monks and the demons. *Tengu* are quite capable of evil deeds. They carry off children, change themselves into false Buddhas (see Japanese Buddhas), kidnap novice monks, and cause anger between individuals and groups. Yet they apparently also do good and are venerated in shrines—either out of respect or fear of what they might do.

Theravāda Buddhism—Theravāda, meaning "teaching of the elders," is a term often used synonymously with Hīnayāna (see Hīnayāna Buddhism) for the early form of Buddhism that accepts only the teachings of Sākyamuni Buddha (see Gautama Buddha) and stresses the ideal of the *arhat* (see *Arhat*), or personal salvation through the Buddha as opposed to the Mahāyāna (see Mahāyāna Buddhism) ideal of the *bodhisattva* (see *Bodhisattva*), who chooses to remain in this world to help others to salvation. Technically, however, Theravāda, the form of Buddhism (see Buddhism) practiced primarily in Southeast Asia and Sri Lanka, is only one branch of Hīnayāna—albeit the only extant branch. The early Hīnayānas, or adherents of the ancient Pāli canon (see Pāli) split into two major factions, in one of which the Theravāda group was dominant. Given the strict adherence to the teachings of the Buddha, mythology beyond that of the life of the Buddha does not play a major part in Theravāda. In southeast Asia (see Southeast Asian entries), however, there is a tendency to absorb indigenous earth spirit and ancestor elements as well as a cosmology (see Three Worlds).

Thraetaona—In the struggle between good and evil in Zoroastrianism (see Zoroastrianism), Thraetaona or Feridun is a hero called upon by the elements to fight against the wicked King Dahaka or Zohak, on whose shoulders are two serpents symbolizing the king's threat to the elements.

Three Worlds—*Loka* is the Sanskrit for "World." In the Hindu (see Hinduism entries) tradition there are three *lokas (triloka)*: Earth, the Atmosphere, and the world of the gods. These worlds represent stages of salvation, Heaven being the *Vedas* (see *Vedas*). The Three Worlds (*trilokya* in Pāli) of Buddhism (see Buddhism) are the lowly *kāmaloka,* the world of Hell and desire; the *rūpaloka,* the world of the gods and of form relieved of desire; and the highest or *arūpaloka,* the world of perfect formlessness (see Buddhist Cosmogony).

Tian—An ancient Chinese term, Tian *(T'ien)* (see Taiyi), used as early as the second millennium BCE by the Chou people, means both Nature and Supreme Deity (see Chinese Deities). The root meaning of the word is "sky"—the place where the gods live. In the Chou period (1111–256 BCE), Tian was a supreme god who interacted personally with the human world. He was also the basis of kingship (see Chinese Emperors). The King was Tian's viceroy on earth and was enthroned or dethroned at his will. Tian probably derives in part from the previous Shang dynasty's concept of the supreme god Di (Ti) or Shangdi (see Di). In fact, during the Chou period the terms Tian and Shangdi were used almost synonymously. In the *Yijing* (see *Yijing*) Tian is Heaven and Di is Earth, the father and mother gods whose union results in creation (see Tiandi). Buddhists saw Tian as impersonal Nature. For Daoists (see Daoism) Tian was related to the Dao (see Dao).

Tiandi—Literally "Heaven-Earth," Tiandi is related etymologically to *Di* (see *Di,* Taiyi, and *Tian),* and is a name for the Supreme God of ancient China (see Chinese Flood, Chinese Mythology).

Tibetan Book of the Dead—See *Bardo Todrol.*

Tibetan Buddhism—The Mahāyāna Buddhism (see Mahāyāna Buddhism, Buddhism) of Tibet, or Lamism, as it is sometimes called because of the importance of the Dalai Lama, is deeply influenced by the Tantric (see Tantrism) aspect of Buddhism or *Vajrayāna* (see *Vajrayāna*), which is itself tied to the tradition of *Sūtrayāna.* In Sūtrayāna one identifies with the suffering of others and works toward the liberation not only of the self but of others. Vajrayāna stresses the possibility of liberation in this life and is a much faster process than *Sūtrayāna* alone. It is said that Buddhism was introduced to Tibet by the Chinese and Nepalese wives of King Songsten Gampo (see Song-sen-gam-po), who reigned in Tibet in the seventh century CE and is, in a sense, the first Dalai Lama; he is considered to have been, like the Dalai Lamas of later periods, an incarnation of Avalokiteśvara (see Avalokiteśvara), with Tārā (see Tārā) the most important of Tibetan *bodhisattvas* (see *Bodhisattva*). Later in the century King Trisong Detsen adopted

Buddhism as the state religion, but subsequent kings turned against Buddhism and persecuted its adherents. It was not until the eleventh century that Buddhism returned in force to Tibet, very much under Indian rather than Chinese influence and with a character all its own, brought about by its Vajrayāna characteristics and its partial assimilation of the indigenous shamanistic (see Shamanism) and animistic (see Animism) religion called Bön (see Bön). The temporal (until the Chinese invasion of 1952) and spiritual leader of Tibet is the Dalai Lama. The next important figure in the Tibetan hierarchy is the Panchen Lama, an emanation of the Buddha Amitābha (see Amida Buddha). The closeness of the two *lamas* is indicated by the fact that Avalokiteśvara is himself an emanation of the Buddha Amitābha (see Tibetan Cosmogony, Tibetan Mythology, Tibetan Wheel of Life).

Tibetan Cosmogony—There are many Tibetan myths of creation via a cosmic egg or eggs (see Tibetan Mythology). One tells how in the beginning the elements became a giant cosmic egg. Its shell was the white cliff of the gods, and within it was a lake with a yolk containing the six classes of life. Out of this center came eighteen smaller eggs, one of which was a white one that produced of its own accord the various parts of a being who became a man, who named himself King Ye-smon.

Other cosmogonic themes in Tibet include an animistic (see Animism) one of creation from the actual body of a primordial goddess. It is said that the Klu Queen who made the world was a child of the Void, that the sky came from her head, the planets from her teeth, the moon from her right eye, the sun from her left, and so forth. It was day when she opened her eyes and night when she closed them. Her voice was thunder, her breath clouds, her tears rain.

Some Tibetan myths say the original being was the "uncreated blue toad of turquoise," some say it was a tigress. In some stories, creation comes from the killing of a primordial being by a young hero. Finally, there are indigenous myths that see Creation as coming from the struggle between the powers of light and those of darkness, or between black light and white light. In this model, the black lord creates all that is antiexistence, while the white lord creates all that is good.

Tibetan Divine Kingship—Until Buddhism (see Tibetan Buddhism) became dominant in Tibet in 842 CE, the people were ruled by a dynasty of sacred kings who traced their ancestry to gNya'khri btsan-po, who came down from the land of the gods as rain that impregnates the earth. All nature celebrated his arrival. After his return to Heaven, this first king was invoked by each of his successors to ratify their divine inheritance (see Tibetan Mythology). In a sense, the rise of Lamaism in Tibet is a continuation in a Buddhist context of this earlier practice.

Tibetan Mythology—In Tibetan mythology there is a distinction between the mythology of the indigenous Bön (see Bön) religion and that of the later Buddhism (see Tibetan Buddhism), although the two sometimes flow together. The myths of the Bön religion are almost always associated with origins, beginning with 'O-lde spu-rgyal, said to have been sent to rule humans by the gods above. Origin myths were told in order to make any ritual effective. If a person was sick, the curing ceremony involved a recitation of origins or Creation. Marriage ceremonies included the retelling of the first marriage—that between the goddess who was daughter of the god of the world and a human man, Ling-dkar. Arguing with the reluctant god for his daughter's hand, the man suggests that the union of man and the gods should mean worship for the gods and protection for humans. Upon leaving Heaven, the goddess is given a third of her parents' inheritance (her brother, as a male, receives two thirds). Her father gives her the masculine arrow and her mother gives her the feminine spindle. In actual Bön wedding ceremonies each action is tied to this origin myth. For instance, the priest presents the groom with a piece of gold and the bride with a piece of turquoise, and then the priest and the couple sing the story of the arrow and the spindle. They sing of how at the beginning of time the union of two immortals resulted in three eggs. From a golden one came a golden male "arrow of life" with turquoise feathers. From a turquoise egg came a turquoise arrow of the female with golden feathers. From a white egg came a golden spindle, and from the sky and the ocean mist came Bön.

A rich mythology surrounds both the Bön and Buddhist religions (see Avalokiteśvera, Bardol Todrol, *Bodhissattva,* Gesar Saga, *Mandala,* Mountain Mythology, Song-sen-gam-po) and, as has been noted, the two religions often blend together in certain myths. One such myth sees the Tibetans as descendants of a monkey (see Monkey) and an ogress. The monkey was sent to Tibet by the Bodhisattva Avalokiteśvara. There, as he meditates on the virtues of the *bodhisattva,* he is confronted by an ogress who takes the form of a woman and asks him to marry her. If he refuses, she will unite with a demon and produce a race of life-destroying demons. The monkey returns to Avalokiteśvara and asks for advice. The *bodhisattva,* with the assent of the goddess Tārā (see Tārā), releases his disciple from his vows of chastity and orders him to marry the ogress, prophesizing the coming of Buddhism to Tibet. The union of Monkey and the ogress results eventually in a tribe of monkeys who then become so populous that they starve, until Avalokiteśvara, from the sacred Mount Meru (see Meru) scatters grains in the world of the monkeys, thus providing crops. Gradually the monkeys lose their tails, and learn to walk upright, to talk, and to wear clothes. Their descendants are the Tibetans. In some versions of this myth, the first monkey's name is Ha-lu-ma-da, which could well be related to the Indian monkey god Hanumān (see Hanumān). In any case, the Monkey is sometimes associated with Avalokiteśvara and worshipped as a *bodhisattva*. There is also a Buddhist tradition that Gautama Buddha (see Gautama Buddha) had been a monkey in one of his former lives.

Tibetan Wheel of Life—One of the most obvious aspects of Tibetan Buddhism (see Tibetan Buddhism) is its reliance on works of art. At the center of this tradition is the depiction of the endless cycle of birth and death known as *saṃsāra* (see *Saṃsāra*) in the Wheel of Life. The wheel is held up by Shinje, the Lord of Death and, therefore, the determiner of Life. The "machine" that turns the wheel is made of ignorance, desire, and hatred, represented by a pig, a cockerel, and a snake. Contained in the Wheel of Life paintings is a rich symbolism depicting the causes of existence and the various possibilities of existence: god, part god, human, animal, ghost, Hell. The Wheel suggests symbolically that it is only through the birth as a human that the individual can move beyond Hell, ghost, and animal forms and begin to achieve liberation from the domain of Death.

Timurid Epic—A Central Asian (see Central Asian Mythology) epic cycle about the conquests of Timur or Tamurlane, the fourteenth-century Turkic (see Turko-Mongol Mythology) warrior-king and founder of the Timurid dynasty.

Tree—See Cosmic Tree.

Trikāya—In Sanskrit, *trikāya* means "Three Forms," and in Mahāyāna Buddhism (see Mahāyāna Buddhism) the term refers to the three forms taken by the Buddha (see Gautama Buddha): the human form, the transcendent enlightened form, the supernatural *yogin* (see *Yoga*) form.

Triloka—See Three Worlds.

Tripiṭaka—Literally the "Triple Basket" in Sanskrit, the *Tripiṭaka* is the collection of Buddhist (see Buddhism) texts traditionally kept in three baskets. The collection differs according to the Buddhist sect (see Xuanzang).

Triśiras—The son of Tvaṣṭṛ (see Tvaṣṭṛ), Triśiras was a three-headed demon killed by the Vedic (see Vedic entries) god Indra (see Indra, Indra and Vṛtra). Triśiras read the *Vedas* (see *Vedas*) with one head, ate with another, and stared into space with the third. Indra became concerned that this powerful ascetic might absorb the whole universe so he killed him with a thunderbolt. But even in death the body gave off power, so Indra had a woodcutter cut off the demon's heads.

Tsukiyomi—Tsukiyomi no Mikoto is the moon god born of the right eye of the Japanese creator god Izanagi (see Izanagi and Izanami, Shinto Mythology, Ukemochi).

Tu'chueh—The Tu'chueh—also known as Kok Turks or Blue Turks—were worshippers of Tengri (see Tengri), the sky god, who inhabits both Heaven and Hell, where good and evil souls, respectively, live. The world between Heaven and Hell is for living humans. The Blue Turks also worshipped Umai (see Umai), the goddess of Childbirth. Tradition has it that the founder of the Blue Turks, like the founders of Rome, was suckled by a she-wolf with whom he eventually mated and produced the first Tu'chueh. The greatest Tu'chueh hero was Bumin, who formed a marriage alliance with the Chinese and defeated the Mongols (see Central Asian Mythology, Turko-Mongol Mythology).

Turko-Mongol Mythology—Turko-Mongolian mythology is essentially monotheistic. The Supreme Being is Tengri (see Tengri), the Sky personified. The Yakuts call him "The White Master Creator." To some Tartars he is Ulgen (Ulgan). His assistant spirits are *tengri* (see Siberian Spirits). Tengri watched over the cosmos and the human social order and later was assimilated into the Muslim (see Islam) concept of the one God or Allah. Other deities were aspects of Tengri, whether Odlek, the personification of Time or Umai (see Umai) the embodiment of the placenta and childbirth and sometimes the Earth itself. Animals, especially the wolf, the bear (a father-man in disguise), and the eagle were important figures. The Turko-Mongols believed in the life of the soul after death and in the power of shamans (see Shamanism) to communicate with spirits (see Siberian Shamanism). Origin myths were popular among the Turko-Mongols. The great Mongol conqueror Gengis Khan, was deified and was said to have been a descendant of the union between the Blue Wolf and a wild doe. The ancient Turko-Mongol ancestor Alp Kara Aslan (Heroic Black Lion) was born of a woman raised by an eagle. He was suckled by a lioness. The hero Uighur Buqu Khan, parented by two trees, was born of a knothole (see Virgin Birth). Other heroes and heroines were miraculously conceived by rays of light and various animal combinations (see Tu'chueh, Central Asian Mythology, Siberian entries).

Tvaṣṭṛ—The great architect of the gods in the ancient Indian *Ṛg Veda* (see *Ṛg Veda*), the demiurge Tvaṣṭṛ resented the Vedic (see Vedic entries) king god Indra's (see Indra) killing of his pious son Triśiras (see Triśiras). To avenge his son's death, Tvaṣṭṛ created the gigantic demon Vṛtra (see Vṛtra, Indra and Vṛtra), who challenged Indra's authority. The fight was earth-shattering, and eventually the demon swallowed Indra. Horrified, the other gods induced a yawn in the monster, and Indra leapt out of the gaping mouth, and the war resumed. When Indra was put to flight, the other gods convinced Viṣṇu (see Viṣṇu) to intervene until such time that Indra was able to kill his foe.

U

Ukemochi—Ukemochi is the Japanese Shinto (see Shinto entries) goddess of food. According to the *Nihongi* (see *Nihongi*), the goddess was created by the first parent gods Izanagi and Izanami (see Izanagi and Izanami) and was sent down to Earth by the sun goddess Amaterasu (see Amaterasu). It is said that boiled rice poured forth from her mouth when she faced the land, seafood when she faced the sea, and game when she faced the mountains. She served up her food first to the moon god Tsukiyomi (see Tsukiyomi). The moon god was disgusted by being fed things that had come from the mouth of the goddess, so he killed his hostess. In anger, Amaterasu refused to look at him again, so to this day the Sun and Moon avoid each other. But out of the dead body of Ukemochi came all of the things that humans now eat.

Umā—An early but post-Vedic (see Vedic entries) Hindu (see Hinduism entries) personification of divine wisdom, Umā like Pārvatī (see Pārvatī), with whom she is identified, is the wife of Śiva (see Śiva). Thus Śiva is sometimes called Umāpati, the spouse of Umā. As the daughter—like Pārvatī—of Himavat, the King of the Himālayas, Umā represents a high state of spiritual being. In the *Kena Upaniṣad* (see *Upaniṣads*), it is Umā who explains to the other gods that the "Supreme Spirit" is Brahman (see *Brahman*).

Umai—A Turko-Mongol goddess of Childbirth (See Tu'chueh, Turko-Mongol Mythology).

Underworld—Most cultures, including Asian ones, have myths of the Underworld where heroes descend for various reasons and where the dead—often the evil dead—reside (see Descent to the Underworld, Siberian Underworld, Siberian Shamanism, Shinto Mythology, Nāga, Jigoku, Emma, Sāvitrī, Monkey, Prahlāda).

Upaniṣads—An extension of early Vedic (see Vedic entries) thought, or *Vedānta* (the "end of the *Vedas*"), but to some extent a reaction against what their eighth- to fourth-century BCE compilers thought of as the somewhat closed-mindedness and action-oriented approach of the *Brāhmaṇas* (see *Brāhmaṇas*), the *Upaniṣads* are sacred Hindu "śruti" (see *Śruti*) texts that are marked by a free-ranging search for the essence of reality (see Vedānta). For the *Upaniṣad* writers, meditation on rituals and thought rather than on rituals and right actions was the true path to salvation. Their emphasis is on inwardness and the spiritual life, a differentiation between the self of the body *(jīva)* and that of the true self, or *Ātman* (see *Ātman*). Understanding that the true Self within must identify with *Brahman* (see *Brahman*)—the ultimate cosmic reality or essential basis of the Universe—the goal of the thinkers in the *Upaniṣads* is *mokṣa* (see *Mokṣa*) or release from the world of physical phenomena. The *Upaniṣads* use myths as teaching tools, as in the famous parable of Prajāpati (see Prajāpati) leading the god-king Indra (see Indra) along the way of truth to the understanding of Ātman as both formless and ultimately real (see Hinduism, Advaita Vedānta, Vairocana, Descent to the Underworld, Hinduism, Hindu Mythology, Upaniṣad Cosmogony).

Upaniṣad Cosmogony—The *Bṛhadāraṇyaka Upaniṣad* (see *Upaniṣads*) tells the following creation story. The Universe began as Self or Ātman (see Ātman) in the body of the primal man, or Puruṣa (see Puruṣa, Hindu Mythology). Looking about and seeing only himself, Puruṣa said "I am." At first, Purusa was afraid but stopped fearing when he realized he was indeed alone and that one could only be afraid of another. Still, he wished for another, and being of two parts in one body, he caused himself to become two: man and woman. The result of the union of the man and the woman was humankind. But the woman was ashamed of incest, of having united with a man who had created her from himself, so she hid from him as a cow. But the man became a bull, mated with the cow, and soon cattle were born. The same thing happened when the woman hid as an ass, as a goat, and so forth. In this way, the world was populated.

Urashima—In Japan, the story is told of the fisherman Urashima who captured a sea tortoise that turned into a young woman. The woman took Urashima to a kingdom under the sea where she was a princess. Urashima and the princess fell in love and were married, and Urashima forgot about his old home and family for many years until one day he missed them. The princess sent him home and gave him a box that she forbade him to open. If he opened it he would never see her again. Suddenly Urashima was home, but in the many hundred earth years that had passed during his three sea-kingdom years he had become a legend of the distant past. Disturbed by the situation, Urashima opened the box and a white mist blew out bearing the diminishing voice of his princess. Urashima then became a wrinkled old man.

Uṣas—Uṣas is the ancient *Ṛg Veda* (see *Ṛg Veda*) goddess of Dawn, who restores life. In the *Veda,* we are told that she brings consciousness.

V

Vairocana—Literally, "one who is sun-like," or "illuminator," Vairocana or Virocana is an *asura* (see *Asuras*) who in the Vedic-Hindu *Upaniṣads* (see Vedic entries, Hindu entries, *Upaniṣads*) attempts with the god Indra (see Indra) to find the essence of self or *ātman* (see *Ātman*). In Buddhism (see Buddhism), he becomes one of the transcendent Buddhas and is called Mahāvairocana—"Great Vairocana"—among Mahāyāna Buddhists (see Mahāyāna Buddhism) in Tibet (see Tibetan Buddhism) and elsewhere in Asia. In Japan he plays a central role in the Shingon sect (see Shingon Sect) as the Dainichi Nyorai (see Dainichi, Japanese Buddhas, Japanese Buddhism).

Vaiṣṇava—A Hindu (see Hinduism entries) worshipper of Viṣṇu (see Viṣṇu) as the supreme god (see Vaiṣṇavism).

Vaiṣṇavism—One of the three major forms of Hindu (see Hinduism entries) *bhakti* (see *Bhakti*), or devotion to a single god—in this case Viṣṇu (see Viṣṇu). The other forms are Śaivism (see Śaivism) and Śaktism (see Śaktism). For many Vaisnavas, Viṣṇu is the manifestation of Brahman (see Brahman). He is popularly worshipped through his avatars (see Avatars of Viṣṇu), especially Rāma (see Rāma) and Kṛṣṇa (see Kṛṣṇa).

Vaiśravaṇa—Also called Kubera, Vaiśravaṇa is associated in Hinduism (see Hinduism entries) with wealth and is a guardian of the

North, one of the four cardinal directions. He is also king of the *yakṣas* (see Yakṣas), the spirits of nature. His evil brother Rāvaṇa (see Rāvaṇa, *Rāmāyaṇa*) stole his home in Lanka causing him to move to Mount Kailāśa to be near the god Śiva (see Śiva, Bishamon).

Vajrayāna—Vajrayāna, which is Sanskrit for "Thunderbolt," is the "Diamond Vehicle," the aspect of Tantric (see Tantrism) Mahāyāna Buddhism (see Mahāyāna Buddhism) that emphasizes the possibility of a swift path to liberation in this life. It develops from *Sūtrayāna,* the identification with the suffering of others and the desire to help others to liberation. Like all of Mahāyāna Buddhism, *Vajrayāna* and *Sutrayāna* are identified with the *bodhisattva* (see *Bodhisattva*) rather than the *arhat* (see *Arhat*) approach to salvation (see Tibetan Buddhism).

Vālmīki—Vālmīki is one of the Homers of ancient India, the legendary author of the *Rāmāyaṇa* (see *Rāmāyaṇa*) and the inventor of poetry (see Vyāsa). When he saw a hunter's arrow kill a mating bird he felt deep sorrow, and out of this sorrow came poetry. A *brahman* (see *Brahmans*) who went astray, he was restored to holiness by the sage Nārada (see Nārada). It is said that Vālmīki, who may, in fact, have been one of many bards who composed the *Rāmāyaṇa*, saw the epic within the sacred texts, the *Vedas* (see *Vedas*). Like Homer, Vālmīki has a community of followers, in this case known as Bālmīkī.

Vāmana—Vāmana, the Dwarf, is the fifth avatar (see Avatar) of the Hindu (see Hinduism entries) god Viṣṇu (See Viṣṇu, Avatars of Viṣṇu). He tricked the demon Bali out of the world he had stolen from the gods. Seeing a mere dwarf before him, Bali agreed to give Vāmana the land he could cover in three steps. Immediately Vāmana changed into a giant so huge that his first two steps encompassed Heaven and Earth. He took Bali's head as payment for the third step.

Varuṇa—In the Indian *Vedas* (see *Vedas*), Varuṇa takes the place of the ancient sky god Dyaus (see Dyaus). He seems likely to have been a chief god of the Aryans (see Aryans), who invaded the

Indian subcontinent in the second millennium BCE. He may also be related to the Greek sky god Ouranos. Blessed with one thousand eyes, Varuṇa watched over humanity for evil doers and was associated with the concept of social order or *dharma* (see *Dharma*). With the development of Vedism (see Vedic entries) and later Hinduism (see Hinduism entries), Varuṇa's importance dwindled. He became the god of the night sky and of the waters and the guardian of the dark west. Varuṇa is closely related to the Iranian Ahura Mazda (see Ahura Mazda). He is referred to in the *Vedas* as an *asura* (see *Asuras*). As an *asura,* in the Indian as opposed to Iranian sense, Varuṇa is to some extent a demon, who possesses the illusory magic of *māyā* (see *Māyā*). With this power, he makes the night dark. Just as the *Vedas'* Mitra is related to Varuṇa, so the Mithra (see Mithra) of the Persian *Avesta* (see *Avesta*) is related to Ahura Mazda. Mitra's eye is the sun, and, with Varuṇa, he becomes the sky god who replaces the older Dyaus. In a sense, Varuṇa, as king of the Ādityas (see Aditi and the Ādityas), is replaced in the *Vedas* by Indra (see Indra). Both are called "king" or "emperor."

Vasudeva—Vasudeva is the earthly father of the Viṣṇu (see Viṣṇu) avatar (see Avatars of Viṣṇu) Kṛṣṇa (see Kṛṣṇa) and Balarāma (see Balarāma, Devakī, Kaṃsa).

Vāsudeva—The creative union of the Hindu (see Hinduism entries) god Viṣṇu (see Viṣṇu) and his *śakti* (see *Śakti*) as Lakṣmī (see Lakṣmī, Pāñcarātra). Vāsudeva is also another name for Kṛṣṇa (see Kṛṣṇa).

Vasuki—As told in the Indian epic the *Mahābhārata* (see *Mahābhārata*), the serpent Vasuki (see Ananta, Śeṣa) serves as the rope used to spin the world axis Mount Mandara (see also Meru), the land mass resting on Viṣṇu (see Viṣṇu) in his form as the tortoise (see Avatars of Viṣṇu) in the depths of the primal Ocean of Milk. The churning of the ocean (see Churning of the Ocean of Milk) brings about aspects of the world's creation and the nectar of immortality called *soma* (see *Soma*).

Vāyu—In the *Ṛg Veda* (see *Ṛg Veda*) Vāyu is the god of the wind, a personification of the breath of the fire god Agni (see Agni). Vāyu is the father of the Pāṇḍava (see Pāṇḍavas) hero Bhīma in the Indian epic, the *Mahābhārata* (see *Mahābhārata*) and of the monkey god Hanumān (see Hanumān), an important figure in Hindu mythology (see Hindu Mythology).

Vedāṅga—*Vedāṅgas* are Hindu (see Hinduism entries) texts written after the *Upaniṣad* (see *Upaniṣads*) period. They were meant to explain aspects of the *Vedas* (see *Vedas*).

Vedānta—Literally meaning end or culmination of the *Vedas* (see *Vedas*), Vedānta is essentially a Hindu (see Hinduism entries) religious tradition based on the *Upaniṣads* (see *Upaniṣads*). Vedānta stresses the inner spiritual life, the presence of Brahman (see Brahman) as the absolute that is everywhere and nowhere and yet present in the material and personal world as the eternal Self, or Ātman (see Ātman). Vedānta also relies on the wisdom contained in the *Brahmā Sūtra,* or *Vedānta Sūtra,* and the great philosophical book of the *Mahābhārata* (see *Mahābhārata*) known as the *Bhagavadgītā* (see *Bhagavadgītā*). In the latter, Kṛṣṇa (see Kṛṣṇa), as the Pāṇḍava (see Pāṇḍavas) hero Arjuna's (see Arjuna) charioteer, explains the relationship between the material world and Brahman and other philosophical aspects of Vedantic thought. One of the greatest of Vedānta philosophers was Śaṅkara, who lived in the late eighth and early ninth centuries CE and who advocated the approach to Vedānta known as Advaita Vedānta (see Advaita Vedānta, Hinduism, Tamil Mythology). In 1896, the Vedanta Society, emphasizing the use of *yoga* (see *yoga*) and the belief in the essential divinity of human nature, was founded in the United States by Swami Vivekananda, a disciple of Sri Ramakrishna.

Vedas—The *Vedas* are the four ancient Indian collections of hymns and ritual formulae of the Samhitā period (c. 2000–1100 BCE), works known as the *Ṛg Veda* (see *Ṛg Veda*), the *Atharva Veda* (see *Atharva Veda*), the *Sāma Veda* (see *Sāma Veda*), and the *Yajur Veda* (see *Yajur Veda*). The word *veda* means "knowledge," and the *Veda,* as a collective noun, has come to mean not only the four *Vedas* themselves, but the commentaries on them. These include the *Brāhmaṇas* (see *Brāhmaṇas*) and *Āraṇyakas* (see *Āraṇyakas*) of the period between c. 100 BCE until c. 800 BCE; the *Upaniṣads* (see *Upaniṣads*), compiled between 800 and 500 BCE; and various *sūtras* (see *Sūtras*) and *Vedāṅgas* (see *Vedāṅgas*). *Vedāṅgas* are technically *smṛti* (see *Sṛuti*)—that is, less sacred—texts rather than sacred *śruti* (see Hinduism, Vedic Mythology, Vedic Cosmogony, Vyāsa, Vālmīki, Nārāyaṇa, Vedism, Sāvitrī, Vedānta).

Vedic Cosmogony—At the center of Vedic creation as expressed particularly in the *Ṛg Veda* (see *Ṛg Veda*) is the idea of creation as separation, or sacrifice, which leads to the ordering of chaos. Incest plays a role in creation. The *Ṛg Veda* tells how the unnamed Creator's phallus reached out to his daughter and how during the act of union some of his seed fell onto the earth resulting in the sacred words, or *Vedas* (see *Vedas*), and the rituals. The Earth itself (see Pṛthivī) may be thought of as the womb or *yoni* (see *Yoni*) of the daughter. Many versions of the incest creation would be told in the *Brāhmaṇas* (see *Brāhmaṇas*), later Vedic (see Vedism, see Vedic Mythology), texts. The *Aitareya Brāhmaṇa,* for instance, names the Creator as Prajāpati (see Prajāpati), who later becomes Brahmā (see Brahmā) and suggests that the daughter might be the Sky or the Dawn (see Uṣas). But unlike the *Ṛg Veda,* the *Brāhmaṇas* tend to stress the importance of ritual and proper action (see *Dharma*). Not surprisingly, therefore, the other gods criticize Prajāpati for committing incest and he is punished, especially by the protector of rituals, Rudra (see Rudra). As in the *Ṛg Veda,* the god of fire, Agni, plays a role in making the god's seed flow, and in the *Kauṣītaki Brāhmaṇa* the sons of Prajāpati are involved with him in creative incest with a now seductive daughter, Dawn (Uṣas). From the spilled seed of Prajāpati and his sons comes the thousand-eyed god Rudra (see Rudra), who resembles the *Ṛg Veda* primal man Puruṣa (see Puruṣa) and who attacks his father and demands to be named. Prajāpati names him Bhava or "Existence." In the *Śatapatha Brāhmaṇa* there is the motif of masturbation as the source of creation. Prajāpati literally "milks" himself, and the butter used for rituals is churned from the milk. This occurs after he creates Agni (see Agni) from his mouth. Agni as fire consumes, and sacrifice must be made to him. In terms of the Brahmanic (see Brahmanism) concern with proper ritual, the symbolism here has to do with the idea that, through sacrifice, Agni, who is Death, is appeased. Even in death the worshipper, who is fed to the fire, is reborn, because only the body is eaten by it.

A more complex *Ṛg Veda* creation story, which is further developed in the more philosophical *Upaniṣads* (see *Upaniṣads*), is that of Purusa, who must unite with the active female principle Prakṛti (see Prakṛti) in order for creation to be realized. In the *Ṛg Veda,* the Puruṣa himself becomes the creation. Three quarters of him is made up of the gods, one quarter is the earthly creation. Puruṣa is divided up as the first sacrifice and from that sacrifice comes the sacred chants and formulae—the *Vedas* (see *Vedas*). His breath becomes the wind (see Vāyu), Indra (see Indra) and Agni (see Agni) come from his mouth, the moon from his brain, the sun from his eye, Heaven from his head, Earth from his two feet, and so on (see Upanisadic Cosmogony, Puranic Cosmogony, Animism).

Vedic Mythology—The first thing that must be said about Vedic mythology (see Vedism) is that it is not an organized corpus of myths moving in a linear path as a "history" of a people. Rather, it is a collection of sometimes confusing and even contradictory fragments in which one deity seems to become another and one action resembles another. The purpose of the brief narratives seems to be more symbolic than historic. Each event suggests many possible interpretations having to do with the centrality of sacrifice and the nature of the Absolute in its multitudinous forms. Still, certain specific figures and events do emerge in fairly clear narrative form from the *Vedas* (see *Vedas*), especially the *Ṛg Veda* (see *Ṛg Veda*). There is the creation story in its several forms (see Vedic Cosmogony, Upanisadic Mythology, Puruṣa), and there are the developing gods of later Hinduism. Among these are the Ādityas (see Aditi and the Ādityas), who were perhaps the sun and planets, but who, in the persons of Varuṇa (see Varuṇa), Mitra (see Mitra), and Aryaman (see Aryaman), were also associated with rulership and social order. Varuṇa especially was the guardian of essential truth. But the fact that Varuṇa also contained a dark *asura* (see *Asuras*), or demonic aspect, meant that he had to be dethroned and replaced by Indra (see Indra) as king of the Vedic gods. While not technically an Āditya, Indra is often associated with that group of deities. A somewhat erratic thunder-warrior god, he sometimes goes astray (see Parade of Ants). Indra is famous for his defeat—with help—of the monstrous demon Vṛtra (see Vṛtra, Indra and Vṛtra). Other Vedic gods include the Maruts and Vāyu (see Vāyu), the storm and wind gods; Rudra (see Rudra), who will develop later into Śiva (see Śiva); an early form of Viṣṇu (see Viṣṇu), who, with Śiva and Devī (see Devī) will eventually dominate Hindu mythology (see Hindu Mythology); and the ritually important gods Agni (see Agni) and Soma (see Soma), who, as fire and the ambrosial and hallucinatory soma, are important to the ritual sacrifices. An interesting aspect of Agni mythology is the god's tendency to hide—as fire hides—and the necessity to find him. As fire he is central to the life of any home and also to the death of any individual, who, on the funeral pyre is a sacrifice that will lead to reincarnation. Soma is also the god of the waters, making him a kind of opposite associate of Agni. Among the female deities of the *Vedas,* there is Uṣas (see Uṣas) who, as Dawn, seduces the creator into materializing the universe by bringing it into the light of day, as it were, through union with her (see Vedic Cosmogony, Prajāpati, Puruṣa). Less individualized forms of this feminine force are Earth, known as Pṛthivi (see Pṛthivi), and Nature in the person of Prakṛti (see Prakṛti). These goddesses, as the materializing vehicles of the creative energy of the male force of the creators, are the forerunners of the later concept of *śakti* (see *Śakti*).

Vedism—Vedism refers to the schools of Indian thought and belief that base their beliefs on *śruti* (see *Śruti*), the sacred texts and rituals of the ancient Vedic tradition that is the *Veda,* that is the particular *Vedas* (see *Vedas*) and their offspring: the *Brāhmaṇas* (see *Brāhmaṇas*), *Āraṇyakas* (see *Āraṇayakas*), and *aniṣads* (see *Upaniṣads*). This pre-Hinduism grows directly out of the religion brought by the Aryan (see Aryans) Indo-Europeans who invaded India in the second millennium BCE. As the invaders moved further south into India, Brahmanism (see Brahmanism) developed as an outgrowth of Vedism and became what we think of as classical Hinduism.

Vietnamese Mythology—Vietnamese mythology is particularly rich in colorful tales, some of them influenced by Chinese mythology (see Chinese Mythology). According to the Vietnamese, there was chaos in the beginning until Kung Lo, a great giant, appeared and separated the sky and the earth (see also Inzanagi and Izanami) with his head before creating a pillar to maintain the separation. At first the giant was creation itself (see also Purusa), his breath the wind and his voice the thunder. When the separation of the sky and earth seemed to be holding, he broke up the pillar and threw the pieces around him to form islands and mountains. Where he had dug out the earth to build the original pillar, oceans were formed, and a giant turtle's breathing caused the tides. When a giant female figure came into being, Kung Lo fell in love with her, but the female resisted him and was the larger and stronger of the two. Before she would agree to marry her suitor, she challenged him to several contests and always won. It was in the course of these frequent earth-changing contests that much of the world as we know it—mountains, rivers, and so forth—were formed. Finally, the giantess accepted the giant's proposal and they were married. On the way to the wedding ceremony, the giant stretched his penis across a river to serve as a bridge for his companions. When one of the friends dropped hot ashes on the penis, the giant jumped, and half of the men fell into the water, only to be rescued by the giantess, who hid them under her dress to dry.

Other stories tell how it was the Ngoc Hoang—the Vietnamese version of the Chinese Jade Emperor (see Chinese Deities, Chinese Emperors)—who, after the separation of Heaven and Earth, created animals out of rough pieces of the sky and earth and humans out of the original chaos. To create the humans he had the help of the twelve heavenly Midwives. The Sun and Moon, daughters of the creator, were assigned to give light and warmth to the world. At first there was a perfect golden age when people were immortal and rice was plentiful. But when the people became lazy and forgot the commands of the creator, it became necessary to work for shelter and sustenance. As for immortality, it was denied humans only because a messenger who was sent by the creator to tell humans they could live forever by shedding their skins when they became old, was convinced by snakes to allow them rather than the humans that privilege.

Sometimes the supreme deity is Ong Troi, Lord Sky—the Sky itself. Sometimes he is Thuong-de. As such, he is the patriarch of a pantheon made up of his family and assistants. Among the most popular members of the pantheon is the goddess Lieu Hanh, who was sent to earth to interact with humans.

The origin of Vietnam is told in several legendary and sometimes quasihistorical epic tales of great antiquity, which were written down in the thirteenth century. The tale of *Lac Long Quang and Au Co* tells of the founding of the nation. It is said that a king called De Minh, who was a descendant of a Chinese emperor-god, fathered Kinh Duong Vuong, king of the Red Demons, with a mountain spirit. Kinh Duong Vuong fathered Lac Long Quang with a princess from the family of the Dragon King of the Sea. Lac Long Quang, also called the Dragon King, is known as the first Vietnamese king. For political reasons, the king married the immortal Au Co, daughter of the enemy Chinese emperor Lai. This union of dragon and immortal blood resulted in one hundred eggs and one hundred sons, half of whom went away as immortals with Au Co to the mountain lands while half remained as mortal dragon people of the lowlands ruled by Lac Long Quang. Eventually Lac Long Quang's son Vuong was named King (Hung, thus Hung Vuong), and it is he who stands at the beginning of the dynasty that was to rule over the land called Van Lang, "home of the tattooed."

In the epic known as *A War between the Gods*, the story is told of a conflict during the period of third century BCE in which reigned the last king of the Hung Vuong dynasty, Hung Vuong XVIII.

It was a conflict between relatives and became the source of Vietnamese monsoons. Son Tinh, the Mountain God, one of the immortal sons of Lac Long Quang and Au Co, joins a fisherman who is talking about an extraordinary fish he has caught. The god buys the fish from the fisherman to save it and returns it to the water. Later a handsome youth comes to Son Tinh in his home on the Vietnamese Olympus and reveals himself as Thuy Tinh, Lord of the Waters, who had lost his immortal powers when he changed himself into a fish. The grateful Thuy Tinh invites his relative to visit him in his Sea kingdom. Son Tinh is impressed by Thuy Tinh's world and he is given a gift of an old book, which he discovers has the power to turn dreams into reality.

When the king, Hung Vuong, holds a contest for the hand of his daughter My Nuong, both Son Tinh and Thuy Tinh compete and become finalists. A final test is assigned to determine the winner. The winner would be the first to bring to the king ten white elephants, ten tigers, ten green pearls, and several other gifts—half from the Mountain world, half from the Sea world. Thuy Tinh gathers the assigned gifts gradually, but Son Tinh makes use of the magical book given him by Thuy Tinh and assembles the gifts long before Thuy Tinh returns to Hung Vuong's palace. When he discovers Son Tinh's trick, Thuy Tinh becomes so angry that every year he pours as much water as he can, from the sea and the sky, on his rival. Son Tinh lives high in the mountains, however, and remains immune to the monsoons and floods.

Another aspect of the Vietnamese cycle tells the quasihistorical story of king An Duong Vuong, one of the one hundred sons of Lac Long Quang and Au Co who ruled Au Lac, a part of what would later become the Vietnamese nation. Au Lac is being threatened by the Chinese general Trieu Da (Chao T'o), so the king tries to build a fortress. But each night evil spirits under the command of an evil 1000-year-old chicken tear down the walls. It is only with the defeat of the chicken by the golden turtle, Kim Quy, that the walls get built. The turtle gives An Duong Vuong one of his toenails as a trigger for a new crossbow made under the turtle's directions.

The use of the new crossbow with the toenail makes it possible for the king to kill many enemies in any given shot. Using the magic bow, An Duong Vuong prevails over his Chinese enemies. But the king is tricked by Trieu Da, who sends his son Trong Thuy as an emissary to Au Lac to find out the source of An Duong Vuong's power. Trong Thuy falls in love with and marries the king's daughter Mi Chau, and she unwittingly destroys her father by revealing the secret of the bow. Trong Thuy substitutes an ordinary bow for the magic one and returns with the latter to his father. Before he leaves, however, he instructs his bride to leave a trail of feathers if for any reason she is forced to leave the palace while he is away. Mi Chau leaves with her father when Trieu Da attacks Au Lac with the magic crossbow. She leaves the trail of feathers behind, a trail that the enemy army can follow easily. When An Duong Vuong prays to the golden turtle for help, Mi Chau's treachery is revealed, and her father cuts off her head. When Trong Thuy, with the pursuing Chinese army, finds the decapitated body of his wife, he buries her and then throws himself into a well. Tieu Da's victory in 207 BCE marked the beginning of a long period of Chinese rule in Vietnam.

Virgin Birth—Although more emphasis is placed on virgin birth in Christianity, there are also Asian versions of the motif, especially if we expand it to include miraculous conceptions in general. Thus, for example, the Persian Zoroaster (see Zoroaster), the Buddha (see Gautama Buddha), the Indian hero Karṇa (see Karṇa), and the Indonesian Hainuwele (see Hainuwele) were all conceived and born miraculously. The significance of the motif seems to lie in the importance it confers on the born hero, who is at once human and somehow divine, both a result of the mortal procreative process and divine immortality beyond that process.

Viṣṇu—The Hindu (see Hinduism entries) god Viṣṇu is both the "pervader" and preserver: he pervades all things and preserves the order of the universe. He is known by his four arms, his conch, his powerful flaming discus weapon, and the lotus. He rides on the eagle Garuḍa and is accompanied by the embodiment of his *śakti* (see *Śakti*), his consort Śrī (see Śrī) or Lakṣmī (see Lakṣmī). For his worshippers or Vaiṣṇavas (see Vaisnava), he is the source of the elements of creation—the Supreme god who becomes incarnate when his presence is required, whether as Kṛṣṇa (see Kṛṣṇa), Rāma (see Rāma) or several other *avatāras* (see Avatars of Viṣṇu). He contains the universe in his being and is the universal Absolute, Brahman (see Brahman, see *Viṣṇu Purāṇa*). As he is the creator, his consort Lakṣmī is the creation, the manifestation of Viṣṇu's energy.

Viṣṇu is infrequently mentioned in the ancient *Vedas* (see *Vedas*), but in the *Ṛg Veda* (see *Ṛg Veda*) it is he who takes the giant steps by which Heaven and Earth are established (see Vāmana). Thus, already in the *Ṛg Veda,* he is the pervasive one, the axis of the cosmos whose ritual pillar—like the *liṅga* (see *Liṅga, Liṅga* Myths) of Śiva (see Śiva) in other myths—reaches from the navel of the earth to the highest heavens. Viṣṇu is the essential sacrifice, he who in the *Mahābhārata* (see *Mahābhārata*) raises up the world in the manner of the earlier version of the creator as Prajāpati (see Prajāpati) and saves it from overcrowding. As Vaiṣṇavism (see Vaiṣṇavism) developed, Viṣṇu assimilated other early creator forms, including the Puruṣa (see Puruṣa) of the *Ṛg Veda* (see Vedic Cosmogony) and the creator god Brahmā (see Brahmā) as the Brahman (see Brahman) within all things or Ātman (see Ātman) and, therefore, as the personification of creative energy itself or Nārāyaṇa (see Nārāyaṇa). Finally, it is Viṣṇu who, as sun, wind, and rain, will absorb the universe at the end of the current age.

The mythology of Viṣṇu is rich. One important myth of the *Jayākhya Saṃhitā* tells how two demons stole the *Veda* (see *Vedas*), plunging the world into disorder. Viṣṇu restores the *Veda* by way of his own knowledge and kills the demons with sacred formulae or *mantras* (see *Mantras*) that reflect his creative energy or *śakti*. One creation story tells how Viṣṇu and Lakṣmī sleep on eternity embodied by the thousand-headed primal serpent Śeṣa or Ananta (see Ananta). During his sleep, the world is "unrealized," that is, it exists only as Viṣṇu's "thought." When he awakens he meditates and begins the process of re-creation. When a lotus springs from his navel, Brahmā appears from it and becomes the actual creator of the world that Viṣṇu will preserve until the next destruction (see also Churning of the Ocean, Viṣṇu Purāṇa).

Viṣṇu Purāṇa—One of the great *Purāṇas* (see *Purāṇas*) of Hinduism (see Hinduism), the *Viṣṇu Purāṇa* is a work of the late third or early fourth century CE. It is a work dedicated essentially to the greatness of the god Viṣṇu (see Viṣṇu) and is, therefore, particularly sacred to Vaiṣṇavas, worshippers of Viṣṇu (see Vaisnavism). In the *Viṣṇu Purāṇa* Viṣṇu is the omnipotent deity. In fact, he is synonymous with the ultimate absolute Brahman (see Brahman) as he is in the *Bhagavadgītā* (see *Bhagavadgītā*). The *Viṣṇu Purāṇa* tells of the creation of the universe by Viṣṇu. The Great God is the navel of the universe and reaches from the heavens to its depths. The *Purāṇa* tells of Viṣṇu's incarnation (see Avatars of Viṣṇu) on earth as the Lord Kṛṣṇa (see Kṛṣṇa) and of the way the universe will be absorbed into Viṣṇu at the end of the age. According to the *Viṣṇu Purāṇa,* God is one and the same with Brahmā (see Brahmā) as he creates, Viṣṇu as he preserves, and Śiva (see Śiva) as he destroys. All are elements of the same universal sacrifice, or process of creation, life, and the destruction that will lead to new life.

Viśvakarman—Meaning "all creating" in Sanskrit, Viśvakarman appears in the *Ṛg Veda* (see *Ṛg Veda*) as the creative power that holds the universe together. In the *Śatapatha Brāhmaṇa* (see *Brāhmaṇas*) he sacrifices himself and his sacrifice becomes the model for all order-sustaining sacrifices to follow. It is clear that Viśvakarman, who is later associated with the divine architect Tvaṣṭṛ (see Tvaṣṭṛ), is also a name for the Vedic (see Vedic entries) creator Prajāpati (see Prajāpati) and the first sacrifice, the primal man, Puruṣa (see Puruṣa).

Vohuman—One of the *Amesa Spentas* (see *Amesa Spentas*) of Iranian mythology, Vohuman, or Vohu Manah, is the personification of the wisdom of the great god Ahura Mazda (see Ahura Mazda). It was he who led Zoroaster (see Zoroaster) in his dream visions to the source of divine power, and it is he who leads good souls to Heaven (see Zoroastrianism).

Vṛtra—Meaning "storm cloud" or "one who restrains" in Sanskrit, Vṛtra is the demon personification of negativity and darkness in Vedism and Hinduism (see Vedic entries, Hinduism entries). In the *Vedas* (see *Vedas*) he is killed by the king of the gods, Indra (see Indra, Indra and Vṛtra, Tvaṣṭṛ).

Vyāsa—Vyāsa was the legendary semidivine dark-skinned sage, or *ṛṣi* (see *Ṛṣi*), who transmitted the Hindu (see Hinduism entries) epic, the *Mahābhārata* (see *Mahābhārata*). According to the story, he dictated the epic of the two families of whom he was himself the progenitor (see Pāṇḍavas, Kauravas), to the elephant-headed god Gaṇeśa (see Gaṇeśa), who wrote it down with one of his tusks. Thus, the story of the Bharatas (India) can be said to have flowed literally from the mind and body of Vyāsa. Like Vālmīki (see Vālmīki), he was one of the Homers of ancient India. He is said to have been the miraculously conceived son of Satyavatī, herself the child of a fish. *Vyāsa* is also the Sanskrit for "collector," and the word can refer in general to collectors of the *Vedas* (see *Vedas*) and other sacred works. Sometimes the collectors are condensed into one Vyāsa, said to have been an incarnation of Viṣṇu (see Viṣṇu) as Nārāyaṇa (see Nārāyaṇa, Avatars of Viṣṇu) and to have been the transmitting vehicle for the *Purāṇas* (see *Purāṇas*) as well as the *Mahābhārata* and the *Vedas* (see *Vedas*).

W

War between Gods—See Vietnamese Mythology.

Wayang Theater and Myths—Wayang is a myth-based ritual shadow puppet theater tradition of Bali and Java in Indonesia (see Indonesian entries). Manipulated by the puppeteer, called a *dalang,* the figures in the dramas are familiar characters from the Hindu (see Hinduism entries) epics, the *Mahābhārata* (see *Mahābhārata*) and the *Rāmāyaṇa* (see *Rāmāyaṇa*). There is some Islamic (see Islam) influence—especially in Java. The *dalang* recites the familiar epic episodes accompanied by a gamelan orchestra and some singers. The most popular divine *wayang* characters are the four-armed Betara Guru or Manikmaya and his old pot-bellied brother Semar. The main heroes are those of the *Mahābhārata*: the Pāṇḍavas (see Pāṇḍavas) and the Kauravas (see Kauravas), the former being much favored.

Woman of Poi-Soya—This *Taming of the Shrew*–type Ainu (see Ainu Mythology) epic takes place in Hidaka, Japan. The hero, Otsam-Un-Kur, has been raised by his two beautiful sisters, who represent all that is valued in Ainu women. But news comes to him of a manly woman named Poi-Soya-Un-Mat, who dresses in men's clothing and hunts, fishes, and steals the game caught by others. When the hero goes hunting and shoots a deer, the bad woman attacks him with some of her servants. Enraged, the hero kills them all, including Poi-Soya-Un-Mat. But the man-woman is revived by her servants. It is then that Ostsam-Un-Kur is informed that he and Poi-Soya-Un-Mat had been betrothed in childhood. Meanwhile, the newly revived Poi-Soya goes on a trading trip, and when approached by would-be suitors, she fights and defeats them to uphold the honor of her fiancée. This manly behavior, however, enrages Otsam-Un-Kur. The epic continues with numerous episodes revealing the inappropriate actions of the woman and the violent anger of the hero. In the end, the hero finds a submissive wife who is willing to cook for him and care for him without complaint.

Woman's Epic: Repunnot-Un-Kur—This is an Ainu work. In the Ainu tradition (see *Woman of Poi-Soya*), the epic is told in the first person by the heroine, Shinutapka-Un-Mat. The heroine, who has been raised by her foster brother, is chosen by him as a wife. The brother leaves for a trading trip to Japan, but not before he captures a bear cub for a bear ceremony (see Ainu Mythology). The bear cub comes to Shinutapka-Un-Mat in a dream and warns her that her foster brother and future husband, Repunnot-Un-Kur, is a villain who had in fact stolen her in childhood and whose jealousy has now been aroused by a rival woman who is claiming that she, Shinutapka, and the bear are having an unnatural relationship. The villain is on his way home with plans of killing his betrothed and the bear. The bear defends the heroine and takes her away to her real brothers. After the bear is sacrificed during the bear ceremony (see Ainu Mythology), he returns as a god and marries Shinutapka-Un-Mat.

X

Xargi—See Siberian Underworld.

Xeglun—Xeglun is the Elk of the heavens, who in Siberian Tungus mythology (see Siberian entries, Central Asian Mythology) is chased on skis by the great hunter Mangi, whose tracks formed the Milky Way.

Xihe—Originally a Chinese goddess (see Chinese Mythology, Chinese Deities) of the ten suns, Xihe came to be thought of as a dual god of Time—a combination of the god Xi and the god He.

Xiyonji—see *Xuanzang*.

Xizi—A book of the fifth century BCE *I Ching* (See *Yijing*), which was in all likelihood composed by scholars not in sympathy with prevailing Daoist (see Daoism) thought. The book stresses mythology such as that of the emperor-god Fuxi (see Fuxi, Chinese Emperors).

Xuanzang—Xuanzang was the Chinese Buddhist monk of the seventh century CE who was the historical source for the legendary traveling master of the *Tripiṭaka* (the *Three Collections of the Buddhist Dharma*), thus Xuanzang is also known as "Tripiṭaka" (see Tripiṭaka). In the legend, he was accompanied by the monkey king (see Monkey) Sun Wukong as narrated in the *Xiyouji (Journey to the West)*.

Y

Yajur Veda—The *Yajur Veda* is one of the four *Vedas* (see *Vedas*) or sacred śruti (see *Śruti*) texts of Vedism (see Vedic entries) and Hinduism (see Hinduism entries).

Yakṣas—The *Yakṣas* are divine beings in Hindu myth (see Hindu Mythology) who can be either benevolent or demonic. They are led by Vaiśravaṇa (see Vaiśravaṇa), also known as Kubera.

Yakushi—A former *bodhisattva* (see *Boddhisttva*), who after long years of practice achieved Enlightenment and the status of Buddha, Yakushi Nyorai is the the Japanese Mahāyāna (see Japanese Buddhism, Japanese Buddhas, Mahāyāna Buddhism) version of Bhaiṣajyagurū, who made twelve vows early on his path to Enlightenment. One of the vows was to become a bright beryl that would illumine the world. So it is that he stands in the East, opposite the Amida Buddha (see Amida Buddha) in the Pure Beryl World. He also vowed to cure illnesses and is called the "king of medicines." It is important to note the Buddha Sākyamuni (see Guatama Buddha) was also seen as a physician; Yakushi thus takes on some of Sākyamuni's importance.

Yama—In both Hinduism (see Hinduism entries) and Buddhism (see Buddhism), Yama is the Lord of Death. In the Indian *Ṛg Veda* (see *Ṛg Veda*), he is lord of the ancestors, and in the *Upaniṣads* (see *Upaniṣads*), he is the bestower of ultimate knowledge, teaching that god and truth are achieved through meditation on the Ātman (see *Ātman*), the god within. In the *Ṛg Veda,* Yama is the son of the Sun as Vivasvat, and he becomes the first human, a fact that associates him with both Puruṣa (see Puruṣa) and Manu (see Manu). In later Hindu mythology, Yama is the more recognizable Lord of the Land of the Dead—a figure to be feared. In Buddhism he is also Lord of the Underworld (see Underworld), sometimes identical to the fiend Māra, who tempted Gautama Buddha (see Gautama Buddha) under the Bodhi Tree (see Bodhi Tree). In Tantric (see Tantrism, Vajrayāna) and Tibetan Buddhism (see Tibetan Buddhism), Yama is a terrifying deity who judges the dead, holding the mirror of *karma* (see *Karman*) in his left hand and the sword of justice and wisdom in his right. In Japanese Buddhism (see Japanese Buddhism), Yama is Emma (see Emma), the demon lord of the Underworld who judges the dead.

Yamabushi—These shamanlike (see Shamanism) Japanese (see Japanese Shamanism) mountain ascetics are associated with spirits; their nature is ambiguous (see Tengu).

Yama no kami—In Japanese Shinto (see Shinto entries), *Yama no kami* is the mountain deity (see *Kami*) who comes down from the mountain and becomes *Ta no kami,* the god of the fields who brings crops (see Mountain Mythology).

Yamato-takeru—See Tales of Yamato.

Yamī—The twin sister of Yama (see Yama), the Vedic-Hindu (see Vedic entries, see Hinduism entries) god of Death, Yamī in the *Ṛg Veda* (see *Ṛg Veda*) proposes an incestuous relationship with her brother and is refused.

Yamunā—The Yamunā or Jumna is a sacred river of the Hindus (see Hinduism entries). It is often personified as Yamī (see Yamī), the daughter of the Sun and twin sister of Yama (see Yama), the god of Death. It flows from the Himālayas into the Ganges (see Ganges).

Yao—The legendary Chinese Emperor Yao (see Chinese Emperors) said to be the Han ancestor was unpretentious and diligent and remains of great importance to Confucianists (see Confucius). He wore simple clothes and during times of starvation and a great flood (see Chinese Flood) he stood firmly with his suffering people. The gods stood behind Yao, making rice out of his horses' straw and leading him to inventions, such as that of the calendar. In this latter endeavor he had the help of Xi and his two brothers and He and his two brothers (see Xihe). Each of these figures was assigned a cardinal direction and a season. Through his organization of time and space, Yao brought about a balance of *Yin* and *Yang* (see *Yinyang*). Many stories are told of the great Yao, including that of the bird with double eyeballs given him by one of his provinces. The bird looked like a rooster but sounded like a phoenix. It was capable of shedding its feathers and flying without them and it could defeat evil spirits. Yao lived for a century. Instead of choosing his evil son Dan Zhu to succeed him, Yao chose the wise Shun (see Shun).

Yasht—*Yashts* (Yásts) are hymns in the Zoroastrian (see Zoroastrianism) *Avesta* (see *Avesta*), containing much of what is known of Iranian mythology.

Yasna—In the Zoroastrian (see Zoroastrianism) sacred book, the *Avesta* (see *Avesta*), *Yasna* is the collection of the seventeen "songs" or "*gāthās*" (see *Gāthās*) of Zoroaster (see Zoroaster) and other longer hymns. The *Yasna* is the part of the *Avesta* used during sacred sacrifices.

Yi—Known as the "Excellent Archer," Yi lived during the time of the Emperor Yao (see Chinese Emperors, Chinese Deities, Yao), when ten suns suddenly rose in the sky, causing a total destruction of crops and great misery for the people. The suns were the offspring of the god of the east, Di Xun, sometimes confused with the Emperor Shun (see Shun), and the goddess Xihe (see Xihe). Ordinarily, the suns lived in the solar Mulberry Tree, or Fusang, and took turns appearing at the top of the tree. But on this day, all of the suns went to the top of the tree. This led to Yao having no choice but to ask the archer, Yi, to shoot down all but one sun. Yi did so, and since then the remaining sun crosses the sky each day in a chariot driven by his mother.

After he shot down the suns, Yi followed the traditional hero's (see Hero Quests) Herculean path by ridding the world of various evil beings.

Another story of Yi concerns the theft by his wife Henge (see Moon Myths) of the elixir of immortality that Yi had obtained. After the theft, Henge fled to the Moon and became a toad there. In this way, the moon contains immortality and is a perpetual body.

Yijing—The *Yijing* (*I Ching*) or *Book of Changes,* probably composed in the fifth century BCE, was, according to legend, made up of elements discovered by the emperor-god Fuxi (see Fuxi). The elements in question are the unbroken line that is *yang* and the broken line which is *yin. Yin* and *Yang* are basic to Chinese mythology (see Yinyang). *Yang* is the masculine principle of Heaven, light, dryness, warmth, and activity. *Yin* is the feminine principle of Earth, darkness, moisture, coldness, and passivity. *Yin* and *Yang* are present in everything everywhere. The whole purpose of the *Yijing,* a collection of omens and oracles, is to demonstrate how *Yin* and *Yang* may be related and balanced in various contexts. Particular combinations in threes of the unbroken *yang* line and the broken *yin* line form symbolic trigrams that have particular meanings. It is said that the original trigrams were used by Wen, the father of Wu, the founder of the Chou dynasty, to form meaningful hexagrams. Wu's son is believed to have been the author of analyses of the hexagrams. Confucius (see Confucius), too, provided explanations. To use the *Yijing* as a divining source, yarrow stalks are cast to form signs, which can then be explained by referring to the *Yijing* itself and making interpretations in connection with the caster of the sticks.

Yima—Yima was an ancient Iranian king of the mythological period. He may bear some relation to the Vedic (see Vedic entries) Yama (see Yama). Like Yama, Yima was associated with death, as he agreed to become subject to that condition as the first human (see Zoroastrian Flood).

Yinyang—In Chinese philosophy, which stresses an organic universe, *Yin* (shadow) and *Yang* (brightness) are opposite energies that interact in such a way as to produce *wuxing*, or the five elements, bringing about the material world and space and time. *Yin* and *Yang* are the opposite boundaries of the absolute source of being, *taiji* (see *Taiji*). The famous *Yinyang* symbol represents the intermingling of the opposites that led to what is essentially the creation of the universe. The interaction is continuous, as is indicated by the dark spot in the light *Yang* and the light spot in the dark *Yin*. Each contains the seed of the other and creates a renewed version of the other. In keeping with this sense of necessary interacting opposites, *Yin* is that which is feminine, passive, and accommodating—the moon, the earth, and wetness; *Yang* is masculine, active, and firm—the sun, the heavens, and dryness. The *Yinyang* model is first mentioned in the first millennium BCE (see Yijing).

Yoga—The term *yoga* is derived from the Sanskrit for "joining" or "yoking." As a discipline, it takes many forms leading to extreme focusing of one's physical and mental powers and to consciousness raising and liberation (see *Mokṣa*) from *saṃsāra* (see *Saṃsāra*) or—ultimately and ideally—to a "joining" with Brahman (see Brahman). *Yoga* seems likely to have been practiced long before the Vedic period (see Vedic entries). There is archeological evidence suggesting its sources, or at least its presence, in Indus Valley civilization (see Indus Valley Mythology), where the practice was perhaps associated with the deity who became Rudra-Śiva (see Rudra, Śiva), himself known as the greatest of *yogis*. A *yogi*, or *yogin* is one who practices *yoga* or who, in a more general sense, is a Hindu (see Hinduism) ascetic. A successful *yogi* is expected to achieve mental control by way of various types of disciplined movement and breathing. The third century CE *Yoga Sūtra* established *yoga* as a *bona fide* Hindu philosophical system, developing ideas originally found in the *Ṛg Veda* (see *Ṛg Veda*) and the *Upaniṣads* (see *Upaniṣads*). In the *Bhagavadgītā* (see *Bhagavadgītā*), Kṛṣṇa (see Kṛṣṇa) becomes the object of meditation for the *yogi*. The clear implication here is that *yoga* can be a form of devotion (see *Bhakti*), or worship.

Yomi No Kuni—See Japanese Afterlife.

Yoni—In Sanskrit, *yoni* means "womb" or "source" and also "vulva," "nest," and even "caste" and "race." Its root meaning, like that of *yoga* (see *Yoga*), is the idea of joining or uniting. In Hinduism (see Hinduism) and Tantrism (see Tantrism), the *yoni* is the generative organ of the Goddess (see Devī). Often it is worshipped in conjunction with the *liṅga* (see *Liṅga*), the generative organ of the god, particularly Śiva (see Śiva). Small models of the joined *liṅga* and *yoni* are found in all parts of India. It is thought that *yoni* worship dates back to the pre-Vedic (see Vedic entries) period in India (see Indus Valley Mythology), to the period from about 4000 BCE to 1000 BCE. Archeological evidence in the south of India suggests a myth in which Śiva takes the form of a buffalo and is sacrificed to the Goddess and reborn from her *yoni*. In southern India there are numerous places where stones with cleavages are worshipped as the Goddess' *yoni*. A popular symbol of the *yoni* is the triangle. The most famous yoni temple in India is Kamakhya in Assam.

Yoon Pai—*Yoon Pai* is an ancient epic of Thailand.

Yorimitsu—A Japanese *samurai* of the tenth and early eleventh centuries CE, Yorimitsu is said to have accomplished many heroic deeds (see Hero Quests), which place him in the category of a legendary-mythic figure. In battling a giant who thrived on human blood, he was victorious, even though the giant's head continued to fight after it was detached from its body. Yorimitsu also defeated a supernatural spider, and performed miraculous feats with his bow and arrows.

Yu—Many mythological (see Chinese Mythology) tales are told in China of the great Yu, sometimes called Gaomi, the man considered to be the first Xia emperor (see Chinese Emperors, Chinese Deities). As a prime example of intelligence, leadership, and adherence to duty, Yu was the epitome of the Chinese ideal hero. It was he who ended the Great Flood (see Chinese Flood). Sometimes Yu is considered a Dragon. There are several myths regarding his birth. According to one, Yu's Mother, after seeing a shooting star, swallows a magic pearl and becomes pregnant (see Virgin Birth). Her chest breaks open to release him. In another version, the mother picks up a seed on a mountain, eats it, becomes pregnant, and gives birth to Yu from her side. Some say Yu, like his son and successor, was born from a rock. Still others say that Yu sprang as a great dragon from the body of his father, Gun (see Gun), who had been put to death for failing to stop the Flood. Gun and his father were associated with mythical aquatic animals. It was they who organized the fields and waterways for agriculture and in so doing organized the world. In effect, Yu became a high god—the god of the soil. He married the daughter of the Earth Mountain, Tushan. When by mistake Tushan saw her husband changed into a bear, she turned into a stone. Yu then had to cut her open to release his son, Qui.

Yudhiṣṭhira—Yudhiṣṭhira was the leader of the Pāṇḍavas (see Pāṇḍavas) in the Indian epic the *Mahābhārata* (see *Mahābhārata*).

Z

Zarathushtra—See Zoroaster.

Zazen—*Zazen* is the Zen Buddhist (see Zen Buddhism) method of meditation. It represents the door to Enlightenment, involving the concentrated attempt to empty the mind of superfluous questions; even those of good and evil or the meaning of scripture or teaching. *Zazen* traditionally takes place in the *zendo,* the meditation hall of Zen monasteries in Japan.

Zen Buddhism—Zen Buddhism is said to have come to Japan by way of Chan, a form of Mahāyāna Buddhism (see Mahāyāna Buddhism) brought to China from India by Bodhidharma (see Bodhidharma), the twenty-eighth successor to Gautama Buddha (see Gautama Buddha), the Buddha Sākyamuni, in the fifth century CE. Chan was a version of what in India was called *dhyāna,* a meditative and ecstatic form of Buddhism. Influenced also by Daoism (see Daoism) when it came to China and various esoteric forms of Buddhism (see Japanese Buddhism) when it came to Japan, it eventually flourished in the Rinzai and Sōtō sects. The monk Dogen is said to have been responsible in the thirteenth century for the rise of Sōto Zen. The monk Hakuin was the leader of a major Rinzai form of Zen in the eighteenth century. Chan and Zen emphasize the possibility for the individual to discover through concentration and meditation the Buddha nature underlying all things, including the self. Zen literally means recognizing the truth that is already there. For the Zen Buddhist, the wisdom to be gained from meditation or from a master who has achieved enlightenment is more important than anything that can be gained from ritual or scripture.

Zhaungzi—Zhaungzi (Chuang-tsu) may have been a contemporary of Laozi, the traditional founder of Daoism (see Daoism). Like Laozi, Zhuangzi was more mystical than his Confucian contemporaries, who preferred to deal with matters of this world. Zhuangzi stressed the possibility of the individual's letting go of the dualities of life in favor of union with the Dao, the "Way," which is all of existence.

Zhurong—In ancient China, Zhurong was the god of fire, the "Brilliant One of the Forge." It was he who defeated Gonggong (see Gonggong) in an epic battle of the gods (see Chinese Mythology).

Zhuzi—Chu-tzu or Chu-ti (The Grand Master) was a fourth-century BCE leader of the Moist school of Chinese philosophy, founded by Modi (Mo Ti) in the fifth century BCE. The Moists followed a doctrine of universal love in opposition to the formalism of Confucianism (see Confucianism). The doctrine is contained in the text called the *Mo-tzu* and in the *Chu-tzu,* which contain a cosmology. The Grand Master apparently believed that the sky was made up of nine levels layered on top of each other, each divided from the other by a gate guarded by beasts. Beyond the space above the top sky there was absolute nothingness, an ultimate void (see Chinese entries).

Zong Belegt Baatar—Zong Belegt is the hero *(baatar)* of this Mongol epic (see Turko-Mongol Mythology, Central Asian Mythology). He is a rich and powerful king who must confront a terrible monster called Khuiten Tomor, who, like many ogres before him, enjoys eating children and laying waste the land of the good—especially that of heroes like Zong Belegt, whom he dreams of destroying. After two marathon struggles with the ogre—one lasting four years, the other seven days, Zong Belegt kills and dismembers his enemy.

Zoroaster—Zoroaster, or Zarathustra, was one of the great prophets of the ancient world. He lived in northeastern Iran, probably late in the second millennium BCE. His concern as a Mazdian (see Mazdaism) priest was the reinterpretation of the ancient Iranian religion and a reestablishment of "good religion" as opposed to the corruption he saw around him. The result of his having "seen God" or Ahura Mazda (see Ahura Mazda) and having interpreted the old teachings was the religious system we now call Zoroastrianism (see Zoroastrianism), based on Zoroaster's preaching in the books called the *Gāthās* (see *Gāthās*). Central to Zoroaster's work is the belief in an essential dualism in the universe, represented by the Wise Lord Ahura Mazda and the evil Angra Mainyu (see Angra Mainyu). Eventually many myths developed around the life of the prophet. It was said that his mother Dughda dreamt that good and evil spirits were fighting for the baby in her womb. At birth the baby laughed. Wise men warned the king, Duransarun, that the baby Zoroaster was a threat to his realm, and the king set off to kill the child. Miraculously the would-be murderer's hand was paralyzed. Demons who stole the child also failed to kill him; his mother found him peacefully sleeping in the wilderness. Later, the king sent a herd of oxen to trample his enemy, but the cattle took care not to hurt Zoroaster. The same thing happened when horses were sent to trample him. And when the king had two wolf cubs killed and the baby Zoroaster put in their place in the den, the mother wolf's anger was quieted by God, and sacred cows were sent to suckle the child. In adulthood, Zoroaster was resented by followers of the old tradition, but he convinced many with his miraculous cures. Zoroaster was killed at an old age by soldiers while he was carrying out a ritual sacrifice, but it is said that he will one day return as a final prophet or *saoshyant* (see *Saoshyant*).

Zoroastrian Afterlife—Zoroastrianism (see Zoroastrianism) preaches the idea that Death is the work of the evil Angra Mainyu (see Angra Mainyu). The religion also asserts the existence of the soul *(Fravasi)* and the resurrection of the body at the time of the Great Renewal that will come one day. The soul, created by Ahura

Mazda (see Ahura Mazda), is immortal and will be judged immediately after the death of the body. At the time of death, the soul must pass over a narrow bridge. At the entrance to the bridge stands the *daenā,* or conscience, a maiden who becomes identified with the individual soul. The good souls see a beautiful and dignified woman, while the evil souls see a witch. The good, led by the maiden, will pass over to the "House of Songs" or Paradise as angel-like beings who will serve as guardians of the living good people. The souls of those who have lived evil lives will be attacked by the witch and will fall as demons into the dark cold ravine or "House of Lies" that is Hell. According to some sources, it is the bridge itself, Chinvat, that decides on the fate of souls. Other sources say Ahura Mazda himself makes the judgment, and still others say that Mithra (see Mithra) presides over an actual trial of the individual, who must plead his or her own case.

Zoroastrian Apocalypse—Zoroastrians (see Zoroastrianism) believe that too few people follow the right path, that the evil ones at present outnumber the good. But they also believe that one day the Wise Lord (see Ahura Mazda) will rectify things at the Great Renewal at the end of the present age (see Zoroastrian Afterlife). Fire, the son of Ahura Mazda, will flow like a river over the universe, as an ultimate sacrifice, destroying all before it—including even Hell—and separating the good from the evil at a "Last Judgment." Then, through ceremonies presided over by the savior, Saoshyant (see Saoshyant), the resurrection of the bodies of the good will take place and a new Golden Age will follow. In some stories it is said that the castle of the primal man, flood survivor (see Zoroastrian Flood), and sacred king Yima (see Yima) is Paradise and that at the Great Renewal, Yima's dominion will encompass the earth itself as the basis of a new Golden Age.

Zoroastrian Cosmogony—Several stories of creation exist in the Iranian tradition. One story tells how Yima (see Yima), the primal man, king of the Golden Age, and later a solar deity, pierced the Earth with a golden arrow, making it pregnant. Yima, who resembles the Indian Vedic god Yama (see Yama), had been created by the sun god Vivahant, a servant of Ahura Mazda (see Ahura Mazda). In the *Avesta* (see *Avesta*), there was only Light—an essential purity—in the beginning. In the Light was the Word and the power of Nature. It was the creator, usually seen as Ahura Mazda himself, who joined together the Word and Nature to make the world (see Zoroastrianism).

Zoroastrian Flood—When the world had become overwhelmed by the constant multiplication of its immortal beings, Ahura Mazda (see Ahura Mazda) decided that the earth must be enlarged and a new beginning made. He warned the faithful king Yima (see Yima, Zoroastrian Cosmogony) that a great flood was coming to cleanse the world and that Yima had to protect himself and two of each species in his castle on top of the highest mountain. The flood came, and the world, except for Yima's castle and its inhabitants, was destroyed. When the flood passed, Yima opened his doors and the world was inhabited again.

Zoroastrian Mythology—In his reform of the old Mazdian (see Mazdaism) religion, Zoroaster (see Zoroaster), in theory, did away with mythology (see Zoroastrianism). The early Aryan (see Aryans) idea of a pantheon of amoral immortals was discarded in favor of an essential duality that lay at the source of existence. There was division between evil spirits or *daevas* led by Angra Mainyu (see Angra Mainyu) and good spirits, or *ahuras*, led by the supreme god, Ahura Mazda (see Ahura Mazda). The choice for humanity and for individuals was between the two sides of the essential duality (see Zoroastrian Cosmogony, Zoroastrian Flood, Zoroastrian Afterlife, Zoroastrian Apocalypse, Zurvan, Amesa Spentas).

Zoroastrianism—Zoroastrianism is a religion that takes its name from the late second millennium BCE Iranian prophet Zarathustra, traditionally called Zoroaster (see Zoroaster) by people in the West. Believing that he had spoken to the ancient Iranian high god Ahura Mazda (see Ahura Mazda), Zoroaster undertook a reform of the old Indo-Iranian religion (see Vedism, Mazdaism) of the Aryan (see Aryans) invaders of India and Iran. At the center of his reformation is an essential dualism, which opposes the good Ahura

Mazda and his heavenly followers, the *asuras* (see *Asuras*), to the evil Angra Mainyu (see Angra Mainyu) and the *daevas,* who in their old Indo-Iranian context were not particularly evil but who in Zoroastrianism become demons, bent on war and destruction (see Zoroastrian Mythology, Zoroastrian Cosmogony). After long years of struggle against the followers of the old religion, Zoroastrianism became the state religion of Iran under Cyrus the Great in the sixth century BCE and remained so until the rise of Islam (see Islam) in the seventh century CE. Important aspects of Zoroastrianism are the belief in the prophet (Zoroaster), a past and future savior (see Saoshyant), an afterlife (see Zoroastrian Afterlife), a Last Judgment (see Zoroastrian Apocalypse, Zoroastrian Flood), and the resurrection of the body. An important aspect of Zoroastrian ritual is fire and fire temples (see Zoroastrian Apocalypse, Parsis), an aspect that dates back to ancient Indo-Iranian roots (see Vedic Mythology) and the centrality of fire sacrifice. An offshoot or "heresy" of Zoroastrianism is Zurvanism (see Zurvan), in which Zurvan, or Time, supplants Ahura Mazda as ultimate reality.

Zurvan—In Zoroastrianism (see Zoroastrianism), Zurvan is the concept of Time. In a Zoroastrian offshoot, Zurvan was considered to be the ultimate reality, the power behind even Ahura Mazda (see Ahura Mazda) and Angra Mainyu (see Angra Mainyu) and thus the source of what was seen as predestination. This "heresy," known as Zurvanism, was at odds with orthodox Zoroastrianism's emphasis on the possibility of choice between good and evil.

Zurvanism—See Zurvan.

Resources

Useful resource books for further study and those that have been particularly helpful in this work include the following:

Bonnefoy, Yves with Wendy Doniger, trans. and ed. *Asian Mythologies.* Chicago: University of Chicago Press, 1993.

Bowker, John, ed. *The Oxford Dictionary of World Religions.* New York: Oxford University Press, 1997.

Campbell, Joseph. *The Masks of God: Oriental Mythology.* New York: Viking, 1970.

Eliade, Mircea, gen. ed. *The Encyclopedia of Religion,* 16 volumes. New York: Macmillan, 1987.

Eliade, Mircea, ed. *Essential Sacred Writings from Around the World.* San Francisco: HarperCollins, 1977.

Grimal, Pierre, ed. *Larousse World Mythology.* London: Hamlyn, 1965.

Jackson, Guida M. *Encyclopedia of Traditional Epics.* Santa Barbara: ABC-CLIO, 1994.

Ke, Yuan. *Dragons and Dynasties: An Introduction to Chinese Mythology.* London: Penguin, 1993.

Leeming, David A. *Mythology: The Voyage of the Hero.* Third Edition. New York: Oxford University Press, 1998.

———. *The World of Myth.* New York: Oxford University Press, 1990.

Leeming, David A. and Margaret Leeming. *A Dictionary of Creation Myths.* New York: Oxford University Press, 1995.

O'Flaherty, Wendy Doniger. *Hindu Myths.* Middlesex, UK: Penguin Books, 1975.

Renard, John. *Responses to 101 Questions on Buddhism.* New York: Paulist Press, 1999.

———. *Responses to 101 Questions on Hinduism.* New York: Paulist Press, 1999.

Rhie, Marylin M. and Robert A. F. Thurman, eds. *Worlds of Transformation: Tibetan Art of Wisdom and Compassion.* New York: Tibet House, 1999.

Sproul, Barbara C. *Primal Myths: Creation Myths Around the World.* San Francisco: HarperCollins, 1979.

Tsunoda, Ryusaku, et al. *Sources of Japanese Tradition.* New York: Columbia University Press, 1958.

Zimmer, Heinrich. *Myths and Symbols in Indian Art and Civilization.* Princeton: Bollingen, 1972.

Index

Boldface page numbers indicate main headings